SEVEN TATTOOS

Also by Peter Trachtenberg
The Casanova Complex

7 TATTOOS

a
memoir
in
the
flesh

PETER TRACHTENBERG

Crown Publishers, Inc.
New York

Published by Crown Publishers, Inc., 201 East 50th Street, New York, New York 10022.
Member of the Crown Publishing Group.

Random House, Inc. New York, Toronto, London, Sydney, Auckland
http://www.randomhouse.com/

CROWN is a trademark of Crown Publishers, Inc.

Printed in the United States of America

Design by Lenny Henderson

Illustrations by Karen Dean
Original tattoos by Sam Peterson, Hanky Panky, and Freddy Corbin

Library of Congress Cataloging-in-Publication Data
is available upon request.

ISBN 0-517-70172-3

10 9 8 7 6 5 4 3

PERMISSIONS

For Mila and Anatole

ACKNOWLEDGMENTS

I thank my agents, Gloria Loomis and Nicole Aragi, for inspiring, coaxing, and occasionally bullying me (in the nicest way possible) into bringing this book to completion. Their assistant Lily Oei was an astute reader and has some impressive ink of her own. Stacy Schwandt and Tracy K. Smith have been of great assistance in the later stages of manuscript preparation. Ever since this manuscript landed on her desk at Crown, Elaine Pfefferblit has been a dream of an editor, not just a literary superego, but at times a surrogate id, who always encouraged me to write from my wildest places. Thanks are also due Ann Patty and Patrick Sheehan; he answered my questions and told the messengers where my apartment is. Shanna Compton has been an ardent and inventive publicist. And thanks, too, to David Tran, Lenny Henderson, Karen Dean, and Christine Rodin for making this book such a visually satisfying object.

James McCourt and Vincent Virga brought invaluable critical perspective to the early drafts of the manuscript, as did Barbara Feinberg, Dan Azulay, Kim Larson, Christiana Bird, Peggy Goodday, and Peter Dimock. Janice Deaner was a dear friend and a generous and sensitive director when I first began to perform sections of this book. Tom Carey has continued to direct me over the past six months, teaching me volumes about the craft of acting and the secrets of Jack Benny's timing. For guiding me in my research, I thank Christina Kreps and Dra. Sri Utami; tattoo artists Henk Schiffmaker, Sam Peterson, and Pat Fish, as well as Chuck Eldridge of the Chuck Eldridge Tattoo Archive in Berkeley and Clayton Patterson of the New York Tattoo Society. Leslie Downer vetted the material on Tibetan Buddhism. Although I have never met Marianna Torgovnick, her book *Gone Primitive: Savage Intellects, Modern Lives* provided me with the conceptual framework for my third chapter.

While writing this book, I actually lived a life, and in all fairness I should thank the people whose presence made it pleasurable and, in the bad times, endurable. I think especially of those who were with me during my mother's final illness and after her death: Sheila Keenan, Kevin Duggan, Erin Clermont, Sheila McManus, Rob Mazze, Karen Petrone, Tina Kacandes, Pamela Grossman, Anne DuPont, Gay Milius, Josine Shapiro, Mara Levi, Bozena Szawrycki, and my cousins Charlotte Weissberg, Natan, Rosa, and Anna Lubinsky and Konstantin Rozenshteyn. Further thanks are due Linda Rosenberg and the staff at Vintage Books for their understanding and flexibility. My profoundest gratitude goes to my late mother and father. I doubt they ever realized they were providing me with stories: They only thought they were teaching me to be a human being. Poor things, they didn't know what they were in for.

CONTENTS

We tell ourselves stories in order to live.
Joan Didion, THE WHITE ALBUM

1

I WALK THROUGH THE MIRROR

The living being is only a species of the dead, and a very rare species.

Nietzsche, THE GAY SCIENCE

I n the fall of 1991 I went to Borneo. What happened was I'd saved some money and I decided to go to the wildest place I could think of. I suppose I was going through a nostalgic phase then, and the thing I was feeling nostalgic for was my younger self. At the time I called this "controlled regression," and one result of regressing in this controlled manner was that I found myself trying to realize the *fantasy* of wildness, of wilderness, that I'd had as a ten-year-old boy in upper Manhattan. I wanted to be an explorer, a guy with a pith helmet and a good jawline hacking his way through a rank, humid, dripping rain forest with all sorts of fauna making ominous background roars and hoots and that weird cackle I associate with no creature I know of but that you always hear in jungle movies and that I actually did hear, years later, in a village on the Mahakam River. I swear on my father's grave. Whatever it is that lives out there really makes that sound.

The other reason I picked Borneo was because of tattoos. I thought I'd find tattooed people there, bowl-coiffed Dayaks who still wore those geometric tattoos, the black, looping, barbed lines and spirals that they call "tribal" on St. Mark's Place. If you go to a tattooist and ask him for a tribal piece, what you'll get will be an imitation of a Bornean, that is to say a Dayak, tattoo. The piece I have on my collarbone—it looks kind of like a set of antlers—is actually adapted from an Iban Dayak pattern from Sarawak, in North Borneo. It was my first tattoo. I'd gotten it a year or so before I went over, and I wanted to see its original, so to speak.

Getting tattooed is one of the few impulses I've ever delayed acting on. Back in the late seventies I was all set to have a forearm piece that was going to be a crucifix made of a pair of syringes wrapped in barbed wire. But the trouble was I didn't know any tattooists then, and by the time I did I had changed my way of life and I no longer cared to advertise my bad habits. I still wanted a tattoo, but everyone kept telling me not to make any major decisions in the beginning. So I waited one year, and then another and another, like somebody in a fairy tale, until almost five years had passed since the last time I'd thought of decorating myself with a picture of crossed syringes. And I figured, What the heck. Live a little.

I got my first tattoo in Amsterdam, where I used to live, from one of the world's all-time great tattooists. His name is Henk Schiffmacher, but he works under the name Hanky Panky. He is one of tattooing's stars—a red giant, I'd call him, a big hot presence at the trade's conventions and in the pages of its glossy magazines, whose photos of freshly decorated body parts have the lush sheen of pornography. Hanky Panky is also an archivist of tattoos, and he's traveled all over the world, hanging out with Hell's Angels in the States and Yakuza in Japan and these big, spooky Samoan guys who do their work with gigantic harpoons that have been known to go right through the skin and puncture spleens and kidneys. His shop was in the Red Light District, overlooking a canal, and it had a little tattoo museum that reminded me of the museums of human oddities they used to have around Times Square when I was a kid: It had that same soothing, musty kind of gruesomeness. The first thing I saw when I came in for my appointment was a glass display case. And inside the case was an entire tattooed human skin from Japan that had been cured like a big sheet of beef jerky and stretched so that you could see its images clearly. And I must have been regressing on all cylinders then, because I wasn't grossed out at all: I thought it was cool.

The next thing I know there's a guy lumbering toward me. He looks like a biker. He's thick all over, not fat, but thick, slabby; he could crush me like a Styrofoam packing peanut, and he's got shoulder-length hair and a beard and his thick, pestle-shaped forearms are covered with very precise, almost dainty patterns that from a distance might almost be knocked off from a Ralph Lauren bedspread. And I'm waiting for him to sneer at me, since what am I but a frail, clean-shaven, unmarked *tourist,* who in all his thirty-six years has done nothing more remarkable to his body than get his earlobe pierced a couple of times? But Hanky Panky is Dutch, and the Dutch are always polite, even when they despise you, and instead he says, in that clipped Dutch accent that's almost impossible to place: "Well. What is it you are looking for, exactly?"

I show Hanky Panky the design that I adapted from a photo in a book of Dayak art, and he has me take off my shirt and he sketches the design on my collarbone with a grease pencil. Then he calls over an assistant to shave my chest. Now, under other circumstances, this could be kind of a turn-on. But in Hanky Panky's tattoo parlor it just reminds me of the shaving I had to undergo before some surgery I once had in the groin region. That one, much to my initial disappointment, had been performed by a male nurse, although actually I *did* see the wisdom of having a man for the job at around the time he began to whisk the razor around my balls. "Hey, be careful. Please!" I begged. And my male nurse answered, "Don't worry, buddy. I'll handle 'em like they were my own."

People are always asking me whether getting tattooed hurts; it's one of the Seven Stupid Questions of the World. True, after a while your endorphins kick in and the sensation of spreading numbness becomes oddly pleasurable, kind of like some Heroin Lite. But in the beginning being tattooed is like being scratched with a safety pin—over and over and over and over. It's irritating and it's boring. And because I'm bored and because it makes me very anxious to sit half-naked with a stranger looming over my prickling flesh, I ask Hanky Panky all these questions: "Say, where did this kooky practice start? Why was it so big with sailors? Can I get AIDS from this?"

When I ask him about AIDS, Hanky Panky glances up from his needle and gives me a cold, gray, gunmetal look. "You should have asked me that earlier." Total, withering disapproval. "I have been working on you for two hours." I turn white. I'm thinking what an indescribable bummer it's going to be to have survived all those years of shooting dope and getting up to all sorts of monkey business in the carnal department only to be killed by a cosmetic procedure. I can just imagine what my father would say if he were still alive: "So, what else did you expect, getting tattooed like some goy sailor?" To my father, there would have been no difference between my getting AIDS from a tattoo gun and my getting it from a syringe I'd shared with half the junkies on Clinton Street. As far as I know, Judaism has no line at all on heroin, while it's got plenty to say about tattoos. At that moment, I remember something my father once told me. I couldn't have been more than five, and he caught me picking my nose. He said, "You know what happens if you stick your finger up there? You want to know what happens, *shmeggege?* The bacteria bores up"—*bores up,* he's saying—"it bores up into your brain and the next thing you know you're dead from infection." And, look, it turned out he was right.

Hanky Panky chuckles. "I am making a joke, heh-heh. We use only new needles. This is Holland, you know." Because of course Holland is the country where hygiene was invented.

Two hours later I get up and I look at myself in the mirror. And there, on that chest that was just a chest, on those shoulders that were just shoulders, is a beautiful, undulant black labyrinth of slender, hooked lines. It's incredibly crisp, the way new tattoos are, and the antibiotic ointment makes it shiny. This is my body, and it's been transfigured. The word that comes to mind is *lithe*. I'm lithe and I'm powerful and I'm wild. This tattoo has turned me into a jungle thing, into a head-hunting Dayak motherfucker. Gone are the timidity, the caution, the doubt, the sniveling Heepish *niceness,* the excruciating self-consciousness that have encysted me since the day I first knew I was an "I," that I dragged around with me through my childhood like some unwanted twin, that I spent twenty years trying to talk away with therapy and wash away with booze and shoot away with dope and fuck away with any woman who was gracious enough to recognize my handicap or dumb enough not to see it, and *look*–it's gone. Four hours under a tattooist's needle and for the first time in my life I can look in the mirror and actually like what I see.

Amazing things, endorphins.

Now, before we get to Borneo, I need to mention that the other reason I'd been so late in getting tattooed was my father. First off, my father was Jewish, and Leviticus 19 says everything there is to say about Jews and tattoos: "Ye shall not make any cuttings in your flesh for the dead, nor print any marks upon you: I am the Lord." That "I am the Lord," I'm convinced, is there as a sort of peevish afterthought, just in case you should have any questions about the basis for these injunctions. It's like one of those T-shirts that says BECAUSE I'M THE MOMMY, THAT'S WHY.

Because he was a nominally observant Jew, my father had no tattoos, but his mother and several other relatives had gotten them when they were herded into Auschwitz. Tattooing had been the Germans' way of keeping track of the Jews they were killing in such huge numbers with such witless method and ingenuity. The only way I can imagine what the Nazis had in mind is to envision an empire of idiot savants who've made it their national project to count to infinity by ones. At the railroad sidings, at the camp entrances, outside the gas chambers and the crematoria, they count and they count. And they tick off each "one" with a number on the wrist, because they don't want to make any mistakes in their idiot progress toward infinity; they want to keep track of all those corpses and those corpses-to-be, of all those "I"s who are about to be transformed into inanimate "its." Because what is a corpse but an I that has become an it?

My father wasn't tattooed, but I grew up among tattooed people. I remember being at a family reunion when I was little and staring at the wrist of my father's cousin S—"S" for Sam or Shmuel or Sandor, the exact name doesn't matter. There, peeking out from under his shirt cuff, are some spidery numbers stitched in blurred blue ink; they look like an old laundry mark. And I was fascinated. Most of the time my father answered questions quickly, in irritated bursts: "What the hell do you mean by asking me anything so stupid?" But when I asked him about his cousin's numbers, my father paused. And he actually thought for a while. I suppose he was wondering what sort of answer would be appropriate for an eight-year-old. And then he said, in that Russian accent that had not yet become so embarrassing to me: "They did that to him in the camps."

So I'm sure that subconscious thoughts of my father had played some part in my earlier hesitation about getting a tattoo. Otherwise it's quite likely that I'd now be talking about a crucifix made of syringes. And the moment I got back from Europe, I fell into a depression. I stepped off the plane in Baltimore and—WHAM!—that old familiar gloom of mine was bludgeoning me like a two-by-four. Because in the back of my mind I was sure I'd betrayed my father and trampled on the memory of the Holocaust. As usual, my depression manifests itself in my body image. Which sucks.

Mornings I stand before the mirror and stare at myself for an hour at a time. I turn in profile. I wring the fat on my waist. I tilt from side to side, checking my love handles. Every woman I've ever gone with has mistaken this custom for some charming vanity, but it's really self-disgust, disgust at the self that is my body. The tattoo? The tattoo changes nothing. No, the tattoo is a beautiful addition to my hideous body, that squat, hairy, clay-colored body that aches and trembles and sweats and shits and stinks. The tattoo is something new for me to feel unworthy of.

But I wouldn't call it a mistake. Or else, the very fact that it *is* a mistake is what makes it so successful. My tattoo may be the first mistake I've ever made that I can't take back. Because up till now I've taken back everything. I was a loving child and I turned my back on my mother and father. I renounced jobs and apartments. I loved people and reneged on them. I got married and divorced so fast it was like something out of *The Time Machine*: Whoops, there goes the Industrial Revolution, there goes the wife! Even drugs and booze, the two great loyalties of my life—I turned my back on them, too, and if you look at me today, you won't see a sign of those abusive love affairs on my entire body. It could be a Mormon who's telling you this. Or at least a lifelong vegetarian.

But isn't this how it's supposed to be for us Americans? For what is the American dream if not the expectation that every shady episode of your life can be erased? Horse-thief uncles, illegitimate kids, old rap sheets—all you have to do is change your zip code and they're history. At the very worst, you hire a media consultant and get him to apply a little spin. You can be driven from the White House in disgrace on national television, but if you wait five years, *Time* magazine will hail you as an elder statesman. I don't know what America Nathaniel Hawthorne lived in, but it sure wasn't the America of Richard Nixon and Oprah Winfrey. Because if Hester Prynne were walking around today with a scarlet *A* on her dress, people would think it stood for Armani.

So what I like about my tattoo is that at last there is some evidence in my life. It may be what I originally meant it to be or it may just be an advertisement of my terminal confusion, like the international symbol for DANGER: BRIDGE OUT. But either way, my tattoo—all my tattoos—are a mistake I can't correct by any means short of laser surgery.

In the middle of my depression, somebody told me about a self-help group for people who wanted to pursue personal visions, and I thought that might be just the thing for me, since I no longer had any. So I went to this Goals Meeting. It was in an Episcopal church in the leafy suburbs, and when I walked inside, a nice lady was explaining that her Goal was to get out of debt and buy a pony for her little daughter.

Then this other fellow got up to share. He was a white boy in a dashiki. He said, "My name is Ira and I have a Goal. Right now I'm unemployed and in debt and I'm living with my parents, who don't understand me at all. But my faith in this program is so huge that I *know* that one year from today I'm going to be traveling across the United States with my Spirit Guide. My Spirit Guide is going to be a white malamute dog named Isis. I mean, I *know* this as clearly as I've known anything in my life. My Goal is for Isis to guide me to the homes of my favorite self-help authors. *Isis is going to take me to meet John Bradshaw and Louise Hay and M. Scott Peck, and I'm going to get them to mentor me!*" He kind of bellowed this. And I wasn't sure whether Ira was exactly what John Bradshaw and Louise Hay and M. Scott Peck deserved or whether I hoped they kept shotguns in their homes. I was honestly torn.

I don't know why I kept on going to this Goals Meeting but I did, and in time I, too, discovered a Goal. My Goal was to go to Borneo. My fantasies of perfect wildness and my fascination with tattoos swiveled into place like the sections of some wacky self-actualization Rubik's Cube, and I started buying guidebooks

1 0

and calling travel agents and learning Indonesian. One of the things I liked about the Indonesian language was that the way you greet a man is *"Apa ada, bung?"* Literally that means "What it is, brother?"

But the closer I got to Borneo, the more preoccupied I was by thoughts of death. Well, a lot of people I knew happened to *be* dead. My grandfather was dead. My old friend Will was dead. And of course my father was dead; he was the number one dead person in my life. One foggy morning as I was Rollerblading around the Lake Montebello reservoir, I had a sudden premonition that as soon as I rounded the next bend I would see him walking toward me through the mist. I knew just how my father would look. He'd still be healthy, and he'd be striding along in that upright way he had, as though he were on his way to an urgent appointment. He'd be wearing the same navy blue windbreaker he has on in a snapshot I have that was taken of him in Atlantic City, in one of those rare moments when he wasn't working: It was a long time ago. Neither of us would stop. I'd go on skating and my father would go on walking. But we'd wave to each other as we passed, as though it were the most natural thing in the world for the living and the dead to be taking their morning constitutionals together around a man-made lake in Baltimore, where my father had never been.

One thing my father had given me, along with an ear for music and a tendency toward hernia, was the idea that death is never all that far away. Witness his views on nose-picking. When I was little, he used to make me wash my hands the moment I got out of bed. At the time I figured it had something to do with hygiene: Who knows where you've put your hands while you were sleeping? But when I finally got around to asking, my father said that hygiene wasn't the point. You had to wash your hands in the morning because in your dreams you had contact with the dead. You might touch them or they might touch you, and unless you washed thoroughly upon rising, their touch might contaminate you. You might be infected. Infected by death.

When my father died, my family sat shivah for seven days. For those of you who aren't Jewish, this is like holding an extended wake, except that shivah begins after the burial and nobody gets drunk. Well, *I* got drunk, but I was the one in my family who always had to be different. You just sit there on a cardboard box covered with wood-grained contact paper. It's not a whole lot of fun. And the misery is compounded by the fact that the men go without shaving and all the mirrors are covered, which at least gives you the consolation of not knowing how bad you look.

I used to think that the point of these procedures was to demonstrate how grief-stricken you were. "Rose was so distraught after Louis passed away that not once did she even check her makeup." But, of course, my father, who'd been raised Orthodox, knew better. "No, no, stupid. Be logical, can't you? Your problem is you're never logical. The reason you don't look in the mirror after someone dies is because you might turn into a dybbuk. You know what a dybbuk is? No, of course you don't. You don't care about tradition. Let me tell you. When someone dies, he doesn't just disappear all at once. His spirit is still hanging around behind the mirror. And if you give just one look, well, I don't believe this, but who knows? If you look in the mirror, the spirit that's waiting there can come into you—whoosh! And then you aren't yourself no more. You're a dybbuk, a live body with a dead person inside."

So when my father died, I knew that a part of him was still somewhere nearby, lingering in the house he'd bought only three years before. He was there in the mirror, on the other side of the mirror, in a place I imagined as a sort of clearinghouse for the recently deceased. Every time I passed one of the covered mirrors, I pictured him standing in a crowd of the silent dead—they'd be milling like commuters in a railway station where all the trains are stalled—waiting for the curtain to be drawn, for the gate to open.

And this thought was not comforting to me. Partly because I had no desire to be possessed by my father's spirit—he'd done quite enough of that while he was still alive. And partly because my father had threatened me on his deathbed, which is a story I don't even want to go into right now.

And in time I came to believe that the death I was anticipating was my own. Borneo seemed like a place with a lot of opportunities along that line. I could catch some pustular jungle fever. My boat could be sucked down in the rapids. My plane could crash. It didn't help to learn that the flight I was scheduled to take from Jakarta was on a Fokker, the plane that was made famous by the Red Baron. And what was really weird was how calm I was about the thought of dying. You see, I believed I was supposed to die, and Borneo seemed like the best place to do it. It would be an Ambrose Bierce–y move. So on the day I left, I folded my mosquito net in my knapsack and imagined I was folding my funeral shroud. I said good-bye to my friends and I thought, This is the last time I will ever say good-bye to them. And when I was finally alone in the airport departure lounge, I skulked over to the tobacco shop and bought my first pack of cigarettes in three months. I'd been miserable the whole time I'd quit smoking, and I figured why not die happy?

Two weeks later I arrived in hell. Hell is situated in Palangkaraya in the province of Kalimantan Tengah in Indonesian Borneo. It's a town of several thousand acutely unhappy souls that was thrown up thirty-odd years ago in the middle of a swamp, like a pup tent erected by a group of drunken campers. Probably the only reason it was built at all was as a pretext for hiring lots of civil servants. But as eager as most Indonesians are for government jobs, it's my impression that the ones who were posted in Palangkaraya got a raw deal. The place is as hot and sodden as an armpit, the air writhes with biting insects, and the architecture consists of concrete bunkers and swaybacked huts made of rattan and corrugated tin. It's a third-rate beach town with no beach.

The only thing I'd learned since arriving in Indonesia was that being tattooed there can get you killed. This isn't mentioned in the guidebooks. Every so often the Indonesian government—that is to say the Indonesian army—sends out semi-secret death squads to mop up the criminal gangs, most of whose members are said to be tattooed. A few years before my trip, hundreds of tattooed bodies turned up bobbing in Java's harbors and nobody raised an eyebrow. To this day I don't know if being tattooed automatically marks one as a member of the Indonesian underworld—if I were a gangster in a country whose style of law enforcement is like one of Daryl Gates's wet dreams, the last thing I'd want to do is walk around advertising it—but never in my life have I seen so many cut-rate skin grafts. Everywhere I went there were men with raw, bubbly-looking spots on their forearms. They looked like they'd been made with a soldering iron. In Borneo I met a nurse and I asked her, "What's with all these skin grafts?"

"For tattoo," she said. "Lot of people come to hospital to take off tattoo. Very popular."

"Well, why would they want to get rid of their tattoos?"

She didn't even blink. "Oh. They might get shot."

So encountering nothing but suspicious stares whenever I so much as said *tattoo,* I ended up in Palangkaraya, mostly because it was located in central Kalimantan and getting there meant taking a six-hour trip by speedboat, which I thought would be fun. Actually, it meant getting slammed endlessly up and down while wedged among twenty-odd other passengers, many of whom kept vomiting in this stoic Eastern way: no tears, no moaning, just a quick *floop* over the side.

When I finally landed, the first person I met was a pretty American anthropologist named Charlotte. She looked something like Inger Stevens from *The Farmer's Daughter,* with the addition of bad heat rash. When I asked Charlotte where I could find some traditionally tattooed Dayaks, she just laughed at me. "You poor, deluded man. No one's been tattooed like that around here for a hundred years."

But I wouldn't believe Charlotte. She didn't even have her doctorate yet. So, very graciously, she took me to visit an old Ngaju Dayak lady who was one of her native informants. We entered the dark house where she lived with her son and grandson and took off our shoes and sat down across from her on the sofa so that we were facing two framed portraits of Indonesia's president and vice-president, who looked like Shriners in their little fezzes, and drank glass after glass of scalding, sugary tea. The whole afternoon reminded me of those times I'd been forced to visit my Russian great-aunts when I was little: the same dark rooms, the same pancreas-destroying tea, the same muttering conversation in a language I couldn't understand.

Charlotte had warned me not to start out asking about tattoos; the old lady would think I was fantastically ill-mannered or a police spy. So I waited a full hour before I said, in the most excruciatingly polite and roundabout way I could think of, "I am very interested in the customs of the Ngaju people, which are very famous throughout America. Everybody in America is very interested in Ngaju medicine and religion and the entire Ngaju way of life, which, I am informed, though perhaps erroneously, includes or once included the practice of drawing pictures on the skin for certain purposes that are not clear to me. Am I being too forward, Mother, to think that you might be able to enlighten me?"

And this very old lady, who was so frail that her neck could barely support the burden of her ancient head, began to laugh. It was a terrible sound, like very dry paper being ripped into tiny pieces. Then she said, and Charlotte translated for me: "You poor, deluded man. No one's been tattooed like that around here for a hundred years."

•   •   •

"Ye shall not make any cuttings in your flesh for the dead, nor print any marks upon you." I've always been intrigued by this verse from Leviticus, and not just because it explains why I can never be buried in a Jewish cemetery (which would be a problem, anyway, since my father is buried in one plot in New Jersey and my mother in another one several miles away, and the last thing I want when I'm dead is another custody fight). No, my real interest in this passage from the book that might be called Yahweh's fine print to the Ten Commandments is the implicit connection it draws between tattoos and death. For it suggests that the peoples of ancient Palestine were in the habit of marking themselves as some sort of offering to, or commemoration of, the dead. This practice is not uncommon. In parts of New Guinea mourners lop off bits of their toes and fingers as offerings to deceased relatives. And if you look at vintage American tattoos, what do you find but coffins, skulls, and tombstones? To me it makes perfect sense. Because a tattoo is a sign of something that is absent or invisible. And what is more absent, less visible, than the dead?

Except, of course, God. Knowing the God of the Hebrews as I do, which, I'll admit, is at some remove. (I relate to God the way I would to an absent father, one who'd run out when I was born but was still somehow remotely in the picture; maybe He sends a child-support check every once in a while, or a birthday card. And He still has expectations. On every check and card there's some ridiculous demand: "And remember, son, thou shalt not commit adultery." "Ye shall make you no idol nor graven image. Fondly, Dad." Oh, it's outrageous, it's outrageous that the Fucker even *thinks* He can ask me for anything. But I always go along. Or disobey Him only at the cost of seething guilt. It's not that I'm scared of what He'll do to me. It's just that I keep hoping that if I do the right thing and go on doing it long enough, one day He'll come back. He'll show Himself to me. There's a sucker born every

minute. As Mona Simpson says, in what may be the truest sentence in the English language, "All you have to do to become
somebody's god is disappear.")

Anyway, knowing Yahweh as I do, I figure that the tattoo rule
had two purposes. The first was to set the Hebrews apart from
their neighbors. Thanks to Leviticus, you could always tell who
we were: the ones who laid off the pork, bobbed their wieners, and
didn't have any tattoos. And the other reason was sheer jealousy.
Tattoos were marks for the dead, and our God wasn't the kind
who shares the limelight with anyone. You aren't even supposed to
send *flowers* to a Jewish funeral; it would be too much like idolatry.

Speaking of the dead, I was very upset after my conversation with
Charlotte and the old Ngaju lady. I felt like one of those bone-
heads who blunders onto an Indian reservation and calls everybody "chief." So to cheer me up Charlotte invited me to a village
further up the Kahayan River, a place called Kasongan, to witness
a *tiwah,* the Ngajus' raucous festival of death. We took the public
boat upriver. Thanks to the logging and oil companies, the landscape we passed through resembled a cross between Jungle Habitat
and Love Canal. The air reeked of forest fires; the water boiled
with industrial pollutants. And over the carnivore snarl of the engine, Charlotte explained what we were about to see:

Most Ngaju are now Muslim or joylessly Protestant, but they
still have a distinctly pagan attitude toward death. They believe
that there's no such thing as a natural one, they're worse than
Kennedy conspiracy theorists. For a long time they lived in terror
of vampirelike beings called *hantuen,* who were thought to steal into
the village when someone died and prey on the survivors. And
they still take it for granted that somebody dies and rivers flood,
crops fail, children wither, grandchildren go mad. Every death is
like a small nuclear explosion: It has a lethal half-life that lasts for
years.

So the moment a Ngaju dies, the survivors take precautions. There are exorcisms. There are taboos. There is a ritual specialist called a *basir* who makes sure that everything and everybody connected with the dead person is spiritually decontaminated. On top of that, the Ngaju inter the body twice. The first time it's in a specially built coffin that they bury outside the village and then more or less abandon: These people are not in the habit of visiting their graveyards any more than we are of picnicking at Three Mile Island. And then, ten or twenty years later, they dig up the bones and carry them back to the village and place them in a family ossuary called a *sandung*. The *sandung* I saw in Kasongan was about the size of a toolshed and covered with what looked like sparkly bathroom tile, and it was equipped with little doors so that the ancestral spirits could wander in and out when they felt like it, like ectoplasmic house cats. It had stairs as well, though these were notched backwards: The Ngaju believe that the dead do everything in reverse.

The festival of secondary interment is called a *tiwah*. It goes on for an entire week, and its purpose is to unite the departed spirit with the bones of his ancestors. You could call it a party, if your idea of partying includes not just drinking and dancing but animal sacrifice and demonic possession. It's a natural way of celebrating for people who've spent the last few decades in a state of exquisite supernatural anxiety, waiting for death's cloud to sprinkle them with its toxic fallout. "A *tiwah*," Charlotte said, "is like an orgy in a graveyard."

At this juncture what came to my mind was George Romero's *Night of the Living Dead,* which used to upset me so badly that I couldn't see it unless I'd shot three bags of dope beforehand. Now, what the Romero movies are, what most horror movies are, generically speaking, are bastard grandchildren of the Gothic, the school of literature that includes *Frankenstein* and *Jane Eyre* and *The Castle of Otranto,* the first Gothic novel, published in 1764.

And it's an eerie coincidence that Gothics, with their ghosts and vampires and dankly haunted crypts, became popular at the same historical moment that the middle classes of western Europe stopped preparing their dead for burial. For thousands of years before that, washing and dressing deceased relatives had been one of those grisly obligations that everybody takes for granted, but toward the middle of the eighteenth century the dead were reclassified. What moments before had been dying people were suddenly cadavers, ex-persons, "I"s who were now "its." And nobody felt much of an obligation to them anymore.

Most historians will tell you that this had something to do with the emergence of the funeral industry, which swaddled death in the sterile batting of professionalism. But there was another reason for this reclassification: The dead had always given the living the creeps. In almost every culture there's a belief that those who have died are jealous of those who are still alive. Their spirits watch us, yearn for us, envy us. They pass among us and wistfully inhale our odors, because to the dead even the rankest life smells as luscious as fresh-baked bread. They stand over our beds at night and warm their hands as though we were so many campfires. They remember what they're missing. And they hate us because we still have it. The Ngaju maintain that *hantuen* lure young people into the forest and gnaw out their livers. Dybbuks possess their closest relatives. Now I ask you, what sane person would want these things in his house?

So about two hundred years ago our ancestors transformed the dead from people into objects, objects that could be buried and then forgotten like old lawn furniture. Except that even as we banished the dead from the sickroom, they popped back up in the library, in the pages of Gothic novels, where they continued to scare the shit out of us. Or some of us. George Romero films aside, I don't find horror horrifying. To me it's just poignant. Because who's really going to believe that the ones who left us so utterly will ever come back? The dead are gone. They're history. And when you really accept the fact that they are absent, *Dracula* begins to seem as hopeless and heartbreaking a piece of wish-fulfillment as *The Velveteen Rabbit*. Or that's what I used to think.

We landed in Kasongan and clambered off the boat and trudged up streets that were really just steaming, muddy trenches. No sooner had we made them than our footprints filled with fetid water that moments later was shimmering with midges. We went over to the house where the *tiwah* was going to be held, a long, roughly timbered structure with few windows and rooms that turned out to be big as bowling alleys when you stepped inside, and we were introduced to the dead man's daughter. At first I thought we'd dragged her out of bed. The poor woman was a mess: hair flying every which way, face caked with yellow rice powder. But Charlotte told me that she was just observing taboo. During *tiwahs* bereaved Ngajus neglect their grooming. "They even cover the mirrors." When Charlotte said this, I seemed to hear the theremin music that they always play in science fiction movies when things are about to get weird: ooo-OOOO-oooh. This was all too Jewish for words.

Jews, even grievously lapsed Jews like myself, are always looking for other Jews. Maybe we want company in case of a pogrom. And all that afternoon, I had the eerie sensation that I'd found some, that I'd stumbled onto an entire outpost of little, brown-skinned, pork-eating Jews with epicanthic folds. The retired schoolmaster who was putting us up for the night looked just like the actor Jack Gilford, and the first thing he wanted to talk about was Einstein: Einstein and God. "They say that Einstein was a religious man, isn't it? He must have been. Only a scientist who believes in God can produce anything of value." I could have been talking with my grandfather.

But as the day went on, I also got the feeling that the recognition went both ways. Soon there were dozens of villagers following us everywhere. They gawked at us as we gawked at the *sandung*. They trailed us into the death house and sat down beside us on the floor, as though we were all waiting for sing-along at summer camp. I started asking about tattoos again. At first nobody even knew what I was talking about, I was so circumspect. But then I said, "With your permission," and I took off my shirt. And I pointed to the tattoo on my collarbone. And I said, "Any of you folks ever see anything like this around here?"

And suddenly all the old people were just buzzing. "Oh, Great-Grandpa used to have tattoo just like that!" "Everybody used to have tattoo, but then the missionaries come and they say they are wicked. And now the government says the same thing: It says we have to be progressive." The marks on my despised body had opened the gates of these people's collective memory. And what was really odd was the fact that my tattoo wasn't exactly authentic. I'd changed it a lot from the original drawing. I was just some Dayak wannabe, a cross-cultural poseur, and here I had traveled twelve thousand miles bearing the key to their past on my skin, without even knowing that was what I was carrying.

Now everybody started drinking a rice-based rotgut flavored with pepper and ginger and galingal. It smelled wonderful, but due to painful past experience I couldn't partake. Which was socially awkward and also a little scary. Because Charlotte had warned me that at *tiwahs* the slightest deviation from ritual etiquette can have repercussions. Months before one of her neighbors in Palangkaraya had gone to a *tiwah* and as he was digging up the bones, he'd cut himself. It was just a little cut, and he didn't think to tell the *basir*. So he goes ahead with the ceremony and then back to the city and a while later he's crossing the street and a bus runs him over, and he's killed instantly. And everybody who hears about this incident shakes his head and says: "Ohhh. It was that cut that got him. Fellow should've told the *basir*."

So if a little tiny cut can get you killed, God knows what happens if you refuse to drink. But as people are brandishing their rotgut at me, and in fact sloshing it all over my clothing, I have one of my rare bursts of intuitive social savvy and yell: *"Tidak minum. Sakit!"* "I can't drink. It makes me sick!"

And here's another way the Ngaju are like Jews: They understand hypochondria. "Oh, he's sick! It'll make him sick. Well, of course he can't drink. What do you think you're doing, Uncle Adi, trying to make him drink? You want to poison the poor guy? Shame on you!"

Even though I wasn't drinking, I was still getting a contact high, plus a mild case of asphyxiation from the smoke of dozens of clove cigarettes. The next thing I knew we'd all moved into another room. Half the village is packed inside. And sitting in the center of the room are the dead man's relatives—I recognized the powdered woman I thought I'd rousted out of bed—and the *basir,* who's a chubby old guy with a crewcut and an eyelid that droops like a broken window shade. The *basir's* wearing a rattan headdress decorated with a hornbill feather. He's dipping his hands into little brass bowls and anointing the family with perfume and oil and hen's blood. And he's chanting in a high, thin voice that a Dayak woman named Sri tells me isn't even his own: It's the ancestors who are speaking through him now.

And what gets me is that nobody is paying any attention. This is the most sacred of sacred events that's going on and these people are acting like it's a cocktail party. They're swigging that rice brandy and smoking those clove cigarettes. Their kids are running around the room and climbing in and out of their parents' laps, and nobody's telling them to shush. Nobody's hissing at them to pipe down and cut out the monkey business or God's gonna send them to hell. Let me tell you, I was shocked.

Because when I was growing up, the Divine was something to be scared of. Or bored by. When you were in church or synagogue you had damned well better pay attention. Even if you didn't have a clue about what you were supposed to be paying attention *to*. Who were these men mumbling at the front of the room? What was inside that Ark? How come you only got one measly sip of wine and one crummy Necco wafer? Why was everybody standing up and sitting down at the same time as in some theological game of Simon Says?

In retrospect I realize that it's all about monotheism: "Ye shall have no other God before me." Ye shall pay no attention to anything except Myself or My stand-in, even if He's speaking a dead language. Even if everything else is so much more *interesting:* the stained-glass windows; those ceilings that look like so many gilded stalactites that might come plunging down and impale you at any second; the *enormous* growth on the neck of the lady in the pew in front of you, which you wonder, Is it filled with pus or is it solid like some horrible malformed sponge? (In every Western house of worship I've ever been in there's always someone with a growth; it's uncanny.) You're not even supposed to be looking. Which is what I discover when my father pinches my arm so hard that I squeal out loud, which only makes him pinch me again. Because the One God is a jealous God, with the glowering, paranoid jealousy of a Father Who suspects that His kids are smirking at Him behind cupped hands, that they're plotting to fuck Mom, scheming to put Him in a home, but they can't fool Him, He knows, He knows what those little snots are up to, and He's just *waiting* for them to try something so He can incinerate them all with one bolt from His dreadful, yellow Eye.

But the Ngaju are animists. They've got deities to spare, a little god curled up in every fallen leaf, enthroned in every hole in the ground. And if monotheism re-creates the patriarchal family at its most aridly dysfunctional, Dayak animism turns the universe into one big, swarming extended family. I'm not saying it's a bed of roses. Think of all the offerings you've got to make. Not to mention being petrified any time you accidentally kick a pebble, not knowing Whom you've pissed off. But at least nobody's jealous, nobody's making exclusive claims on your allegiance. Kids want to run around? Let 'em. You want a cigarette? Go ahead and have one, for God's sake. I mean it. He's probably hovering nearby, waiting to get a whiff of your smoke.

At around this time I realized that there was someone interested in me. His name was Pak Tari, and he was a thin little cricket of a guy, in his sixties, I'd say, with big, horn-rimmed glasses and a huge, white grin that made him look indiscriminately delighted. At least he was delighted with me. He was delighted that I spoke a little Indonesian and he was just tickled that I didn't drink. Possibly because that left more booze for him; he was putting that stuff away. And the drunker he got, the more friendly he got. When Pak Tari found out that I spoke Dutch, he clapped me on the shoulder and crowed, *"Bahasa balanda!"* "Dutch language!" I asked him if he spoke Dutch, too, but he just shook his head and yelled *"Bahasa balanda!"* again. In all the time I lived in Holland, I never met anybody who was so happy to hear me speak Dutch. I'd gargle off a sentence in the most impeccable accent and the Dutch would just look at me like "Why would you *bother?*"

Not Pak Tari. He clasped my hand in both of his and asked me something that made Charlotte blush. "What did he say?"

"Pak Tari is begging you to stay here in Kasongan so that you can teach his grandchildren how to live progressively."

Now, if you're an American traveling in the Fourth World, you've got to resist the temptation to play Great White Father. Because people will want you to do it. They may want you to be the good, providing father, or they may want you to be the Bad Dad, with his coups and his Contras and his CIA. But, regardless of your actual respective ages, the stance they take toward you will be distinctly Oedipal. I could have asked Pak Tari what he meant by progress. A six-lane highway with a McDonald's on one side and a Burger King on the other? A performing arts space? But I was in no position to rhapsodize about the "Ngaju way of life." No one has any business congratulating other people for all the things they don't have. It was so much simpler when I was still drinking: I would have just mumbled something like "Always use the right drill bit for the job," and everyone would've been happy.

Whatever I said couldn't have been too gauche, because the next thing I knew Pak Tari was crushing me to his meager bosom and making my eyes water with rotgut fumes. And he was yelling, in what might have been Ngaju or Indonesian or maybe even English—though I'd have sworn he didn't speak a word of it—he was yelling: *"I father you! I father you!"*

And I thought, Oh, Jesus, not again! Because ever since I stopped drinking, I've become a magnet for drunks. Drunks find me deliriously attractive. Drunks waylay me at parties. Drunks enlist me as their priest, their shrink, their marriage counselor; if they're women, drunks want me for their boyfriend. And now I had reached some new depth of involuntary co-alcoholism: I had found a drunk who wanted me for a son. I looked wildly over Pak Tari's shoulder for a rescuer, and what I saw was an entire roomful of people grinning back at me and, I was certain, trying not to laugh in my face. At that moment I remembered the Ngajus' legendary reputation for practical jokes. During their wakes, these people are known to soak a cloth in the juices that drip from the decaying corpse and then wring it out over the face of an unwary sleeper. They think that's hysterical.

This moment, thank God, didn't last too long, because some people came up to the front of the enormous room and began playing the gongs and drums. The music was a bubbling hybrid of salsa and gamelan: You could dance to it or you could trance to it. The Ngaju started dancing. They formed two circles, men on the outside, women on the inside, and then they shuffled rhythmically from side to side with their arms held out like wings. The women held their shawls stretched out behind them, so they looked like large wading birds. And every so often they'd all dip their knees, drop their arms, and then jerk upright with a shrill whoop and a highly explicit pelvic thrust. Skinny grandmas with betel-stained teeth, old men in deep-dish trousers—they were all doing it, along with their children and their grandchildren.

Of course, Pak Tari wanted me to join in. "Don't be shy!" He kept yanking my arm, and he was strong for someone so thin, and I didn't want to be rude, so I let him drag me to my feet and into the men's circle and I held on to his leathery hand as he nudged me first one way and then the other, and when he dropped down and did that funky little grind, I did, too. He was overjoyed. "I father you!" he kept yelling. "Dutch language!" I was about to ask him to stop shouting, but all of a sudden I thought, What the fuck. The old guy wanted to father me, he could father me. It was no big deal. And, anyway, I could use a father. God knows, I'd been missing mine lately, blundering through this strange country where everything seemed designed to make me feel as lonely and incompetent as an eight-year-old.

And the fact is, my last conversation with my father hadn't gone too well. All my life he'd treated me with a mixture of love and anger. The love was because I was his and the anger, I guess, was because I wasn't more like him. When I was still little, he used to cuff me and then kiss me on the spot he'd cuffed and groan, "Ach. What am I supposed to do with you?" But he'd been sick a long time, and in the course of his sickness the love had burned away, it had burned away along with his flesh until all that was left was a skeleton, a skeleton with a fierce, gnashing grin and a hard pebble of anger rattling around inside it. It's hard to express love, it's even hard to feel it, when you're in pain, and my father was in agony. And he couldn't even take painkillers because the cancer had fucked his liver. One Dilaudid would've been enough to send him straight into a coma. So he hurt all the time, and his pain made him angry. He was enraged at his body and everything connected with it: at the sandpaper sheets, at the light that drilled through his eyes. And, I'm pretty sure, at the son he'd fathered thirty-one years before, who was still alive while he was dying. And what's more, taking all the narcotics he couldn't; I was taking enough dope for the two of us. And when I came to visit him that last day, my pupils must have been so pinned that they looked like the periods in the *Oxford English Dictionary,* the one that comes with a magnifying glass.

I leaned over my father's bed—the ambulance hadn't yet come to relay him to the hospital—and he bared his teeth at me. "You stink from cigarettes," he hissed. "You stink like the plague. You better stop smoking, or I'll kill you. I'll kill you! You hear me?" I could feel his breath on my face. "You're a mess. Your whole life is a mess. You got to stop fucking up your life."

I tried to argue with him, in the same teary, ineffectual way I'd argued with him when I was little. But even if he hadn't been right, there would have been no point. You can't argue with dying people. They see things, from the edge of their high cliff, more clearly than you ever will.

I don't know how long we went on dancing. Different groups of musicians kept coming up to play, but they seemed to be playing the same song; they might have played it all through the night. At one point I realized that we had drifted out of the house and into the yard and were now circling what I can only describe as a totem pole that was carved in the likeness of a gigantic woman. Her hair was painted black and her mouth was a stern slot. She looked like a great primal Mom waiting for her kids to pick up their toys. Back in the darkness you could hear the animals that were tethered by the *sandung,* animals that in a day or so would be butchered as of-

ferings to the dead. The pigs, especially, sounded horrible, squeal-
ing as though their throats were already being slit. In the torchlight
everyone looked red-faced and drunk and sweaty. I suppose most
of us were. I looked down and saw that I was dancing barefoot in
the mud, in the layered, impacted shit of chickens and pigs and
water buffalo. And it seemed to me that I'd read a warning in the
travelers' advisory against doing just such a thing. The situation
embodied every one of my father's hygienic nightmares.

But the one who'd adopted me that night was barefoot, too. His
hair was askew. His glasses dangled uselessly from one earpiece.
Pak Tari was really far gone. He still wanted to dance, even
though all he could manage were a few gasping steps before he
had to rest. I was scared the poor guy was going to have a heart attack. "Take it easy, Pak. You're getting overexcited." It's unbeliev-
able, the things you hear coming out of your own mouth.

"Don't you worry about me, son. I'm doing fine, I'm doing fine.
Just steer me to that rice brandy and I'll dance all night. You're the
one I'm worried about. How're *you* holding up?"

And he gave me that look that fathers always give sons, that
look that says "I ain't dead yet. I can beat you at this any day."

Luckily, some of the old man's relatives came to collect him before he danced one of us into the grave. But before he went off with
them, Pak Tari walked over to me and he hugged me and I hugged
him back. I was struck again by how small he was. His head barely
reached my shoulder. And then, as Pak Tari stumbled off in the di-
rection of his hut, I called out, "Sleep well, Father," and I bowed to
him and folded my hands across my forehead in the gesture of respect that is called the *wai* in Thailand but that is probably unknown in Borneo, at least I never saw it my whole time there. If Pak
Tari had looked back at me at that moment, he would have been
very confused. It's hard to describe what I was feeling. Part of me
was appalled at my shameless habit of milking drama from every
conceivable situation. And at the same time my cheeks were wet.

"Well," Charlotte said. She'd been watching from the shadows. "That was quite a performance! I felt so sorry for you, getting stuck with that old guy. But you were so patient with him. You must be a very good actor."

I just nodded.

We were drenched with sweat and our clothes reeked of rice brandy and clove cigarettes, so Charlotte and I and her Ngaju friends Sri and Clarence decided to bathe down by the river. The bank was steep and slick. The dark water moved silently below, but if you stepped in past your waist, you felt the current suck you greedily downstream. We stayed in the shallows, holding on to the pilings that supported a flimsy landing that felt as though it might give way at any moment.

Later, as we tiptoe back into the village and approach the open kitchen behind the house where we're going to spend the night, we hear something scream. I don't know what else to call the sound. It starts low, it seems to bubble out of the mud itself, and then it gets high and rasping and livid. It might have burst from the center of the earth, from some underground clearinghouse of the dead. It's a voice and it's forming words, but I wouldn't call it human. There are moments when you realize what a limited category human is.

There's a light burning inside the kitchen, and by the light we can see three men grappling. Or, really, it's two men—one of them's the old schoolteacher who looks like Jack Gilford—holding on to a third, a young man, who's writhing in their arms. His head is flopping back and forth, his chest is heaving. He looks like he's vomiting: *projectile* vomiting. But what spews out of him is that voice, that ravenous, homicidal voice, a voice that might be issuing from an open wound. "Let's not mention this," Charlotte whispers. She's doing her best to sound calm. "When we go back inside, pretend you didn't see anything."

Now, I for one was not about to go back inside. We sent poor

Sri into the hut as our delegate to the old man. When she came back out, she said, "He apologizes. He says his son drank too much. He got sick."

We just stared at her.

"He wasn't drunk." Her voice became confiding. "Maybe somebody slips a poison in his liquor. This happens at *tiwahs*. But he is not regular drunk. You know every family has a spirit that watches it and helps it and protects it. These people, they have a spirit that lives in the river. They make it offerings and the spirit gives them favors. But this boy, he does not give his offerings for a long time. Maybe he doesn't believe anymore. People want to be modern." She shook her head.

Charlotte wanted to know if the kid had been possessed.

"I don't know. The voice that came out of him, it was talking in Ngaju, so I knew what it was saying. It was saying"—she tried to imitate the voice but could do so no more accurately than she could have imitated an earthquake or a falling star—"It was saying 'I'm here. I'm here and I want what's mine.' "

This was only the first night of the *tiwah*. In the days that followed there'd be a ritual attack by villagers from further up the river and a mass slaughter of sacrificial animals, the entire village slashing away with honed machetes, men and women spattering themselves with blood as blithely as children playing beneath a water sprinkler. And then one morning the dead man's relatives would return to the graveyard and cut through the underbrush and dig up the bones they'd buried so long ago. They would wash them and anoint them with scented oil and wrap them in scarlet cloth and then again in white cloth. And at last they'd carry the bones back to the village, back to the *sandung;* they'd carry the remains of their father or grandfather the same way he'd carried them when they were small children. And although all human bones look more or less the same, and they aren't exactly the kind of thing that makes you feel sentimental, everyone would reach to touch them as they passed. And they'd all be weeping.

I know about this part of the *tiwah* from my conversations with Charlotte and from reading; I did a lot of reading after I came back. But I saw none of it. I left Kasongan the next morning and a week later I was back in Baltimore. I didn't die in Borneo. But the strange thing was that after I returned, Baltimore no longer felt like home to me. It no longer felt real. Thanksgiving was a few days later, and when I sat down to that big dinner with my dearest friends, I had the persistent feeling that I wasn't looking at them, but *through* them, as though they'd become transparent while I was gone. I've always heard that ghosts are supposed to be transparent, but I wonder whether the opposite isn't true: that to the dead it's the living who seem sketchy and insubstantial. I had no doubt that my friends were still alive. But I wondered about myself. Because from that time on I was never happy in my old home, though I tried and tried to be. And I left a year later.

I wish I were an anthropologist. It seems like the only profession that would let me legitimately realize those fantasies I had when I was ten, those dreams of traveling in remote places with a pith helmet and a notebook. But I'm not an anthropologist. I don't have the patience to sit invisibly in one place and watch things happen. I lack the precision and humility. I'm the classic unreliable witness: All the time I'm watching those other people, I'm also watching myself. I watch myself watching and I watch myself thinking and I watch myself doing what is so often exactly the wrong thing at exactly the wrong moment. And I probably don't have the courage to be an anthropologist, either. Because on the night I heard that voice, that voice that might have been a man's or a woman's, that might have been shrieking "I'll kill you!" I was very scared. And, after spending six agonizing hours lying on the floor of the hut and waiting to hear that voice again, I caught a boat back to Palangkaraya with Clarence, who had business there.

He was glad for my company. He hadn't met many Westerners before, and none who had tattoos like the ones his great-grandparents had worn. He wanted to know how I'd learned about them and where I'd gotten them. He wanted to know how much they'd cost. He wanted to know if being tattooed in America could get you shot. At last he asked me, "Does your father like them?"

And I said, "My father's dead."

"I am sorry. Did he die at home?"

"No," I said. "Very few Americans die at home anymore."

And I told Clarence that on the day my father died, I'd come to visit him at his house in New Jersey, where the hospital had dispatched him after it became clear that there was nothing more that could be done for him. As I've said, he was in a great deal of pain and he was thrashing feebly on his bed and he was weeping. I'd seen my father weep only one or two times before, when I was little, and it seemed to me, as I watched him now, that those times had been rehearsals for this moment, and that was why they had been so frightening to me. Because even then, my father's tears had told me that he would one day die.

I called my father's doctor and asked him how long he'd have to go on suffering. And the doctor said that we could take my father back to the hospital, and they would give him a room and hook him up to a morphine drip and make him—the word he used was "comfortable." Then he said, "Of course he'll go straight into coma. You have to realize that." And I said I did.

I told my stepmother and my stepbrothers what the doctor had told me. I told my father. I asked him, "Do you understand what this will mean?" Which was my code for "Do you understand that this will kill you?" My father nodded, but I didn't trust myself to interpret that. "You're sure this is what you want?"

And my father looked up from his bed and said, "What else is there left for me?"

So we took my father back to the hospital, where for once they admitted him quickly. I don't even remember anyone asking me if he had insurance. The room they put him in was tiny and green and it had no window: I would have liked my father to have had a view of some kind. But then I would have liked it if my father could have died smoking a cigar and listening to the Verdi *Requiem*. That would have been a good death for him. I turned my back as the nurse undressed him, and when I turned once more he was wearing that thin gown they always give you, and he had a battery of tubes plugged into his arms and nose and groin. He looked like something caught in a spiderweb.

As out of it as I was then, at least I had the clearheadedness to tell the old man I loved him. And I heard him say that he loved me, too. Then he asked me if I'd eaten, which of course I hadn't. I hadn't had time or appetite to eat that day.

"You told me you were going to eat earlier and you didn't." He was too tired to yell anymore. "Why do you always have to disappoint me?"

Then I left. We all did. I went back to the city and scored my dope for that night. And the next morning I learned that my father was dead. He was seventy-three years old but, as I told Clarence, the Ngaju would have called his death "unripe" because it was accompanied by so much pain and such great bitterness. We buried him in an Orthodox Jewish ceremony, though I'd never thought of my father as being Orthodox. And afterward the family sat shivah for seven days. And we kept all the mirrors covered.

After I returned from Borneo, I did a great deal of reading on the Ngaju. I learned that their sacred bird is the hornbill: That dance I took part in is called the hornbill dance. And the Ngaju believe that it's the Hornbill god that bears the dead man's spirit down the river to a paradise that they picture as a prosperous village whose sand is made of gold and whose beaches are diamonds. But although the Ngaju imagine the next world as a perfect village, it doesn't mean they aren't sad when they leave the imperfect ones they lived in. In one of the books I read I found a song that the dead man is supposed to sing as he sails away in the ship of souls and turns back for his last glimpse of his former home:

> *I can still not express my innermost thoughts properly*
> *Nor is it possible for me to speak what fills my heart.*
> *I have thrown away the village lent by the Hornbill,*
>> *as one discards a useless plate.*
> *I have pushed away the place where the hornbills live*
> *widely scattered, as one rejects an unusable dish,*
> *And I have myself become like a cast stone, never to return*
> *I am like a clod of earth thrown away, never to come home again.*

2

I ACQUIRE A WOUND

"They ought to make it a binding clause that if you find God you get to keep Him."

I'd give anything to say I wrote that, but it's Philip K. Dick from *VALIS,* a book that may be science fiction or a direct transcription of one of its author's many nervous breakdowns or a theological masterpiece on the order of *Fear and Trembling* and *The Imitation of Christ*. I cite this phrase sometimes to explain a tattoo I have on my right side, between my rib cage and my hipbone. This tattoo seems to call for an explanation. At least people are always asking for one: "Excuse me, but what *is* that thing?"

I acquired this tattoo about nine months after I got my first one, in between my last trip to Amsterdam and my first trip to Borneo. It was like one of those shoeshines you get while killing time between trains at railroad stations—a stopover tattoo. Actually, a great deal of thought went into it and not a little anguish of the emotional or spiritual variety. Compared to that, I barely noticed the physical discomfort of the tattoo itself. A tattoo, I've always believed, is a visual reminder of pain, which has the tendency to be forgotten quickly and so sometimes requires documentation. This tattoo was my document of a particular kind of suffering, suffering

I wanted to keep in mind and was afraid I wouldn't: I knew what a fickle slut my memory can be.

It also happened to be a pain to get, mostly because it took me such a long time to find anyone who was willing to touch the job. Tattooists are supposed to be a permissive bunch, perfect laissez-faire capitalists. Swastikas, Confederate flags, there's nothing they won't do. But when I went around to tattoo parlors in Maryland, which is where I lived then, asking if anyone could execute the design I had in mind, people acted as if I was asking them to tattoo "666" on a baby that had been freshly butchered as an offering to the devil. There was one guy—he was on retainer to a biker gang in West Baltimore; he used to do little skulls on the members' arms so they could keep track of all the people they'd killed—who took one look at my sketch and said, "No, no, man. That's sick. You're gonna have to go to New York for that."

So I went up to New York and I found this woman named Slam. No last name. She worked out of a tenement in my old neighborhood on the Lower East Side; the only other business in the building was a mom-and-pop heroin dealership. She smelled of the clove cigarettes that she chain-smoked like a Malay pirate and her hair was dyed the black of black shoe polish, but she had a straightforward manner and a generous, gummy smile that made me think of a small-town cheerleader who'd been dropped down a chute into a black leather motorcycle jacket and a full set of arm tattoos. What drew me to Slam was her utter lack of squeamishness. Once she'd tattooed a fastidiously realistic snake—it had little slit-pupiled eyes and little scales with *slime* shining on them—on a client's penis and followed that up by inscribing the words "BUTT SLUT" on his girlfriend's ass. And Slam happens to be a very political lesbian.

When I told Slam what I wanted, she said, "Fabulous! I've never done one of *those* before! What kind do you have in mind?"

"Kind? What do you mean, 'what kind'? How many kinds are there, for God's sake?"

"Well, you could be looking for something like da Vinci's or Mantegna's. They're so gorgeous. Or maybe you want something medieval, you know? They're more primitive, but the plus is anyone who looks at them won't immediately be thinking 'trauma ward.' Here, let me show you."

And she brought out some art books and the two of us began to flip through them, looking for the right . . . *example*.

"Honey, the first time you show this thing to a priest, you are going to be excommunicated. I guarantee you. There's not a church in this town that'll let you in."

"I wish," I said. "I always wanted to be excommunicated. Too bad I'm Jewish."

"No! *Jewish?* Too fucking much!"

And I said, "Yes it is. Ask any Jew."

The fact is, what I wanted tattooed on my right flank, there where the skin was as taut as the head of a new snare drum, was a stigma. From the Greek *stizein,* meaning, interestingly enough, "to tattoo." I wanted one of Christ's wounds. You'll admit this is an outré thing for a Jew to want.

Slam asked me if I was trying to convert and I said, No, so many of my ancestors had been killed in horrible ways by people who were trying to convert them that I just couldn't. Call it loyalty or retrospective historical spite: "FUCK YOU, POPE URBAN II! FUCK YOU, TSAR ALEXANDER! YEAH, YEAH, AND YOU TOO, TORQUEMADA! YOU'RE SUCH A BIG CASTILIAN HARD-ASS, LET ME HEAR YA SAY 'SYNAGOGUE' WITHOUT A LISP!"

And with very few exceptions, conversion strikes me as a kind of social climbing. It's always the high churches that get the wannabes, those Catholics and Episcopalians with their heart-stopping cathedrals and their mitered muckety-mucks. You don't hear of too many Catholics converting to, say, Presbyterianism: "I wanted a God I could picture buying whole-life insurance from." And you want to know who converts to Judaism? People in show business, that's who. Sammy Davis, Jr. Because for *him,* turning Jewish was a positive career move.

I told Slam, "I think I may already have *been* converted, only I'm not sure to what. And I'm not sure it's what I would have chosen. Assuming I had a choice. Do you know what I mean?"

But Slam just looked at me.

So I told her about something that happened to me when I was little. On the day I entered first grade, a kid named Georgie Torres told me about a movie he'd just seen. It was called *The Tingler*. It starred the great Vincent Price, which is something I discovered only when I finally saw it many years later. The movie's central premise was this: Inside every person is a creature called a Tingler. It looks something like a lobster and something like a scorpion, and it lives on the spinal column. Ordinarily a Tingler is very small, but when you get scared, it grows. It thrives on fear. The more scared you get the bigger it grows, like a mosquito ballooning up with blood, until at last it grows big enough to sever your spine with those claws that are now the size of garden shears. Unless, that is, you scream. Screaming is the only thing that will keep the Tingler from killing you.

I was six years old, and I hadn't yet learned to distinguish movies from real life, and I was highly upset by Georgie's story. I remember interrupting him: "Wait, wait, wait. You're saying it lives *inside* you? Where? Show me!" "I dunno, down there someplace. In your back." "No! You're making this up!" "I am not. It says so right in the picture! You don't believe me, go see it yourself. Get your mom to take you." "No, I don't wanna see it! My *mom* doesn't want to see it!"

I brooded about the Tingler on and off for that whole year. I didn't like the sound of it at all. And the next summer my parents took me to a resort in the Catskills, where I spent the days in play group, getting ready for sleep-away camp, while they got ready for their divorce. (And I have to say I was a faster learner than they were, because I was ready for sleep-away camp the next summer while it took my parents another five years of raised voices and slamming doors before they finally split up.) In the evening we'd eat dinner together and then they'd deposit me in the hotel room before they went down to the nightclub to catch Buddy Hackett or Mimi Hines. I think it was the last summer they pretended to have fun together.

Anyway, one night as I lay in bed I found myself thinking about what Georgie Torres had told me. And my back began to itch. It was one of those wily itches that always manages to elude your fingers. And it seemed to me that what I felt was the movement of something scuttling beneath my skin, clawing its way up the rungs of my spine, blindly undulating like some killer grub. And I could feel it growing. I told myself not to be scared, I couldn't be scared, but you know how futile that is. I started breathing in shallow gulps. I was pulling the blanket over my head and yanking it back down. Because of course the thing I was scared of was *inside* me. And finally there was nothing for me to do but scream. It was either that or have my neck snapped like kindling. So I did. I screamed and screamed in my pathetic six-year-old falsetto, and at last someone opened the door—I suppose it must've been un-locked—and came in.

"What's the matter, sweetie?"

Whoever it was didn't turn on the light, but I was pretty sure it was a woman.

"Did you have a bad dream? You must've had a bad dream. I'll bet it was just awful. But you're awake now. Don't be scared. Nothing's going to hurt you. I'm right here."

I never bothered asking who it was, standing by my bed there in the dark. I suppose I was too grateful. It was just a stranger.

Does this explain anything?

But Slam just smiled her charming, gummy smile. She didn't even say, "I'm afraid not." And this silence made me nervous. So I started talking more quickly. I said: Now, if you're a Christian, getting one of Jesus's wounds might be considered a laudable thing to do. You know the *Imitatio Christi*? *The Imitation of Christ*? But if you're a Jew, it's just sacrilege. Let me refer you to Leviticus 19, which forbids the Hebrews to make any markings on their flesh. So here I am: I'm breaking a lesser commandment, I'm defaming Jesus. And I'm violating the tacit rule that Jews do nothing—*nothing*—to chafe the sensibilities of the people whose tolerance we literally depend on for our lives.

I know what you're thinking: Get over it, buddy, this ain't Germany! But let me tell you something. Wherever we go, Jews are like guppies swimming in an ocean filled with sharks. Or with big, unidentified fish that may turn out to *be* sharks, we're never sure. Oh yeah, from a distance that grinning blimp of a thing scudding toward you looks harmless, but don't swim too close, don't be too vivid, whatever you do, don't get too aggressively, outlandishly *offensive,* because that fish has pretty teeth, dear, and he keeps them pearly white.

And we try, we try. Jews do everything they can to sustain the fiction that they're either (a) lovable ethnics who swill down the matzo ball soup and say things like "Enjoy!" or "Enough already!" or (b) just WASPS with yarmulkes and high SAT scores. (Which we are and we aren't. Because your god is a god of Love, and our god is a god of Justice. Or so they say.) The thing is, Jews have this *problem* with God. It's practically a matter of doctrine. Open the Old Testament and what do you find on every page? Indignation, doubt, lamentation, outcry. In Byzantine art the saints are always depicted making a distinctive gesture: palm out, thumb bent, and the first two fingers raised, like a Boy Scout salute. Well, it's a good thing that Judaism prohibits representations of the human form, because otherwise every synagogue would have a ceiling fresco showing the prophets rending their garments with one hand and shaking the other fist at heaven. And it would be generally accepted that the meaning of the gesture was: *This I Need?*

And what else should we be saying, considering the Jewish tendency to become a bloody footnote in other people's history? (Enslaved in Egypt, exiled in Babylon, banished from England, tortured in Spain, lynched in Russia, machine-gunned in Germany, starved in Germany, flayed in Germany, gassed in Germany, frozen in Germany, burned in Germany, burned in Germany, burned in Germany. Smoke over Europe.) Especially if you buy the notion that we were *chosen.* Just try to translate it into human terms. Say you're a small-businessman who agrees to buy protection from a racketeer. Actually, from the *capo di tutti capi.* As long as you make your payments, the Boss will take care of you. And you feel pretty safe, because there's no other Boss before Him and you are the only one He's chosen. But no sooner have you signed up than your shop burns down, your car is bombed, and your kids are snatched from the playground and mailed back to you in pieces. And you might very well ask—as Moses asked, as Job asked, as Jesus asked when he cried out on the cross, *Eli, Eli, lama sabbacthani!*—you might very well ask: Chosen for what?

So I came to the concept of God with what amounted to a genetic memory of grievance. And my family circumstances didn't help. My mother was, to put it mildly, an anxious woman, and she put about as much faith in a Higher Power as she did in whichever doctor she happened to be seeing. My mother saw a lot of doctors and she was always sure that they were lying to her: "What kind of idiot does he think I am, can you tell me? Because he's saying there's nothing wrong with me, when right over the man's shoulder I can see my X ray and there's a spot on it this big! This big, I'm saying!"

And my father? Well, as a young man in Vienna, he'd been a socialist and a hell-raiser, but by the time I was born, my father was forty-one years old, a refugee from three countries and an orphan, since his parents had died in the Holocaust. Along with millions of other people whose entire way of life had been based on the premise that they were Chosen. All those losses had made him not religious, but grudgingly respectful. He'd made his peace with God the same way medieval serfs must have made their peace with the local baron after their last uprising had ended in impaled corpses and burning fields. I doubt they were waving any flags when the guy came riding through to inspect the fiefdom: "How's the Missus, Otho?" "Not well, Sire. Your knights gang-raped her last spring." "Oh, that's right. How terrible for you." That's how it was with my father: He showed up dutifully in synagogue on High Holy Days, he sent me to Hebrew school as a sort of offering, but you couldn't say he loved God; he just knew when he was beaten.

I've always felt that a person's optimism is a measure of one of two basic beliefs: Either he thinks God is good or he thinks that it's possible to get over Him. My parents had no optimism. None. I remember telling them once that all I wanted from life was to be happy. It's one of the last times I remember us sitting together, in the cavernous Upper West Side apartment where the three of us rattled for twelve years like the last three grains of salt in an empty salt cellar. I'm wearing pajamas that make me look like a bit player on *Star Trek,* the plump, bland-faced crewman who gets killed off in the first act. My parents are wearing a blue silk bathrobe with white polka dots and a quilted bed jacket of champagne-colored satin, the kind of outfits Nick and Nora Charles might have on when they were entertaining At Home. We've been fighting. I yell, "All I want is to be happy!" My mother looks over at my father and says, "Then you should never marry someone who doesn't love you." My father doesn't look back. He fumes: "You think life is about being happy? Let me tell you, *shmeggege,* life isn't fun and games and *The Three Stooges* on the television. Life is work. Life is working hard so you can put a bit of bread in your children's mouth. You want to know what happiness is? I'll tell you: Father dies, son dies, grandson dies. That's happiness."

So this was what I grew up believing: that God was there, omnipotent, omniscient, and indifferent, if not actually malign. You were fucked from the beginning and the only reason you observed any of the commandments was you'd be fucked even worse if you didn't. If I'd been a stronger child, I would've been an atheist by age six. But I wasn't strong; I wasn't strong at all. I believed in God the same way I later came to believe in cancer, and when I disobeyed Him it was in more or less the same way I'd light a Camel. I didn't think I was getting away with anything. I just said, "Fuck it," "Fuck *You,*" sullenly, fearfully, with one hand raised against the holy microwaves that were about to blast me to a heap of ash. "Fuck You, God." "Fuck you," when I nursed a hard-on in synagogue, staring at the bosom of Shari Bobrow; "Fuck you," when I played hooky from Hebrew school; "Fuck you," the night before my bar mitzvah, when I went to dinner with my sweet, adoring, infinitely patient grandfather and his very pious brother, who'd come down all the way from western Canada, and they told me to order anything I wanted and I said I'd have the pork chops.

"VAT? VAT ARE YOU SAYING?"

"Pork chops. I want the pork chops."

"Shhh, Peter! You don't know what you're saying! He doesn't know what he's saying, Ziama."

"I do too know what I'm saying. I want pork chops."

"Pfui! You can't eat this . . . this *chazerai!*"

"It's not *chazerai*. It says 'select,' doesn't it? It says it right here on the menu, Uncle Ziama. 'Two of our luscious, select pork chops.' "

"What's wrong with him, Leo? He's getting bar mitzvah and he doesn't know kosher?"

"Sure, he knows kosher. His mother and father keep kosher!"

"Not outside, Grandpa. They let me have whatever I want when we eat out."

"He's making a joke. All the time he's joking, this boy."

"I'm not joking." I'm starting to whine. "I just want the pork chops."

"Have something else, *boychik*. Have the chopped steak. It's just like hamburger. Don't make a *shondah* for the *goyim*."

It was like a highly limited sit-down strike. Except that principle had very little to do with it. God or no God, I really did want the pork chops. And whatever drama my sacrilege might have possessed was sorely diminished by the fact that I wasn't facing down the lowering demiurge of Job, the Author of Suffering Who boils across the horizon like the Father of all Thunderclouds and roars in a voice that splits the rock. (I wasn't even up against my father, who'd once had the power to scare the shit out of me. Before he left.) No, I was arguing with two reedy old men with skin like cracked porcelain and hands that trembled when they got excited, and when I gave in, which of course I did, eventually, it was because I was scared that my blasphemy would kill them.

But sacrilege is a drug. Fear doesn't deter you; it lashes you forward. I went ahead with my bar mitzvah, I let myself be piped into the dwindling ranks of Jewish manhood, and within weeks I'm doing my best to get drummed out. I have no more interest in being part of this *minyan* than I have in belonging to any of the other ones you get press-ganged into as a kid: the Cub Scouts, the Ice Munchkins, the fifth-grade Tonetteers. Fuck 'em all.

One night I'm alone with my resentment and the telephone, and I think of Joshua Mandel. He is the smallest kid in my junior-high-school class. Which gives us something in common, since I happen to be the fattest. We barely know each other, Joshua and I, but we are secretly competing for the status of Eighth Grade Goat. At this point we're running just about neck and neck, except Joshua is slightly ahead since his voice hasn't changed yet and he has the unlucky habit of crying at the least provocation. Joshua Mandel misses a foul shot on the basketball court, he gives a wrong answer in algebra, and the tears spurt out of him like seawater jetting through the rivet holes of a sinking submarine. Joshua, too, has recently been bar mitzvahed, but he's actually proud of it. I think it has less to do with piety than with the fact that he now has some tangible proof that he's not eight years old.

I look up Joshua's phone number in my class list and dial it and when he answers, I put on my deepest, most unctuously authoritative grown-up voice, and I say:

"Am I speaking to Mr. Mandel? Mr. Joshua Mandel?"

"Y-y-yes. That's me." He can't believe he's getting a telephone call from an actual grown-up. It's just like they said it would be: You get bar mitzvahed and the next thing you know grown-ups are calling you on the telephone. You really *are* a man!

"Splendid, splendid. I'm delighted to speak with you. My name is Ariel Himmelfarb. Rabbi Ariel Himmelfarb from the American Council of Rabbis. I'm sure you've heard of us."

"Oh, yes, Rabbi." Not just a grown-up, but a rabbi! Representing an entire council of rabbis!

"Now, Joshua—do you mind if I call you Joshua?—I'm going to tell you something that you can't tell anyone else. Because if it ever reached the wrong ears, it could be very harmful to the Jewish people. Recently we've learned that some unscrupulous person has been impersonating rabbis in the metropolitan area. And he's been performing religious ceremonies under false pretenses. Do you understand what I'm saying, Joshua? It's a terrible, terrible thing I'm talking about here. This individual must be some kind of a madman, another Hitler. Now, what the council is trying to do, Joshua, is find out how much damage he's done. So what I need to ask you, Joshua, is what was the name of the rabbi who did your bar mitzvah? You were recently bar mitzvah, am I correct?"

"Y-y-yes. Two weeks ago. By Rabbi Fishbech."

"And where did this 'Rabbi Fishbech' perform this so-called 'bar mitzvah'?"

"At Sha'are Tefilah, Rabbi. In Larchmont."

I fall silent. Mostly because I'm trying not to laugh. And then I say, "Oh. This is serious. This is very, very serious."

"Wh-wh-what is it, Rabbi? Did I do something wrong?"

"Oh no, not you, my boy. You've done nothing wrong. No, my son, it's *you* who has been wronged. Deeply. Heinously." (I pronounce this word as though it were derived from "heinie," but luckily Joshua's vocabulary isn't any better than my own.) "But it's my regrettable duty to inform you that your 'Rabbi Fishbech' is no rabbi at all. The man who called himself Rabbi Fishbech was an impostor. And your bar mitzvah, I'm afraid, was invalid under Jewish law. Do you know what this means, Joshua? Surely you understand what this means?"

"What, Rabbi? What, what? What does it mean?"

"It means, Joshua, that according to Jewish law"—and now I'm practically vomiting with repressed laughter—"going by Jewish law, YOU ARE NOT A MAN!"

I'm going to go to hell for this. If you were God, wouldn't you send me to hell? Of course you would. Wouldn't you?

But Slam was busy pouring ink into a cup the size of a doll's thimble. For such a macho craft, tattooing has something suspiciously dainty about it: teeny-tiny needles like the points of superfine calligraphy pens, flash that looks like the decals on a third-grader's looseleaf notebook. I had a sudden understanding of tattooing's true appeal: It's Troll-collecting for biker types.

I said, Let me tell you something about this stigma business. In the Gospel of John, Chapter 19, Verse 34, we learn that when Jesus was hanging from the cross, some Roman soldiers came to him and "one of the soldiers with a spear pierced his side, and forthwith came there out blood and water." The next we hear it's three days later and Christ has risen from the tomb and revealed himself to his disciples. And among the disciples is Thomas, the skeptic, the doubter. And Thomas says, "Except I shall see in his hands the print of the nails, and put my finger into the print of the nails, and thrust my hand into his side, I will not believe." You can almost hear the whispers and the indignant rustle of apostolic robes. Oooh, that Thomas is really asking for it! But Jesus grants Thomas's request. He proffers his flank with its mysterious, tear-shaped rent, like something made not in flesh but in canvas, and he—I don't quite know how to say this—he lets Thomas *fist* him.

I'm not making this up. Read the Gospel of John. Or look at the Caravaggio painting that illustrates this verse. It makes Robert Mapplethorpe look like a photographer for Hallmark greeting cards. But I find Thomas's exchange with Jesus extremely moving. In all the other Gospels the risen Christ displays himself in tawdry majesty, like a comic book superhero: TAAA-DAAAH! Personally, if you don't mind a Jew saying so, I find this tacky. No, no, give me John, any day. Because it's here that the Son of God acknowledges the normal skepticism of one of his followers, who has seen him die and wants to be sure that he isn't dreaming or hallucinating. And Christ proves his divinity by presenting Thomas with the bloody evidence of his mortality, by letting him rummage in the flesh that was rent and harrowed like the flesh of the humblest thief. All the eroticism, sado- and homo-, of this scene aside, what I find most affecting about it is its humility. Because there aren't many moments in the literature of any of the world's religions in which God submits to the dispassionate scrutiny of man. In which he lets himself be *seen*.

And of course it's fitting that out of all the apostles it would be Thomas whom Christ permitted that extraordinary touch. Since, according to some Gnostic gospels, Thomas was Jesus's twin. Which, as I'll get around to explaining, is something we have in common.

You'll be happy to know that after that phone call to Joshua Mandel my days of sacrilege were over. I'd finally realized that it's impossible to piss God off. You can't even get His *attention*. Any idiot who's even heard of the Holocaust ought to know that much. So the next thing you know, I'm sixteen and I'm doing a lot of drugs and I'm reading Jack Kerouac and Alan Watts and D. T. Suzuki, and I've decided that what I am is a Zen Buddhist. Zen Buddhism is very attractive to me, (a) because in Zen they don't even mention God, it's all Void and whatnot; and (b) because in my limited understanding a Zen Buddhist can smoke grass and drink Boone's Farm Apple Wine and boff, or try to boff, fifteen-year-old girls. As long as he doesn't make the mistake of believing that they actually *exist*.

Twice a week after school I faithfully make my way to the New York Zen Center, this cool, whitewashed island of silence that floats above the heat and filth and hammering, blatting chaos of upper Manhattan. I take off my shoes in the vestibule and bow to the monk. The monk is Japanese, which means he has the same prestige as a Viennese shrink; you can't get any better. And even though my hair hangs down to the middle of my back and has the consistency of something tossed in a light vinaigrette, the monk bows back to me. He may even smile, though with these cats it's hard to tell: They're so serene they're like minerals. And I step with reverent care between the tatami mats where dozens of other people are silently sitting zazen, and I find one that's vacant and I fold myself down onto a cushion with my legs crossed and my hands resting loosely open on my knees. I cup them to receive the pure white liquid of satori. And I lower my eyes until they are gaz-

ing at a point on the floor precisely six feet before me. And I begin
to meditate.

Except that before leaving school that afternoon, I sneaked into
the boys' bathroom and in one of the stalls shot up some crystal
methedrine; this is a skill I've recently acquired. And it turns out to
be very difficult to be both a practicing Zen Buddhist and a speed
freak, because the goal of Zen meditation is to put the mind in neutral, and speed stomps down on the brain's accelerator like some
crazed redneck Richard Petty wannabe. So here I am, sitting in the
prescribed Zenly posture, feeling each Zenly breath percolate
down into the pit of my Zenly being and then puff slowly outward
into the universe, gazing at Nothing. And in the meanwhile my
blood is pounding, my eyeballs are pinwheeling. And my brain is
fizzing with random ideation:

"Say, just how far does my breath travel when it leaves my
mouth? How far before it stops being *my* breath and becomes just
air? Oxygen, nitrogen, carbon dioxide . . . But if it's been inside
me, it must have little bits of me mixed up in it. Dead skin. *Mucous*
membrane. Tiny invisible flakes of mucous membrane, and somebody else is breathing them in at this very moment! Maybe the
master. Maybe that cute chick over there. Millions of particles,
whole *nebulae* of nasal slough, which of course she realizes, only
she's too enlightened to show how disgusted she is. Oh, man, now
she'll never have anything to do with me!"

And then the observing part of me bellows: "STOP IT! STOP
IT RIGHT THERE! LOOK AT YOU, ALL YOU EVER
THINK ABOUT IS SEX AND SNOT! YOU'RE SUPPOSED
TO BE BLANK, YOU SCHMUCK! BLANK! BLANK!
BLANK!"

The trouble with Buddhism—apart from its basic incompatibility
with speed—is desire. A Buddhist isn't supposed to desire *anything*.
And at sixteen I was a highly desiring being. As I am now. But at

that age the desire was so much fiercer and more ruthless, more global, more devouring. At sixteen I was a seething Jell-O of want thinly contained in skin. What did I want? I wanted to be happy. Yeah, I still wanted that. I wanted to have a body like Keith Richards's and a voice like Jim Morrison's and hair like Big Brother and the Holding Company's—the entire band's. I wanted not to miss my father. I wanted him to take me away to live with him. I wanted him to leave me alone. I wanted my mother to stop crying all the time. I wanted not to feel like crying when she yelled at me. I wanted Kathleen Kenneally to love me. I wanted to overthrow the fascist government of Amerika and march down Pennsylvania Avenue brandishing the Viet Cong flag and a Kalashnikov rifle. I wanted to be the one acidhead who stays calm enough to coax the other heads down from their solitary crags of panic, like Bruce Dern in *The Trip:* "Be cool, be cool, man. *Flow with the fear.*" I wanted Kathleen Kenneally to go to bed with me. I wanted Laura Ross to go to bed with me, too, though I didn't much care if she loved me. And I wanted not to want so constantly and hopelessly, like someone out of those torch songs I hadn't yet learned to love but found myself responding to with a shameful thrill of recognition every time I heard them. Shameful because their tone of unappeasable yearning seemed somehow womanly, and of course they were always sung by women, women appealing to or raging at or grieving over men who were always halfway out the door—men who were totally unlike me. Because the moment a girl showed the least bit of interest in me, I practically haunted her and I panted for her touch in a way that would have disgraced a Labrador retriever.

By the time I was in my sophomore year of college, I'd fallen in love with dozens of girls who told me that they wished other guys were as sensitive as I was just before they rejected me. Well, "rejec-tion" is a value judgment. Let's say that those girls and I had diverging interests. I just wasn't their cup of tea. And what I want to do now is provide a partial list of their names, just in case one of them is reading this: Lisa Todaro, Page Soltvedt, Lindsay Huffman, Jan Fisher, Lisa Leibman, Rebecca Smith, Margy Kaplan, I could go on all day. These were the untouchable objects of my longing, the innocent tinder of my misery. Every time I tried to see through the veil of desire, what I saw was them. Their faces shimmered before me. Their voices sang in my head. I swear, once I was meditating in a meadow upstate and I began to smell Margy Kaplan's perfume, though there was no one around for miles. And if you're a Buddhist who's devoted every waking second to shrugging off attachment, this is like being Satanically possessed.

But around this time I came across *The Interior Castle* by Saint Teresa of Avila, who experienced God's love as a lance driven into her heart and whose mystical classic reads like the log of a lover's vigil. And I identified. I identified with her holy lechery, with her heartsickness. I identified with the times she loses patience with her fickle heavenly lust-muffin (See? See? Even *He* won't commit!) and snaps, "If this is how you treat your friends, no wonder you don't have many!" I identified with the futile hope that kept her waiting night after night for his return, kneeling alone in her cell in a Carmelite convent like a teenaged girl waiting for the phone to ring on a Saturday night.

And I suddenly realized that Buddhism just wasn't me. Instead of trying to negate desire, why not go with it? Why not just direct it to a more appropriate object? Because in some inarticulate way I understood that my desire was a kind of Platonic form—I *had* taken freshman philosophy—and those girls were just the shadows it cast on the walls of my cave. And as long as I was going to go on yearning for someone who would never give a shit about me, I might as well go the whole nine yards: I might as well long for God.

This is how I decided to become a Catholic.

Except that all I knew from Catholicism was scarlet robes, confessionals, burning incense, and Gregorian chants. And, of course, that sexy saint, whose notorious statue, the one by Bernini, I'd seen in my art history class and couldn't help noticing depicted its subject laid out in an orgasmic swoon. And since in those days I sexualized *everything,* I ended up confusing the Triune God with Saint Teresa herself. She was the one I prayed to nightly for the next six months, an earnest, long-haired, somewhat chunky kid, dressed in denim overalls, if I remember correctly, with a tie-dyed headband cutting off the blood flow to my brain, kneeling in my dorm room before a homemade shrine containing some holy candles I'd bought on a shopping trip to the Lower East Side (along with three grams of methedrine and one of my very first bags of heroin): "Most revered saint who speaks in the language of orgasm, reveal yourself to the one who adores you. Comfort me in my loneliness. Succor me in my faithlessness. O Teresa, let me feel your love!"

Before I took the leap of formally converting, I decided to make a pilgrimage to Avila. I was also trying to get over Tamara Janicki, a tall, gorgeously cheekboned, damson-mouthed weaving major who'd actually slept with me a couple times before she dumped me. She did it in the kindest way possible ("Oh, Pete, you're such a *great* guy!") but it still hurt. And as I passed among the flayed ocher hills and melancholy roadside towns of northern Spain, as I prayed before innumerable statues in innumerable churches that smelled as though they had just been dredged from beneath the sea, as I got drunk on Rioja and passed out beneath the olive trees and woke at dusk to buy over-the-counter speed at dusty village *farmacias,* pursued by thrilled urchins who crowed, *"Jipi, jipi, jipi,"* at me on account of my ponytail—I kept thinking of her, of Tamara, of Teresa, the two blurred together, as Teresa had already blurred with God, into one luminous image of loss and impossible redemption, Slavic cheekbones and Spanish eyes, lipsticked cigarette butts and a halo, I was like some God-stricken, drug-addled Gatsby gazing at the green light on the far shore, I was heartsick, I was swooning with nostalgia for a past I couldn't remember, for a body I had barely brushed against, I was wigging, I was *gone*. And I finally came to Avila, the one long-haired American—and, I am sure, the only Jew—in a file of elderly pilgrims. I had to help the guide trundle them down the narrow stairway that led beneath the convent to a crypt where the saint's heart was preserved in a glass case. It was a dark, parched thing the size of a fist, and it was encased in a gilded reliquary that looked like an exquisite life-support device built for a dying millionaire. Up until then I'd been ignoring the guide's multilingual spiel, but just then I heard her say, in English that was all the more dignified because of its accent: "And if you look closely at the saint's heart, you will see the wounds God made there." I burst into noisy tears. I don't know whether my fellow pilgrims were moved or horrified, because I staggered up the stairs and out of the church and across the street into a cantina, where I spent the rest of the afternoon getting loaded.

I went on doing this for the next thirteen years.

I asked Slam, Have you ever wondered why opiate addiction is a disease endemic to Christian and Muslim societies? (Forget all those slanders of the poor Confucian Chinese; they never would've started kicking the gong around if the British hadn't forced opium down their throats in the 1840s.) I'll tell you why. It's because the opium high corresponds almost exactly to our innate schema of heaven. That same gliding, disembodied bliss. That magnanimous indifference to hunger or the need for bowel movements. So when someone who grew up in this culture gets his first taste, there's a "ping" of subconscious recognition, a fit between that chastely voluptuous junk high and buried memories of hymns, church sermons, Sunday school lessons. And a voice in-side whispers: *Don't be scared. Nothing's going to hurt you. I'm right here.*

Philip K. Dick—you remember me talking about him?—was al-ways exploring the subterranean connections between drugs and religion. In one novel he has Martian colonists taking a pill that in-duces transubstantiation: You drop it and God is suddenly literally inside you. Which turns out to be not so pleasant. Drugs play a minor role in *VALIS,* whose title is an acronym for "Vast Active Living Intelligence System." In that novel God, or the aforemen-tioned Vast Active Living et cetera, takes the form of a beam of pink light, which strikes the protagonist in the middle of his fore-head, endowing him with, among other things, a sudden inexplica-ble fluency in Biblical Greek. Unfortunately, anyone who apprehends God in this manner ends up dying of brain cancer or stroke. The thing that makes *VALIS* such an unnerving book is that it's so blatantly autobiographical. Dick starts out pretending that the events are happening to another character, but by the book's end he's abandoned that conceit and unveiled himself as his own protagonist. He's writing about a divine visitation experienced by a writer named Philip K. Dick in 1974, following years of drug abuse, the suicide of a woman friend, and his own nervous collapse. In his letters Dick claimed to have had a theophany exactly like the one he describes in *VALIS.* He also acknowledged that he might be absolutely batshit. He may very well have been. And it may be a coincidence that Dick died at an early age, barely a year after he fin-ished *VALIS.* And that the cause of death was a stroke.

In justifying my addiction, I often cited the fact that none of the Western religions specifically prohibits drug use. I'd say, "Look. They've got rules against pork, they've got rules against fucking, they've got rules against *astrology,* for Christ's sake. If any of those guys had had something against dope, don't you think they would've said so?" Later, of course, I realized that the ban is implicit. It's subsumed in the commandment "Thou shalt have no other God before me."

One night during this period, I was dope-sick and trying to cop. This was on the Lower East Side. Late fall, cold, damp. Tuberculosis weather. No one was holding anywhere. And I was finally reduced to giving thirty bucks to some sleazebag I barely knew who said he could get me something. And although I was pretty sure he was going to rip me off, I went ahead with the deal because by this time my addiction had spiraled to the point where I *had* to give money to somebody two or three times a day, no matter what the odds of a return: It was a sort of compulsive charity. I sat down to wait on a bench in the Pitt Street park. It isn't much of a bench. The slats are splintered. The backrest's completely torn away. I look down and where grass ought to be growing I see broken gimmicks and torn glassine envelopes and charred bottle caps. The reason I happen to be looking down is that I've begun to double over with withdrawal cramps, and right on schedule I start vomiting in an acrid stream between my feet.

At this moment I hear someone behind me say, "I am begging your pardon, sir. You are waiting to purchase some heroin?" I look up and there, standing beside my seat of misery, are these two Indian—*East* Indian—guys. They look like engineering students. "My name is Prakyash and my friend is called Sanjay. We are wanting to *cop some shit*." You can tell how proud he is to have remembered this phrase. "You will be able to be assisting us?"

I start to say something but I have to heave again. "Come, come, my friend. Don't be shy with us. Do you think we are narcs?"

"Ha ha ha ha!! Oh Prakyash, you naughty boy! We are not chaffing you, my friend. We are the real McCoy."

I groan like one of the damned.

"We will be tipping you handsomely."

They keep pestering me, practically tugging my sleeves, but they no longer bother me. Because suddenly I am coolly, almost serenely, aware that I am exactly where I belong. I'm not trying to accomplish anything. I'm not pretending to be anything. I'm not trying to convince anyone that I have anything to offer. No skill, no money, no power, no sex, no wit, no love, none of the currencies I've used to pay for my leasehold upon the earth. And at that moment I realize that up till now my entire life has been the life of a guppy, churning its tiny fins to stay afloat, darting ceaselessly to stay out of the jaws of sharks. And what a relief, what an incredible relief it is finally to sink to the bottom.

Now, I'm not sure about the next part; I'm not sure whether it was real or a very elaborate hallucination, though hallucinations aren't a common symptom of heroin withdrawal. Somehow I managed to get up from the bench and away from my new chums and I wandered around the Lower East Side, north to Houston, south to Delancey, and deep into the projects along the East River. And on one of the side streets in between I come across a line of junkies—you recognize your own kind—filing into a ruined warehouse. And I figure I've hit the jackpot. I walk to the end of the line and I ask the guy ahead of me, "What've they got?"

"Is God, man."

And I say, "No shit. Is it decent?" Because I figure he's talking about a brand name, like Suicide or Poison. "God": It's the work of a marketing genius.

But inside the warehouse there are rows of pews. And every pew is filled with junkies. There are black junkies and Anglo junkies and Latino junkies. There are twelve-year-old boys sniffling from their first training-wheel habits and stooped veterans with hands like waterlogged sponges, those hands that everyone calls "New York mittens." There are fashion models with the faces of drowsy angels who've been chauffeured down from townhouses in the East Sixties and who'll powder their tracks with Lancôme before the next day's photo shoot. There are cadaverous, crook-backed junkies who've crawled from beneath rain-soaked packing crates in Tompkins Square Park and whose bodies are gruesome *exempla* of their disease: every vein collapsed, every limb cratered, eyes jaundiced, teeth rotten, dicks gone flaccid as the peeled shrimp in a fishmonger's window—the kind of junkies you always look at and think, At least I'm not *that* bad.

And they're all praying. They pray to statues that stand at the front of the room, amid rows of burning candles. Over there is Saint Sebastian; those arrows are a dead giveaway. And next to him is Saint Barbara, who is invoked against bad habits, and Saint Dymphna, the patroness of nervous disorders and sexual madness. There's the good thief Dismas, and Gestas, the bad thief, who cursed Jesus as he hung dying by his side. There's Dominic Savio, guardian of choirboys and juvenile delinquents. And, naturally, Saint Jude. People pray out loud, one at a time, while the rest of the congregation calls out a response:

"O Lord, hear my prayer. May the man be holding good shit tonight and not dummy."

"Amen."

"May his dope be white as sugar and strong as lye."

"Amen."

"May his coke make me speak with the tongues of parrots."

"Amen."

"Lord, protect me from the pigs of the Ninth Precinct."

"Amen."

"Protect me from those trigger-happy crackheads. Fuckers are crazy."

"Amen."

"Protect me from AIDS."

"Amen."

"Tonight let me find a good vein right away."

"Amen."

"And let me hit it the first time."

"Amen, amen."

As I said, I don't know if this really happened. I never found that church again. I wish I could say that I prayed to get straight and was cured from that night forward: It would make a great story. But I wasn't big on praying then. And I went on using for another year or so, anything I could melt down in a teaspoon and draw up through a syringe. I passed in and out of detoxes and emergency rooms and moved to another city, where I gave up my last illusions of being able to lead anything like a normal life. I spent the six days between Christmas and New Year's Eve of 1985 without speaking to another human being. And then I had a change of heart. Or maybe I should say my heart was changed, since it took place against my will. If you want to know the truth, it was like being shaken mercilessly awake from a long sleep. A sleep in which I was inclined to linger.

You know what that's like. Don't you?

This time the smile Slam gave me struck me as being at least somewhat apologetic. It was the smile you get from well-meaning people who know that the commission of their tasks may have painful consequences for you and have the decency to wish it could be otherwise: the gatekeeper who shrugs as he bars your entry; the cop who clicks her tongue as she writes your ticket; the doctor who sighs as he tells you that your test came back positive.

This is what I discovered when I awoke. My father was dead of cancer. Dead, too, the grandfather and great-uncle I'd shocked so badly twenty years before. Of the people I'd used with, Miguel was dead of AIDS, Frankie had plowed through his car's windshield, Will had killed himself. My mother was still alive, but she was sick and afraid, and more and more it looked as though she was right when she accused her doctors of lying to her. The women I'd suffered over had wisely married other men. Everyone else was a stranger.

My new acquaintances told me that I was unlikely to stay alive without a belief in some sort of deity, something I could appeal to. They'd suggest, "You could say that God got you clean." And I'd answer, "I could say that He fucked me up in the first place." And I'd smile at them. I was very pleased with myself, in a bleak way. The philosopher Berkeley claimed that everything in the universe exists solely as a thought in the mind of God. In response to this Samuel Johnson is supposed to have kicked a stone and said, "I refute him thus!" I was a lot like Johnson in those days, only not as clever. Any time anybody urged me to appeal to a heavenly father, I'd point to the corpse of my earthly one; I'd point to the skull cities erected by the Khmer Rouge; I'd point to the fever that kept me hungering for what had nearly killed me so that I woke up night after night from dreams of heroin with hopeless tears in my eyes: "I refute Him thus!"

Nowhere is it written that Johnson stubbed his toe when he kicked that stone. But he probably did and it probably hurt.

Actually, I was desperate for something to believe in. I was combing through everything from the Book of Job to the Diamond Sutra. I was half crazy with teleological longing piled on top of chemical withdrawal. And I think that's why I reacted as violently as I did late one night, a year or two after I stopped using, when I came across these words: "From loss and grief the Mind has become deranged. Therefore we, as parts of the universe, the Brain, are partly deranged." I literally felt a chill crawl up my spine. Let me say them again: "From loss and grief the Mind has become deranged. Therefore we, as parts of the universe, the Brain, are partly deranged."

This was in *VALIS*, which I'd been reading in a vain effort to entertain myself in my insomnia. And it says something about the nature of revelation that mine came to me in one of the rare moments that I wasn't looking for it, in what I'd thought was a science fiction novel.

As I said, *VALIS* is the story of a man who is either going elaborately crazy or being bombarded with information from something that may be God. And one of the first things he learns is that *God is crazy*. Behind this universe, generating it, infecting it, ticks an unhinged Mind that destroys what it creates, cruelly and purposelessly, over and over and over. This explanation made perfect sense to me. Remember how I told you that being Jewish is like agreeing to buy protection from a racketeer, and then finding out that what you get is just the opposite? You ask an Orthodox why the *capo* isn't standing up for you and he says, "Oh, the boss is very particular. You was supposed to leave the dough in a *manila* envelope! Nine by thirteen." You ask a Kabbalist and he'll tell you, "The boss withdrew from the material universe; he wants you should be self-sufficient." That night I realized: "You wanna know why the boss isn't taking care of you? He can't take care of himself is why! He's too busy trying to catch the butterflies on the fucking wallpaper!"

I read on, drenched with sweat, quivering with nicotine poisoning. The idea of a deranged God, I learned, originates with the Gnostic Christians, who claimed to possess the secret teachings of Jesus. Their gospels portray the Creator as a vengeful paranoid and Christ the Son as His adversary and healer, a divine rabble-rouser who stands with man against God in the prison yard of the world. Some Gnostics go so far as to suggest that the serpent who tempted our ancestors in the Garden was Jesus in another form. "You shall not die," he reassures them. "Rather, your eyes shall open, and you shall become like gods, recognizing evil and good."

And among the Gnostic gospels I found one that purports to be the secret testament of Thomas, who was Jesus's twin. If you accept that Thomas and Jesus were twins, the whole wound business is a little less grisly. Twins, after all, are the sundered halves of a single egg, of a primordial One that drifted in the womb. So when Thomas placed his hand in the rift in Jesus's side he was touching his other self. That second self had once been human, but it had been cast into a furnace and what was merely human in it had been consumed. All that remained of its former nature were the wounds in its hands and feet and side, where blood still flowed. In touching Jesus, Thomas was touching himself made God. But he was touching him in the last place where he remained human.

Reading this, alone in my house at two in the morning in a city whose wholesome nightlife effectively ends at midnight, I remembered something. I was an only child, but when I was a little boy there was a story my mother used to tell me. She'd say, "Before you were born, I had twins. Their names were Ricky and Sacky and they looked just like you. But they wouldn't behave, so I threw them in the river and they drowned." To this day I don't know whether she was trying to entertain me or make an oblique threat—"Shape up, darling, or tonight you sleep with the fishes"—but as a kid I was half convinced that there had once been others like me, other selves who were now gone. Maybe this feeling is common to all children of Holocaust survivors. Maybe we have the equivalent of an amputee's phantom limb syndrome: a pain that emanates from absence. *From loss and grief the Mind has become deranged. Therefore we, as parts of the universe, the Brain, are partly deranged.*

Speaking of those deranged from loss, Philip K. Dick had a twin sister, Jane, who died when they were small children. He went on grieving for Jane long after she had faded from his immediate memory and become only a pervasive sadness and the story that explained it. "Once you had a twin. Then she died and there was just you." As a grown man, Dick kept falling in love with younger women whom he associated with the twin whose death had left him so maimed and incomplete. He married four or five times, but he died alone and he was buried beside the remains of his first companion. I found a photograph of their grave that night and what struck me was that they share a single headstone. The epitaph reads: "Jane Dick. Philip K. Dick. Twins."

All of this, you've got to understand, was racing through me at the nauseating speed of insomniac thought as I sat before my ziggurat of reference books. The protagonist of *VALIS* receives his divine transmissions in sudden, epileptic bursts, information as seizure. That's what it was like for me: "*VALIS*. Gnostics. God. Jesus. Madness. Wounds. Thomas. Twins." Bang, bang, bang, bang, bang. And by the time I had seen the sun rise over the alley, with its tiny, valiant gardens and its stiff-tailed cats marching home for breakfast after the night's prowl, this is what I'd decided: that what I'd suffered from all my life was the loss of a twin, not the ones my mother had made up, but a twin who had died before I was born, maybe in another lifetime, though the idea of reincarnation has never appealed to me. I wasn't the only person to have been bereft in this manner. There'd been others like me, others who'd been anchored to this second self and then cut loose, unmoored from him—or her: I had the idea that the absent one had different genders at different times. One, I was pretty sure, had been Philip K. Dick. Even in his fiction his sadness and wistful fantasies of restitution seemed so much like my own. And of course there was Thomas, whose longing for his sundered twin had been so fierce, so unhinging, that it had driven him to plunge his hand into the other's riven flesh. What I'm trying to say is that sometime that morning I came to the conclusion—though I don't know if you can call it that, "conclusion" sounds so *reasonable*—I came to the conclusion that I was Jesus's secret twin.

Don't stop me. There's more.

I was very discreet in my madness. I didn't go out and declare myself. I just cherished the glow of my private knowledge. I practiced Gratitude, Modesty, Compassion: I hoped that if I did so long enough I might stop thinking of them in capital letters. I hoped that if I did so long enough I might somehow become worthy of my twin.

For a while I volunteered in a children's hospital, where once a week I'd work with kids whose bodies were living evidence that the Creator of this universe was insane. Many of them suffered from dwarfism, which can be partially corrected these days, but only at the cost of an excruciating procedure that entails breaking and setting the legs over and over and over again for a period of months or years. The kids with dwarfism had their broken limbs encased in vicious-looking steel birdcages that held the ends of the bone an inch or so apart so that they'd lengthen as they grew together. They were in constant pain. It was an effort to get them to do anything, and you wouldn't have dreamed of suggesting that they play.

There were three boys who'd been burned hideously in a tenement fire. At first I could barely stand to look at them: Their faces were noseless masks; their hands were gauze-wrapped talons. But at the same time they were tough little boys from Baltimore's inner city. They called me "Yo" and when we played cards, they cheated. They cheated me and they cheated each other, and if I called them on it they looked at me with what I eventually realized were grins of defiance. Even burned like that, they could still grin.

One day I was working with a group in the art studio and one of the three—I think his name was Elvin—began to rub his head against my side. It was a totally unexpected gesture of love and trust. I felt myself choke with tenderness. I reached down and patted Elvin on the head. And he scowled up at me; I could tell he was scowling for the same reason that at other times I could tell he was grinning. He said, "Who the fuck you touching, man?" And I realized that the only reason Elvin had rubbed against me was because his head itched and he couldn't scratch it with those mummified claws of his. Love and trust had nothing to do with it.

And in that moment I was cured. My delusion ended. I'm not

crazy anymore. Or not crazy in the same way. I have no twin. Not Jesus. Not Philip K. Dick. It was pretty to think so, but the truth is I'm an only child and I've spent most of my life alone and if my heavenly double were to show up on my doorstep tomorrow and say, "Did you miss me?" I wouldn't know what to do. Probably the same thing I used to do when friends came over for dinner or a girlfriend stayed overnight. As glad as I was for their company, the moment they'd leave I'd find myself stowing their plates in the dishwasher, mopping their footprints—footprints I couldn't even *see*—off the floor.

What stayed with me from that time was the habit of prayer. I pray most nights, the way you see children pray: on my knees at the foot of the bed, with my hands folded before me. The way I see it, the fact that I'm praying at all is so weird that I might as well go the whole nine yards. I have no idea Who I'm praying to. For a while there I'd begin by saying "Father." But one night, not too long ago, I slipped and what came out was "Fucker." I didn't apologize. It sounded right. I went on: "Fucker, why have you forsaken me? Don't pretend you don't know what I'm talking about. Fucker, why did you burn my grandparents in ovens? What about all those other grandparents? The ones who are still burning. Why did you make my father so sad? Why did he and my mother hate each other? Why did you give him that cancer? Why couldn't you have killed Ronald Reagan? They were exactly the same age! Believe me, Fucker, a lot of Nicaraguans would be thanking you. Why did you kill Will and Miguel and Frankie? Why did you spare me? Thanks a lot, Fucker, but why couldn't you have cured me while you were at it? Why did you make me so greedy and sniveling and self-pitying and morose? Why did you put a hole in my nature? Why am I thirty-four and alone? Why don't I know how to love anybody? Why won't you make me good? Answer me! Why the fuck won't you answer me? Answer me!"

• • •

Oh, I hate to repeat all the things I yelled. Because by now I was yelling for real, there in that apartment that had steel gates on its windows and three locks on its door to keep out the larcenous armies of my fellow sufferers. I ranted on as poor Slam washed me with Hibiclens and transferred the design she'd copied from a Dürer woodcut onto my skin, starting at my rib cage and ending just above the waistband of my jeans. She never complained, though I was only paying her for a tattoo.

"Try to hold still," she said, and she turned on the motor of her tattoo gun. "This may hurt."

3

I GO PRIMITIVE

Now that the Polynesian islands have been smothered in concrete and turned into aircraft carriers solidly anchored in the southern seas, when the whole of Asia is beginning to look like a dingy suburb, when shanty towns are spreading across Africa, when civil and military aircraft blight the primeval innocence of the American or Melanesian forests even before destroying their virginity, what else can the so-called escapism of travelling do than confront us with the more unfortunate aspects of our history? The first thing we see as we travel round the world is our own filth, thrown into the face of mankind.

Claude Lévi-Strauss, TRISTES TROPIQUES

I'll tell you something. You can be traveling to any destination on the surface of the earth—Burkina Faso, Kazakhstan, the Falkland Islands—and if your flight originated in the United States, there will always be one asshole on board who's wearing the grown-up counterpart of rompers: a Day-Glo baseball cap and matching shorts or golf slacks, and maybe a sweatshirt in some snuggly, washable fabric that looks suspiciously like terry cloth. It's as though the government of the world's most powerful and trigger-happy republic were secretly instructing a select group of its citizens to dress like three-year-olds whenever they went abroad. To reassure the natives. "Don't be scared, amigos. We're harmless."

It was 1992 and I was on my second flight to Indonesia, and I'm relieved to say that I was not the asshole with the Day-Glo baseball cap. I was the asshole with the Banana Republic "correspondent's vest," the kind that has enough cargo pockets to accommodate the newsroom of a small Midwestern daily, and a pair of army-surplus fatigue pants that had even more pockets, along with eight earrings and three tattoos. My friend Dean was the guy with the same vest and a red bandanna tied dashingly around his forehead. My friend Flipper *was* wearing a baseball cap, but it was olive-drab, and it accessorized a seersucker jacket, so that all in all he looked like a low-level civilian employee—a defoliants expert, say—of the U.S. Army during its doomed adventure in Vietnam. Which is where Flipper would have preferred to be going. "Why do you have to go back to Borneo? There's nothing to buy there. You said so yourself."

"I never said there's nothing."

"Okay, they've got trading beads. Big deal. In Vietnam they've got mortar shells. They've got mortars! That *work!* They've got engraved cigarette lighters that say 'Da Nang, 1968 to 1969. When I die I'll go to heaven, 'cause I've spent my time in hell.' Do you know what those things go for at the flea market? Do you have any idea?"

The guy with the Day-Glo baseball cap had boarded in L.A. and was now sitting in the aisle across from us. He was named Buddy. His cap was the color of Gatorade, the original lime flavor, and his shorts were the same color. I'd say that his sport shirt was more of a lemon shade. Fashion sense is not a window onto the soul, and you couldn't blame Buddy for not having any. He was thirty-six years old and had spent almost every minute of it in Opelousas, Louisiana. A couple times he'd been over to Shreveport and Baton Rouge. Never to New Orleans. "Ugly things go on in that town," he told me. "Lord, you wouldn't believe."

Up until a few months before, Buddy had been a demolitions technician in a salt mine. It sounded like a decent job, getting paid to gratify the manly instinct for blowing things up without any loss of life or property. "What it is is you plant these charges in these big old salt domes and you set 'em off by remote. Them domes is rock-solid, but when one of those bad boys goes off, that salt comes raining down like Morton's. I'll tell you boys, it's good pay, but it's hell on the skin. Feel my arm. Skin's just like some old grandmama's."

Under normal circumstances Buddy would have spent the rest of his life blowing up salt domes and rubbing Vaseline Intensive Care Lotion into his ravaged skin and praying at his Assemblies of God church. But a while ago he'd fucked up his back on the work site, and disability had given him a check for a hundred thousand dollars. Don't tell me America isn't an amazing country, or that its people aren't capable of turning their lives 180 degrees on a dime. Because Buddy was using that money to go to Indonesia and, even more incredibly, to Kalimantan in Borneo, a place that's commonly portrayed as the heart of darkness, impassable jungle and reeking swamp, trees like prehistoric megaliths, vines like strangling malignant growths, beetles big as fists, spiders fat as goose-down pillows, man-eating tigers, shrieking viral monkeys, and a populace of stunted Dayak headhunters who'd grin like crackers at a Fourth of July pig barbecue as they scooped the hot pulp from your brainpan and slopped it out to their dogs. I don't know whether Buddy had this exact mental schema. Mine was gleaned from Conrad, Tarzan, Lowell Thomas, *Bomba the Jungle Boy,* and the pseudo-documentary *Shocking Asia.* But he was going to Borneo to join up with an Assemblies of God mission there and spread the gospel to the same natives I'd once imagined using human skulls for a xylophone.

"They tell me there's still cannibals over there. They tell me there's people there ain't never even *heard* of Jesus."

"Yeah, but they've heard of Matlock," Flipper snickered; he always cracks up at his own jokes. "Peter, didn't you say all those Dayaks watch *Matlock*?"

I said, "No, they all watch *MacGyver*."

When I'd traveled through Kalimantan the year before, I'd seen hundreds of people wearing MacGyver T-shirts. They might have been some kind of foreign aid. You passed someone in a village and he'd call out the equivalent of "Where're you from?" and if you said "America," he'd give you the thumbs-up and yell "MacGyver!" At the time I didn't know who MacGyver was. I think the show went off the air in this country in the 1970s.

I was pissed at Flipper, who'll talk to anybody. I really didn't want Buddy to know that I'd been in Kalimantan or that the three of us were on our way back there. I was scared he'd want to make friends. And I didn't want to make friends with an eager, tubby peckerwood—a delegate from a region that in my own benighted way I thought of as *a prehistoric earth, an earth that wore the aspect of an unknown planet*—a peckerwood, moreover, who dressed like a guest on *Barney the Dinosaur* and was going off to evangelize blameless heathens with two dozen copies of the *Good News Bible*. I wanted to lecture Buddy on the evil wrought by missionaries, from smallpox to shanty towns where drunken Apache or Yupik or Walbiri squatted numbly amid the wreckage of their cultures, wondering what the hell had happened. I wanted to ask him if he thought he'd be doing the Dayaks a favor by getting them to trade a multitude of indulgent little gods for one big jealous one. I wanted to tell him that religion—any religion—is to spirituality what prostitution is to sex. But I said nothing. I just glared at Buddy—and at Flipper—as the two of them argued about salvation. Flipper will argue about anything. He had just asked Buddy who'd want to convert to a faith that had Tammy Bakker for a spokeswoman. And Buddy was chuckling, "Flipper—what kind of name is that anyway?—

where'd you ever get the idea that Christians is perfect people? Lord, you don't have to be perfect to be a Christian. All you got to do is be willing to follow the One who is."

Borneo is not a stopover to anywhere. Nobody goes there without a reason. Buddy was on his way to harvest souls. Flipper was going because he was my oldest friend and he thought I was too dumb to go wandering through the rain forest without a keeper: "I know you, you'll come back with a motorboat's propeller pin through your dick. You'll pay some *witch doctor* to do it!"

Dean was going to detox from one of those insanely destructive love affairs that make a man and a woman taunt and harry and degrade each other every moment that they aren't fucking. He couldn't say his girlfriend's name without it coming out as a groan, and if you ran into the two of them in public, he would give you the look of a captive gazing up from a pit, a look that simultaneously conveyed two messages: "For God's sake, get me away from this woman!" And "For God's sake, leave us alone!" I could identify: Sexual anguish is my natural habitat.

I was going—well, at the time I thought I was going to Kalimantan to correct a mistake I'd made on my last visit, when my anthropologist friend Charlotte had invited me to a village called Kasongan to take part in a *tiwah,* the ceremony that is as sacred to the Ngaju Dayaks as Easter Mass is to devout Catholics. It may be even more sacred, since at *tiwahs* the supernatural manifests itself not just symbolically but tangibly. When a Catholic priest gives Communion, the wine he sips is supposed to turn into God's blood, but how are you supposed to tell? It's not as if he sprouts a halo. When the Ngaju ritual specialist goes into a trance, he starts speaking in the voices of the ancestors who were present at the midwifing of the world. And you actually hear it: a drowsy, high-pitched keening that sounds uncannily like one of those old-time bluegrass singers, the ones you can listen to only on 78s so scratched that they seem to be calling out from a dust storm in the moment before it swallows them forever:

> *Well, I've done all I could do*
> *To try and get along with you*
> *And I ain't gonna be treated this way.*

At the *tiwah* I attended, as I've said, I actually heard the voice of what I can describe only as a demon—either a demon or an extremely nasty anima projection—howling from the throat of a young man who had been possessed. He writhed and gibbered, he convulsed with supernatural electricity, and the sound that came out of him was no more human than the shriek of some prehistoric bird. *The commonest sort of fortitude prevents us from becoming criminals in a legal sense; it is from weaknesses unknown, but perhaps suspected, as in some parts of the world you suspect a deadly snake in every bush—from weakness that may lie hidden, watched or unwatched, prayed against or manfully scorned, repressed or maybe ignored more than half a lifetime, not one of us is safe.* On the night of the *tiwah* I came face-to-face with my weakness, and it drove me from Kasongan on the next boat. If I'd stayed, I might have seen and heard things that would have changed my life—that would have set it right. *I may look as genuine as a new dime, but there is some infernal alloy in my metal.* I have spent years trying to smelt it out.

When I came back to the States, I was like someone under a curse. Everything that had been familiar now felt strange to me, and constricting and false. I was lonely but I avoided friends. I didn't know how to be around women: I forgot how to make small talk; I forgot how to kiss. Or, really, it was more that I could imagine kissing only one person, who was all but dead to me, and the few times I tried to practice with others—I'd once thought of kissing as a nice thing to do—it was all wrong. *Every day I was in dispute with an invisible personality, an antagonistic and inseparable partner of my existence.* And it kept nagging me: *What a chance missed! My God! What a chance missed!* I don't know. Maybe I couldn't tolerate the evidence of my own cowardice. Maybe leaving a *tiwah* before you're supposed to is like turning off a computer in the middle of an application: Something crashes. Maybe I had just succumbed to the malady that Lévi-Strauss says is endemic among anthropologists, though God knows I'm hardly an anthropologist: *Through being exposed to such complete and sudden changes of environment, he acquires a kind of chronic rootlessness; eventually, he comes to feel at home nowhere, and he remains psychologically maimed.*

And then one day I got a letter from Charlotte, who was still sweltering over her fieldwork in a malarial entrepôt in central Kalimantan and, I imagined, gravely shaking her head at the recollection of my unsoundness. "Most irregular," I pictured her telling her cronies over a round of gin-and-tonics at the club (though Charlotte wasn't English, and the closest thing to a club in the hellhole where she was living was a "luxury" hotel that served weak beer to lonely civil servants from Jakarta). *There never was a man so mercilessly shown up by his own natural impulse. A single moment had stripped him of his discretion—of that discretion that is more necessary to the decencies of our inner being than clothing is to the decorum of our body.* But in her letter, Charlotte told me that she'd met a Dayak ethnologist who'd offered to guide her up the Mahakam River, in the eastern part of the island, up into regions where the roads dwindle into footpaths that wind through soaring ironwood forests and the inhabitants still stretch their earlobes with heavy brass rings and embroider their flesh with fantastically ornate tattoos. Would I like to join her?

And I thought, *Ah what a chance! My God! What a chance!*

So I decided to go back to Borneo, and Dean and Flipper announced they were going with me. But before I left, I went up to New York to see my tattooist. It sounds so bourgeois to say "my

tattooist"—it's like saying "my hairdresser," or "my color consultant"—but by now that's how I thought of her. Tattooing *is* an inti-
mate transaction, and the fact is that while getting tattooed I'd also
burdened Slam with the story of most of my life. I'd told the poor
woman more in two hours than I have most psychiatrists, and I've
been in one kind of psychotherapy or another for close to twenty
years. I suppose Slam had become that thing I have never quite believed exists: a safe person. I trusted that she would never disfigure
me or infect me with hepatitis or fall in love with me (she was a lesbian, after all) or suffer me to fall in love with her. And I knew that
she would bear my confidences not just stoically but with at least a
pretense of enthusiasm. This last is a rare quality among tattooists,
who as a group are as cynical as vice cops and as omniscient as
Stephen Hawking. Whatever you may have to tell them they already know. And they couldn't be less interested.

When I walked into Slam's tenement studio, she poured me
some goldenseal tea (good for the immune system) and had me admire the scrawny butterscotch kitten she'd rescued from a neighborhood Dumpster. She had three more cats, and to some of her
colleagues their presence in the studio would have marked Slam as
a dirty woman. But tattooists are always bad-mouthing one another, and the cats didn't bother me at all. Then she said, "You
going to get another stigma? I've been telling everybody about
your last. You're famous as the Jewish guy with a Jesus tat—I think
you're the only one on the East Coast. So what's it going to be
today? The hands or the feet?"

I said, "Oh, one's enough for me. This time I was thinking of
something pagan." And I showed her the design that she subse-
quently inked on my left ancient biceps. It looks something like a
cross between a wheel and a swastika (a symbol that a Canadian
performance artist calling himself ManWoman has sought to de-
liver from its unwholesome connotations by having dozens tattooed on his person. This is what's known as sacrificing oneself for

an idea). But to the Iban and Punan Dayaks of northern Borneo it's known as "the Dragon Dog," and it expresses the cosmic unity of male and female principles. Slam thought the Iban and Punan must be groovy, gender-sensitive people. I didn't tell her that until quite recently they had also been avid headhunters.

Most tattoos are signifiers of the past, commemorating events that have already transpired. That's how I see most of mine. They are the snapshots I was too slow to take, the journals I was too lazy to keep. But tattoos may also act upon the future, protect the body from impending danger or consecrate it for some arduous task ahead. The Iban employed certain designs as talismans against evil spirits. In Thailand you come across men who have verses from the sutras tattooed on their chests. They're veterans, mostly, and they got their markings before they crossed the border to fight in Vietnam or Laos back in the 1960s. They believed that the tattoos would make them bulletproof, and they may have done the trick, since the guys I saw were all alive. I told Slam that I saw my new tattoo as preparation. I didn't specify what for. I was pretty sure that Borneo was no more dangerous than many other places I'd been. But having lost my nerve there once, I wanted at any cost to avoid a further occasion for regret, and I was desperate enough to try a tattoo on the same principle that someone else might resort to prayer or aromatherapy.

Slam liked the idea of me walking into an Iban village sporting her version of a traditional Iban tattoo. "You'll be the first West-erner these people have ever seen, and you'll be carrying my ink. I feel like a *goodwill ambassador!* Remind me to give you some of my business cards. You never know." As I said, I found her enthusiasm attractive, but at that moment I almost wished she'd been more jaded. You don't want too much enthusiasm from someone who's drilling an intricate pattern into your upper arm.

"I just hope they don't take it the wrong way," she added. It was the first time I'd ever seen her look sad. "That happened to me once." And then she told me this story while she worked on me, the tattoo gun connecting us with its thread of current and distress. Every so often she'd pause to clean the tip and swab up my blood with a gauze pad. Tattooing isn't an especially gory business and I'm not a heavy bleeder, but there's always some blood involved.

The summer she was eight, Slam's parents had packed her and her brothers in the station wagon and driven across the country. And one of the places they'd stopped was a Sioux reservation in South Dakota, near Mt. Rushmore. They stayed in a motel that had a huge neon war bonnet out in front and a souvenir shop next door. Slam's father bought all sorts of junk for the kids, and they drove onto the reservation wearing moccasins and headdresses, the old man included. "My dad's a really decent guy," Slam confessed, "but he can be kind of a doofus."

Right away Slam Senior—I still don't know their last name—started talking to some men who were lounging outside a store. They looked just like television Indians, Slam recalled, except for their cowboy boots and flannel shirts. As young as she was, it was pretty clear to her that they wanted nothing to do with white people—"They looked at us like we were shit"—so she was surprised when the Sioux asked her father if he and his kids—Mrs. Slam was pointedly not included—would like to watch something they called a "secret sunrise ceremony" at dawn the next day.

Slam didn't want to go, but once her father got an idea in his head, the whole family had to submit to it for fear of hurting his feelings. So at four the next morning they were waiting by the trading post, their breath steaming in the cold, and although she'd expected the worst, the Indians did show up with a pickup truck, and they clambered in and drove off into the hills. They ended up at the foot of Mt. Rushmore. "Have you ever been to Mt. Rushmore?" Slam asked me. "It's really amazing. You think, What could be tackier than a bunch of politicians' heads hacked into the side of a mountain, right? But when you look up the slope, you can't tell who they are, not even what race. They could be those stone heads on Easter Island. They could be gods."

They climbed and they climbed until they were at the summit, gazing down at the Presidents' big stone foreheads and the entire state of South Dakota. And the Indians began the ceremony. They told the family to watch them and copy their movements exactly, it was very important, and then they began to chant in that groaning way we all know from television and dance around the observation deck. Slam and her father and brothers sang and danced right along with them. "And then," she said, "these Sioux guys danced over to the guardrail, with the four of us following. And they all unzipped their jeans and whipped out their dicks—I'd never seen a grown-up's dick before—and they pissed down the side of the mountain, onto the faces of Washington, Lincoln, Jefferson, and I guess Teddy Roosevelt. They hosed them all down. If it had been just him, I'm sure my dad would've whizzed along with them, but I was there. And just as he was apologizing—he really felt terrible about it—we saw that the Indians were laughing at us. I mean *roaring*. They were laughing their heads off at these stupid white people who'd been ready to piss on their own Presidents."

Twenty years later I could tell that Slam was still bitter about this incident, and her bitterness felt like a reproach. I told her, "I had a Shoshone friend once."

She said, "Well, for your sake, I hope she had a nicer sense of humor."

Actually, my friend Dinah *did* have a nasty sense of humor, but it was democratically nasty. She used to call her own people "Kai-yais"—as in "Kai-yai-yai!" And she had cruel things to say about the strangers who were always coming up to her and announcing, out of nowhere, "You know, I'm one-sixteenth Indian myself." "Do perfect strangers come up and tell *you* that they're one-sixteenth Jewish, or is it just us who've got to put up with this shit? This bitch is blond as Meg Ryan, and she's telling me she's Indian. What is it with white people? One day they're exterminating you, the next they're adopting you."

I don't remember how I answered Dinah at the time. I might have said that wherever they go, whites always view the natives with terror and disgust until they've eradicated them, at which point they can *afford* to feel nostalgic. I might have compared it to the way men think fondly, even longingly, of women they once treated like shit. I might have told her the story of the first white men who came to what is now Yosemite National Park in 1851. They were soldiers, naturally, and they were hunting down a band of Indians led by the chief Ten-ie-ya, whom they eventually captured by the lake that now bears his name: Lake Tenaya. Recalling these events afterward, one soldier wrote: "When Ten-ie-ya reached the summit, he left his people and approached where the captain and a few of us were halting. . . . I called him up to us, and told him that we had given his name to the lake and the river. At first he seemed unable to comprehend our purpose, and pointing to the group of glistening peaks near the head of the lake, said, 'It already has a name; we call it Py-we-ack.' Upon my telling him that we had named it Ten-ie-ya, because it was upon the shores of the lake that we had found his people, who would never return to it to live, his countenance fell and he at once left our group and joined his family circle. His countenance indicated that he thought the naming of the lake no equivalent for his loss of territory."

I believe Dinah would have appreciated this story, with its laminae of romantic melancholy, imperial guilt, and postmodern irony. She would have especially enjoyed hearing it from me. *Ours was one of those strange, profound, rare friendships between brown and white, in which the very difference of race seems to draw two human beings closer by some mystic element of sympathy.*

I met her in Baltimore, where we were both displaced persons. I'd come there fleeing the uglier aspects of my life in New York.

Dinah had moved there from Chicago to go to graduate school, with a husband who left her a month later. One summer she moved down the block from me. I couldn't help noticing her. No other woman in that neighborhood had black hair—hair so black it suggested a cloak of invisibility, a cloak of night—worn straight down to midback, or such a heavy, sullen jaw, or skin like speckled bronze, or a way of looking at you that was at once hostile and fearful and amorous, as though she wanted you but was scared of the consequences, and angry at you for arousing her. All of which turned out to be true.

I suppose you think it is a story that you can imagine for yourselves. We have heard so many such stories, and the majority of us don't believe them to be stories of love at all. For the most part we look upon them as stories of opportunities: episodes of passion at best, or perhaps only of youth and temptation, doomed to forgetfulness in the end, even if they pass through the reality of tenderness and regret. The truth is I wanted Dinah before I knew I wanted her. At the time I met her I was sporadically involved with a woman who lived in Paris and whom I saw every few months, and I was living at a continuous low boil of yearning and resentment. *All you have to do to become somebody's god is disappear.* But I was at least theoretically attached and loyalty meant a great deal to me in those days, so I did a lot of repressing. And I told myself that I wasn't interested in Dinah except as someone to chat with when I ran into her at the farmer's market, swishing between the stalls in her big gypsy skirt. I told myself I just liked her kids: She had two little boys she was raising on her own. And on the snowy morning I found myself shoveling her front walk, I told myself that I was just being—oh, neighborly. There were three other neighbors living between Dinah's house and mine, and I didn't touch a single one of *their* front walks—they could have frozen to death in a snowdrift for all I cared.

Then one evening I asked Dinah over for coffee. And she told me the story of her life. She'd been born in Nevada, to an alcoholic mother and a father Dinah strongly suspected was white: How many Indians have freckles? An Anglo couple had adopted her—this was before there were laws against whites adopting Indian babies—and taken her to live in Illinois. They might as well have taken her to the surface of the moon.

She said, "There've been studies made of Indian children raised in white families, and we all suffer from this thing social workers call Broken Feather Syndrome. We don't know who we are. We don't know where we belong. When I was little, I wouldn't look people in the eye. My mother was always on my case about it. 'Honey, how many times do I have to tell you? People won't like you if you always look down like that. It makes you look shifty.' When I finally met other Indians, I found out that *none* of us look people in the eye. It's something we just don't do. But for years I thought there was something wrong with me."

What can such beginnings prepare you for? I had a picture of Dinah as a little girl balanced on a seesaw, with some shadow self squatting heavily on the other side. It would be too pat to say that one self was Indian and the other white; the fault lines in her character went deeper than that. She'd spent her life being swung unpredictably between hard ground and thin air, too frightened to jump off and always at risk of falling. There'd been booze, drugs, poverty, a husband who beat her, another who'd kept calling her his "savage" long after it had stopped sounding fond or funny. But then she'd also gotten sober and put herself through school and raised those kids. They were good kids.

There are people—they are the people who run this country—who'd cite Dinah as proof that American lives are endlessly renewable, that color, class, and gender mean nothing. They'd be overlooking the fact that she got where she was with the help of welfare and affirmative action scholarships and that if she'd been born higher up on the American money-river, she'd probably have been a department head by now instead of a debt-ridden doctoral candidate in comparative literature. They'd be overlooking the threadbare clothes, the stacks of unpaid bills. And they'd be overlooking the costs of her ascent. "Look at me: this hair, these eyes, this big old Indian torso—I look like every other Shoshone at Wind River. But when I finally tracked down my birth mother, we had nothing to say to each other. I embarrassed her. Shit, she embarrassed *me*." *Through being exposed to such complete and sudden changes of environment, she acquires a kind of chronic rootlessness; eventually, she comes to feel at home nowhere, and she remains psychologically maimed.*

For some people a story like Dinah's would have been a red flag, a sign saying "Abandon hope all ye who enter here." For me *it was as horribly urgent as a hand reaching out of the sea.* That evening I somehow managed to get through coffee without compromising my vows to the girlfriend I never saw, and I walked Dinah back to her house like a perfect gentleman, repressing like hell the whole time. And just as she climbed the stairs, I looked up and saw her pause beneath the moonlight, which was almost tropical, a cool liquid spilled over the panting surfaces of the world. *All I could see were the flowing lines of her gown, the oval of her face, with the white flash of her teeth, and, turned toward me, the big sombre orbits of her eyes, where there seemed to be a faint stir, such as you fancy you can detect when you plunge your gaze to the bottom of an immensely deep well. What is it that moves there? you ask yourself. Is it a blind monster or only a lost gleam from the universe?* And I told Dinah, "I've got to tell you: You're one gone little kitten and I'm terribly attracted to you. But there's nothing I can do about it."

And from that moment we were doomed.

Our plane landed in Jakarta, which is where Charlotte had agreed to meet us. And right away, everything is going wrong. We can't telephone her hostel. Jakarta has two separate telephone systems: One is licensed to the President's daughter and the other to one of his in-laws, and these phone systems are totally incompatible. It's easier to call the States than it is to ring someone on the other side of town. So Dean and Flipper and I spend half the day looking for Charlotte, even though we're stupid from jet lag and the instant we step outside we feel the water boil out of our cells to become part of the general humidity. Jakarta's boulevards are a war zone of cars and trucks and buses and flimsy motorized rickshas, all hurtling at suicidal speeds, weaving as frantically as bees and fouling the air with Lord knows what kind of effluvia, the emissions of fuels that were banned in this country thirty years ago, *coal oil,* I'm saying. The back alleys called *gangs* are passable, if you can bear walking, but just barely, and there's nothing resembling a street sign. We wander for hours among endlessly ramifying warrens of fried-tofu vendors, little boys selling loose cigarettes and hard candy (that spring they have one called SCUD that has a picture of a missile on the wrapper in honor of Sadaam Hussein), women shouldering dripping baskets of fish, bicycles festooned with bolts of cloth and braces of limp-necked ducks, metalsmiths pounding away at the ruined bits of vehicles that didn't make it through the traffic on the main drag. We are lost in a squalid postindustrial megalopolis whose innards have been hollowed out to make room for a thousand transplanted feudal villages. When we surface, Dean clutches my wrist: "I'll tell you right now, I can't take it here too long. This city is my definition of hell."

"Well, of course it is," Flipper says. "Hell is Peter's *Club Med!* At least the exchange rate's not bad."

When we finally find Charlotte, this pretty, strapping American whose misfortune it is to live among people so exquisitely fine-boned that they make her feel like a sweating, thudding, doughy-fleshed circus fat lady, she says, "I'm afraid we're going to be stuck here for a while." Because being an anthropologist in the 1990s means you spend most of your time in the capital, pleading with bureaucrats to approve your visits to the interior. For the next three days Charlotte trudges back and forth between government offices while I look up ethnographic documents at the library and in my spare time tag along with Flipper and Dean as they shop—or, really, as Flipper shops; Dean and I are merely his porters. He wants to hire some street urchins to lug his purchases, but I threaten to leave right then if he's going to act like some hog of an American tourist. Which he does anyway. In the market by the old harbor he scoops up hundreds of little tin boats that have been hammered together from sardine cans by the maimed and halt: He claims he can sell them for ten bucks apiece at the Sixth Avenue flea market. He pays with fistfuls of crisp new dollar bills. Who knows what it comes out to per boat? The nutritious green of fresh American currency drives these emaciated wretches crazy. They throng to Flipper like disciples; they call him *Tuan,* "Lord." He pretends to be irritated, but you can tell he's in heaven; irritation is the camouflage of this man's bliss. I still see him in an antiques stall on the Jalan Surabaya, scolding a guy who's haggling with him over a pair of brass diving helmets, the kind you see in old movies. Only Flipper would travel all the way to Indonesia to buy diving helmets. "You don't understand!" he yells. In English. "I know all about flea markets. I'm one of you guys!"

On the night our visitors' permits for East Kalimantan finally come through, we go out with Charlotte to eat at a Sumatran restaurant. There's no menu. You just sit down at your table and within seconds the waiters whisk out an assortment of bowls filled with unidentifiable curries or gnarled carcasses that might be a minimalist's idea of a chicken or a very fit rat (in one of the Sherlock Holmes stories there's a reference to "the giant rat of Sumatra," and I think this is it). And just as we begin to eat, someone hollers "Compadres!" and it's Buddy, Buddy the missionary. He's still wearing that green baseball cap. He sits down at our table without waiting for us to invite him and gives Charlotte the eye. "Oooh, honey, ain't you somebody's answered prayer! Which one of these lucky fellas is your boyfriend?"

Charlotte says, "None of them, thank you."

"Well, what's wrong with them? What's wrong with you guys? A pretty little fox like this and ain't none of you snapped her up? You boys ain't queer, are you? What's that y'all are eating? Looks good. I'll have the same." He gets this across to the waiter by shouting it very loudly, opening his mouth very wide, and jabbing a finger inside, as though he were trying to bring on vomiting.

All through dinner Buddy comes onto Charlotte; she glowers at him and then at me when I try to intervene out of some absurd reflex of chivalry. Laser beams of dislike are shooting back and forth across the table. The only relief comes when Buddy finds out that Charlotte lives in Borneo. He gets businesslike: "Okay, these Dayaks of yours, that's what you call 'em?"

"Actually, they call themselves Ngajus."

"Jews! They got Jews in Borneo?"

"*Ngaju,* Buddy!" I snap. "Ngaju, Kenyah, Kelabit, Ot-Danum. Think of Indian tribes."

"Okay, okay, Jews, Ngajus, Indians, who cares? I was asking the lady. These Dayaks, they believe in God?"

"They believe in several."

"Several gods." He says this like a doctor repeating a patient's symptom: *Bloody stool. Fascinating.* "What about Satan? They believe in Satan?"

This makes Charlotte think. "Well, the Christians do. And the animists believe in all kinds of evil spirits. You can't walk ten feet without running into an offering flag. But Satan? I don't think so. Not in the sense of one omnipotent evil being. No."

"Well, what's their problem? Don't they know about sin?"

"I don't think they believe in that either. Just bad behavior."

He bursts out laughing. "Oh, honey, honey, honey. You must not know these folks as good as you think you do! Hell, everybody's got sin. 'By one man sin entered into the world, and death by sin; and so death passed upon all men, for that all have sinned.' It says so right in Romans." He glances over at Dean, who's staring at a dripping lump of meat that he's just pried out of his mouth. "What's the matter? Don't you like it?"

"It's weird. It's got a texture like a sweetbread or something, but look, it's got a *bone* in the middle."

"They got raccoons in Indonesia? It could be a raccoon's peen. They say *they* got a bone in the middle." He winks. "Bet y'all wish you were raccoons."

I don't know whether Dayaks possess a sense of sin, but Westerners do. And ours is sufficiently vast and dark and looming to cast a shadow over every primitive people we encounter. (I don't like using the word *primitive,* but it's the best we've got: tactful synonyms like *archaic* or *traditional* turn out to be just as loaded and far more cumbersome.) When Europeans first set foot in what we now call the Third World, they carried their sense of sin with them like a virus that had lived inside them for so long that they'd come to take its ravages for granted. They noticed it again only when they had passed it along to—projected it onto—new hosts. Spaniards who had serenely tortured heretics in the courts of the Inquisition suddenly blanched at the cruelty of the Aztecs. The English sailors who'd whored their way from Cheapside to Naples marveled at the sight of Orinoco Indians fornicating in the open air. I'm not saying the natives were sinless. Who knows what those people did to one another in the centuries before they were conquered by white armies and subsumed by white imaginations? We *can't* know. The native Americans had syphilis long before they infected some horny conquistador. But we shouldn't forget that it was our great-great-grandfathers who gave them smallpox.

Read your Conrad: Kurtz goes to Africa and right away he "goes primitive." That is, he succumbs to a madness that is supposedly local in origin but sounds an awful lot like the old European sickness, the invisible horror that becomes visible only beneath the black light of the equator. Lust, envy, anger, sloth: You'd think they were endemic to that "primordial" landscape, those "primordial" peoples, like AIDS, like Ebola; that they wait to infect the unwary white traveler, who is all the more vulnerable because he is *civilized*.

Sometimes the primitive works the other way: It may be a state of *sinlessness*, populated by cavorting natives as naked and cuddly and guileless as hippies at a rock festival. In another novel Conrad uses Patusan, a fictional principality in the East Indies, as a kind of moral sanatorium, the one place where a disgraced white man can go to be cured of his scurvy of cowardice: *He had, of course, another name, but he was anxious that it should not be pronounced. His incognito, which had as many holes as a sieve, was not meant to hide a personality but a fact. . . . Afterwards, when his keen perception of the Intolerable drove him away for good from seaports and white men, even into the virgin forest, the Malays of the jungle village, where he had elected to conceal his deplorable faculty, added a word to the monosyllable of his incognito. They called him Tuan Jim: as one might say—Lord Jim.*

In the face of the primitive a Westerner has two choices: predator or penitent, beast or angel.

Conrad is supposed to have based Patusan on Borneo, and for the past several pages I have been liberally quoting—or stealing—*Lord Jim*'s gorgeous colonial prose. Forgive me, *Pani* Korzeniowski, but all the passages in italics are yours. Plagiarism is another Western illness, only by now it's so common that we had to start calling it "appropriation" to make ourselves feel better. The truth is that I was feeling a lot like Lord Jim on this trip, another white wuss trying to bury his conscience in a Bornean grave. But if Borneo was the scene of my original transgression, why did I feel compelled to go back there?

Dinah once told me that I had the most hyperactive conscience she'd ever seen. "It must be because you're Jewish. You think your ancestors killed Christ."

I said, "My ancestors did not kill Christ. Read your Bible. It was the Romans."

"You don't have to get defensive with me, baby. I grew up believing that *my* ancestors had killed America's frontier heroes. Of course, they *did*. Anyway, when I was little I wanted to be Jewish. I wanted to be that girl in *Fiddler on the Roof*. What's her name? Zeitel. I wanted to be Zeitel."

These were the kinds of conversations we had in our calmer moments, when I wasn't breaking up with her. What made me keep breaking up with Dinah was exactly the thing she complained about: my ridiculously pumped-up conscience. I couldn't forgive myself for having become Dinah's lover while I still had a girlfriend on the other side of the Atlantic. And not only couldn't I forgive myself for falling into her bed (actually, it was *my* bed we first fell into, but it sounds better the other way): I couldn't forgive *her*.

The morning after we became lovers, I wrote her a letter. "Dear Dinah, it pains me to write this, but I have made a dreadful mistake. As much as I care for you—and I do, more than it is wise for me to say—I cannot bring myself to . . ." It was disgusting. But I wrote it and put it in an envelope and slipped it under her door. And an hour later I heard a knock and she was standing outside in her black skirt, with her black hair shining like wet coal in the pale November light and her black eyes coldly glaring. "I don't want to be anybody's mistake," she said. I watched her tear up my letter and let the pieces fall from between her outspread fingers, as though anything more forceful would be a waste of her strength and feeling. Then she peeled off one of her black gloves and threw it at me where I stood in the open doorway. It may have hit me, but if it did I scarcely felt it. I remember looking out my window hours later and seeing it lying on the porch like something dropped by the mailman, a black letter.

I wished I could die. . . . There was no going back. It was as if I had jumped into a well—into an everlasting deep hole. Dinah's glove might as well have been one of those malign charms that are supposed to be common in Haiti and the East Indies, a headless black rooster or a bottle filled with poisonous vermin and the skulls of rats. It imprisoned me in my house, where I spent the next few days pacing and smoking and cringing at my loathsomeness. I wanted to drink again. I wanted to kill myself. For one silent hour I sat holding a kitchen knife with its point against my chest, trying to access whatever was necessary—courage, despondency, thanatotic ardor—for me to carve out my heart. It wasn't my French girlfriend I felt the worst for. It was Dinah. When you cheat, it's not just your steady partner whom you fuck over, it's the person you cheat with, the one you use as an instrument of your infidelity, an agency, a *tool*. Moreover, I had this idea, I still half believe it, that every sexual encounter is a kind of promise. And it seemed particularly heartless to break a promise I'd made to an Indian. Dinah must have had centuries of broken promises, stratum after stratum of them, fossilized in her genetic memory.

In time I called a friend, who talked some sense into me, and I put the knife back on the knife rack and got some sleep. It could have ended that way, with Dinah and me resuming our old lives and avoiding each other ruefully on the street. But a while later I called her or she called me, and we both apologized for being stupid and melodramatic and we talked about being friends again and within days we were crawling back into each other's bodies, thrashing stickily on sheets and floors; we were neglecting work and children; we were drinking and breathing each other; we were calling out each other's names; we were bathing each other in salt and honey; we were deep-sea diving in each other's eyes and staying down longer and longer, twining rapturously in those depths in which I'd once imagined a blind monster or a lost gleam from the universe, in which she'd imagined God knows what, because I never knew what Dinah imagined. For all she told me, I never knew.

Afterward I always said, "I'm sorry." And she'd say, "Me, too."

"I should have more control."

"If you ask me, you've got a little too much."

"You deserve better."

"Please don't give me that shit."

"Well, wouldn't you prefer someone who's actually *there?*"

She'd take a drag of her cigarette; oh, she was as tough as a gunslinger. "Peter, you live halfway down the block. What could be more there?"

On Thanksgiving after one of these conversations, she called and said, "I'm sorry. I swore I wasn't going to call you, but this is an emergency." Her older boy had a bad headache that sounded a lot like meningitis. So I drove them to the hospital and waited with them in the emergency room. I was such a conscientious philanderer. I told Hunter stories to keep him calm. I took down notes of everything the doctor said so Dinah wouldn't have to remember. She was one of those people who doesn't show her fear, who just sits silently with her hands folded in her lap, hunched forward as though she were bracing herself against the next gust of bad news. It was another trait I thought of as Indian. Sitting there, I felt my heart grow huge, turn into a room big enough to hold them both, the mother and the little boy. I wanted them to live in it forever. *You take a different view of your actions when you come to understand, when you are made to understand every day that your existence is necessary—you see, absolutely necessary—to another person. . . . But only try to think what her life had been. It is too extravagantly awful. . . . And me finding her here like this—as you may go for a stroll and come suddenly upon someone drowning in a lonely dark place.*

I'd promised my friends that things would be better in Borneo. But when we got to Palangkaraya, which is where Charlotte lived, the professor who was supposed to guide us had left, no message, nothing. Such departures were standard practice there. So we caught a speedboat to Banjarmasin, and from there a plane to Balikpapan, and then an even tinier and more makeshift aircraft to the logging city of Samarinda, on the mouth of the Mahakam River, the avenue to the tribal regions. Although the landscape we flew over was unmistakably Conrad's—*We could see below us in the declining light the vast expanse of the forest country, a dark sleeping sea of sombre green undulating as far as the violet and purple range of mountains; the shining sinuosity of the river like an immense letter S of beaten silver*—Samarinda itself might have been invented by J. G. Ballard. It's a cross between an equatorial frontier town and a cesspit. Between the riverbanks felled trees scud so thickly you could almost walk across. The lumber mills spew out a poisonous slurry that's the exact green of Buddy's baseball cap. You watch it unfurling in the water, this color never seen in nature, and you realize that its very presence here signifies that nature is ending, nature is defunct. Everyone who stays in Samarinda comes down with diarrhea and skin infections. The hotel lobbies are full of big, drunken Texan and German and Australian logging engineers with tiny prostitutes dangling from their arms like purses, so they can get laid between making deals. *The first thing we see as we travel round the world is our own filth, thrown into the face of mankind.*

Dean's excited because he figures that where there's Texans there's got to be steaks. And bread. He's dying for rubbery, cotton-white American sandwich loaves. Flipper wants to look for more diving helmets. But by now I'm crazy to find tattooed Dayaks; I want to squat by a fire with the great-grandsons of headhunters, listening to the stories of their markings and telling them the story of my own. "No time," I start yelling. "Fuck the Silver Cup, forget the diving helmets. We've got to find a guide!"

The guide we find is a citified Kenyah Dayak named Petrus. He looks like an evil dance instructor: pomade, gold chains, translucent patterned socks. He calls me "my friend." "You want to see primitive peoples? No problem, my friend, where I am taking you is very primitive. But comfortable. Deluxe hot-and-cold running water. Gourmet cooking, my friend."

It may be the p-word, it may be those patterned socks, but right away I've got an attitude. "Wait a second. You're saying that these people are . . . are . . . 'primitive' and they've got hot and cold running water?"

"Sure, running water. Sanitary flushing toilet, too."

"I don't want to go to some tourist village." The Indonesian ministry of tourism has herded Dayaks into hoked-up reproductions of traditional settlements: prefab longhouses, "authentic" ceremonies performed three times a day. Charlotte tries to calm me down, but I shake her hand off my arm. "I mean it, no tourist villages! *Tidak desa turis!*"

"On my boat is all kind running water. You come look."

The whole deal sounds bogus, but Dean and I follow Petrus across town and down to the river landing, to check out his "boat." At one point we have to walk single file across a footbridge some thirty feet above the Mahakam. It's pitch dark and absolutely deserted and I think, This would be the perfect setup for an ambush. All little Petrus has to do is whistle and four brawny Lascars will pop out of the weeds to gut us with their *krisses. Our fate, whatever it was, would be ignored, because the country, for all its rotten state, was not judged ripe for interference. . . . It would be for the outside world as though we had never existed.*

Actually there *is* a boat, a reconditioned tug that was used to trawl logs out to the freighters in the harbor. Steel bulkheads, a big, greasy, clanking engine. The shower's just a closet with a drain in the floor; the tap emits a broken thread of lukewarm water. Petrus starts apologizing. "No, no, it's perfect. We'll take it."

We leave early the next morning. The look Petrus gives us when he lowers the gangplank is like the look doormen give East Side matrons when they come back from a good day at Bloomingdale's. Among the four of us we're carrying three cameras, fifty-odd rolls of film, a microcassette recorder with two weeks' worth of tapes, one laptop computer with surge protector, AC adapter and spare NiCad battery, ten high-density diskettes, Flipper's scuba gear, which includes two full-sized oxygen tanks, a clip-on reading lamp, five mosquito nets, insect repellent, a first-aid kit, three machetes and one K-bar knife, the kind used by serial killers, twenty-five packages of ramen noodles, seven cases of bottled water, five pounds of ground coffee, sugar, condensed milk, sweet soy sauce, two ten-pound sacks of rice, four loaves of Indonesia's version of Wonder Bread, marked PROPERTY OF DEAN MEYERS, fresh mangoes, papayas, and bananas, a battery-operated toothbrush, bags of loose tobacco and hard candy to bribe the locals with, and an odd pumplike apparatus that Flipper claims is a combination water purifier and enema. "Don't laugh," he scolds. "Last night when I was packing it, I suddenly thought, This may be the thing that saves our lives."

We toil upriver between booms and derricks, past brontosaur freighters with rust-streaked hulls and huts that tilt queasily on wooden pilings (you can't imagine that they were actually *built;* they just seem to have been deposited there by the last flood to be swept away by the next one, on loan, the lives inside them on loan). Battens of dressed logs come sailing past, thirty, forty, fifty feet long, thirty logs across, whole cities of plundered forest, metropolises of luxury office furniture, with hard-hatted Dayaks stationed at either end, surveying the river traffic above folded arms.

The crew treats us with mortifying delicacy. If you're a man, you know how it is when you travel by boat: You immediately feel compromised by the sailors, those paradigms of stolid, spitting, greasy-fingernailed maleness. And you overcompensate. Dean and I rip off our shirts and strut around in our combat vests like two extras from *Apocalypse Now.* Nobody comments on my tattoos except for the stammering sixteen-year-old mate; he wants to know if by any chance I'm friends with the members of Guns 'N Roses.

We stop in a village where a hand-lettered sign advertises SRI BUAYA—*Lord Crocodile*. Inside a hut a proud fisherman and his wife sit beside a six-foot gavial that lies despondently at their feet, with its needle snout propped against a wall. They show me a photograph of Sri Buaya with three children riding on its back. It must have been taken in happier days. Flipper wants to know how they managed to tame the reptile. The fisherman is indignant. Petrus translates, "Oh no, he is not making Mr. Crocodile tame! He is saying Mr. Crocodile is his *uncle!*" He takes in Flipper's blank look and giggles. "He is reincarnation of dead person."

Dinah used to say that we'd been married in a former life. It was why I couldn't leave her. "We belong together," she'd say. "You're my *beshert*."

"*Beshert?*"

"*Beshert, beshert!* It's Jewish, you ought to know what it means. It means you're my Other, my destined one."

I didn't want to believe in destiny. It sounded so *primitive*. My qualms had nothing to do with my other girlfriend. By now there was no other girlfriend. There was only Dinah. She was the late-night ring on my telephone, the tapping at my door. "Forgive me," she'd whisper. Her face was like something glimpsed in a forest. "I couldn't sleep." She was terrifying. She was inescapable. Or maybe I never really tried to escape. No matter what we'd last said to each other, no matter how bloodily we'd ripped apart, I always answered. I always let her in.

I told myself it was guilt that kept me attached to her, guilt transferred from the woman I'd betrayed to the one with whom I'd betrayed her: *You take a different view of your actions when you come to understand, when you are made to understand every day that your existence is necessary—you see, absolutely necessary—to another person.* Life had been bad to Dinah. Her house was cold; her heart was faulty, with a prolapsed mitral valve; it terrified me to hear its arrhythmic kick.

There was always a sick child, a job she was about to lose. She was never surprised when I told her we had to stop seeing each other, which was my euphemism for "I have to stop seeing you." "I knew you'd say that. I fucking knew it!" There was a kind of triumph in it, the bitter satisfaction of pessimism fulfilled. I thought of this pessimism as the natural consequence of growing up on the dark side of history, where the meteors of war and famine, exile and slaughter, plunge from the airless sky, unremarked by anyone but those they crush. It was like the way Jews revel in bad luck. It was my father saying, "I told you that job wouldn't last"; it was my mother crowing, "See? See? I knew it was malignant!"

Or am I just conning myself, like those Victorians who justified the rape of Africa as their civilizing mission? Am I making Dinah my white man's burden? Oh, guilt *can* be a deterrent against bad behavior, but my experience is that it's more often just the price you pay for it, the sin tax you shell out as a tariff for the next binge. The soldiers who captured Chief Ten-ie-ya must have felt guilty, since the first thing they did after he surrendered was name a lake after him. Only then could they march his people off to a parched reservation in the San Joaquin Valley. The first thing I said after I took off Dinah's clothes (she dressed in layers—that long skirt, flannel shirt, dyed long johns, startling silky scraps of underwear—and removing these always reminded me of peeling some tricky tropical fruit, the kind whose flesh makes you feel like a cannibal and whose fragrance makes you drunk)—the first thing I said was always, "We shouldn't be doing this."

"Oh, why not?" I hear her say—I am arguing with her as I write this. She is lying on my bed on a Sunday morning with turquoise on her fingers and a rawhide medicine bag hanging from a cord between her breasts and bars of sun and shadow tattooing the knoll of her stomach. Otherwise, she is a body in a state of nature. Well, not quite: On her belly Dinah has a cesarean scar, a dark pleat I love to kiss, even though I get queasy at the thought that this was where a surgeon sliced her open and pulled life out of her. "What's your problem, Peter? What do you have against me?"

What *do* I have against loving her? It's bad enough I feel guilty without having to feel like an idiot, too. Which I do in the worst way. What kind of moron denies himself the pleasure of loving someone who loves him? A woman he can't give up without weeping? Every time I tell Dinah to leave and she actually does, I cry so hard I fall to my knees.

"I've told you a hundred times," I say through clenched teeth. "This isn't how I want to be. All my life I've gone from one relationship to the next, and they don't last. They're drugs. I don't want to use you as a drug, but I'm afraid I will. I am already! I shouldn't be with anyone right now. I should be alone."

She props herself up on an elbow. "Give me a break! You're not that principled. You don't *fuck* like someone principled. What is it, Peter? What's your real reason? You think I'm not good enough for you?"

"Don't be ridiculous!"

"What is it, I'm too fat? Too neurotic? I don't have my degree yet?"

"Will you stop? Will you stop doing this to yourself!"

"Just tell me. Is it because I'm not white?"

You prophesied for him the disaster of weariness and of disgust . . . with the self-appointed task, with the love sprung from pity and youth. You had said you knew so well "that kind of thing," its illusory satisfaction, its unavoidable deception. You said also . . . that "giving your life up to them" (them meaning all of mankind with skins brown, yellow, or black in colour) "was like selling your soul to a brute."

"Oh, Dinah, I'm not white either. Jews are just honorary."

I want to make her laugh—I love to hear her laugh—but for once she doesn't. Her face hardens into a mask in which I see all the attributes I think of as "Indian": the broad cheekbones; the eyes with their shrouding lids and irises black as agates; the blunt, pugnacious nose. It's more than just physical. "Fury," "grief," "stoicism," "wildness"—her face is a pure signifier, like a stop sign, like a red light flashing before a washed-out bridge, and it's beautiful because it *is* so pure. And it's terrible because it's just a signifier, because behind that Shoshone mask, the mask I gave her, I can no longer see Dinah. I don't know if I ever did.

She dresses. The mask vanishes behind black hair as she bends to pull up her long johns. At the door she turns to me and squeaks, "Oh Mama, don't leave me!" Now I'm the one who doesn't laugh. "Don't let me go," she says sadly. "I swear this time I won't come back."

If only I could explain myself to her. I want to tell Dinah about a dream I had around the time we first became lovers. In that dream I'm in my house, only its rooms are laid out the way the rooms are at Dinah's. I'm sitting in what I think of as "my" office but is clearly hers, a little alcove that used to be a pantry. And on the desk before me is not my computer, but Dinah's prehistoric Remington. (Is it just coincidence that Remington is both a brand of typewriter and a painter famous for his depiction of vanquished red men?) I am writing something when I feel her standing behind me. You're not supposed to be able to smell in dreams—I've never heard anyone else describe it—but I can smell Dinah's perfume, which always reminded me of the smell beneath a grape arbor, the sweetness of things fallen and crushed. I can smell it now. "Can I have the typewriter?" she asks me.

I say, "Darling, you can have anything."

I turn and she is beaming at me. "Anything?"

"Anything."

"Can I make you pregnant?" she asks. "Can I give you my baby?"

And I say, "Of course you can."

I want to tell Dinah about this dream so badly. I want to tell her how fearful it is to love someone so much that you'd change your sex for her, so wildly that you can deny her nothing. Unless, that is, you deny her everything. But Dinah has already closed the door behind her. And she's told me not to call.

"You always leave us—for your own ends." Her face was set. All the heat of life seemed withdrawn within some inaccessible spot in her breast. . . . "Ah! You are hard, treacherous, without truth, without compassion. What makes you so wicked? Or is it that you are all mad?"

We passed through Tenggarong and Muara Kaman, Muara Muntai and Long Iram. And on our third day up the Mahakam we lost Flipper and the boat. "I've had it," he said. His nose was peeling, his eyes bloodshot from squinting at the sunlit river. "I don't care, you can go on looking for headhunters as long as you want, but you aren't going to find any. There aren't any tattooed people around here. There's nothing. There's a bunch of kids in *Charlie's Angels* T-shirts following us around and screaming 'Good morning, mister!' I've never seen so many kids in my life. Haven't these people ever heard of birth control? I've used up all my film taking pictures of the little bastards. I'm going back to Samarinda."

"Fine! Go back to Samarinda. Go back and buy some more diving helmets, it gets your rocks off. You can have the tug. Tell Petrus to take you back and I'll hire a *longbot*. See if I care!"

I suppose I was hurt. If I'd gone a tad more primitive, I might have ordered Petrus to whack Flipper's head off with a machete and plant it on a stake by the riverbank: "This is the fate awaiting those who defect from the Mission."

Dean and Charlotte and I located a motorized canoe with a crabby pilot who kept warning us that the engine was about to fail at any minute, and we waved good-bye to Flipper and our former crew and set off farther upriver. We broiled in the sun or gasped beneath the canopy and gazed dopily at the jungle as it slid past: green, green, green, green, green, and every so often the gouged red mud and blackened tree stumps of a logging encampment. We slept on the floors of mission houses. We ate bowls of watery noo-dle soup in shops run by Javanese emigrés who hated Kalimantan and despised their Dayak customers. They called them *orang hutan,* which means "forest people," but is also the origin of the word *orangutan.* In some villages we found meetinghouses decorated with traditional Kenyah murals—tusked demonic faces, pop-eyed war-riors with dangling earlobes—but the buildings were empty unless there was a television inside, hooked up to a satellite dish and a generator whose throb made it necessary for viewers to crank up the volume to full blast when they gathered to watch *MacGyver* or the Indonesian version of *Three's Company.* At night you could hear the canned laughter a mile out on the water.

After two days we came to a place called Long Bagun. We tied up at the dock and picked our way across some floating logs and then up a steep slope; one wrong step and we'd have skidded thirty feet down into the noisome shallows by the outhouses. As we were looking for a place to sleep, I saw an elderly woman inch past us. There were blue markings on her hands. "Christ, I've found one!" I hissed, and I motioned to Dean and Charlotte and we followed her. She was very slow, so we had no trouble keeping up. At last we turned a corner and found her squatting outside a hut beside an old man who I guessed was her husband. The two of them might have been an ancient farm couple rocking on their front porch in some wind-blasted Kansas prairie town. The old woman's hands and feet resembled old Delft china, the tattoos were so faded. Time had blurred them into a pattern as random as the fretwork of veins and wrinkles. She was an heirloom.

And after coming all this way, I'm too scared to approach her. She is so tiny and fragile and self-contained, and I'm so big and thuggish and blundering. I'm a dinosaur in a combat vest and tat-toos that cost more than these people earn in ten years. "I can't," I wail. And Charlotte says, "If you don't talk to that woman, I'm going to disgrace you. I'll publish a paper on you in *The Journal of Borneo Studies*."

"What am I supposed to say?"

"You could say hello."

So I walk up to the old lady and drop into my creaky approximation of a squat. "Hello, Mother."

"Hello," she says, but she doesn't look up. The whole time we talk she barely glances at me.

"I am a teacher from America." I haven't taught a class in six years, but it's a respected profession in Indonesia, whereas every foreign writer is seen as a spy.

"Far away."

"Yes, very far. Very far." I look despairingly back at Dean and Charlotte. "I was admiring your tattoos. I myself"—I tap my arms, my chest—"am tattooed. They are based on the tattoos of your people."

"They're not from here." She sniffs with contempt. "My people are Kayan."

"Forgive me, I was mistaken. It is kind of you to instruct me. May I ask you some questions about your tattoos?"

It would be torture to reproduce our entire interview, as it was torture to conduct it. I couldn't say a word without stammering and I chopped every question into cautious morsels, as though I were dicing up food for a feeble aunt in a nursing home. The old lady told me that she had gotten the tattoos on her feet when she came of age and the ones on her hands when she married. The first set announced that she was eligible; the second, that she was taken. The designs were also supposed to protect her from leprosy, but she quickly added that this had been a belief in "the old times"; now everybody went to a clinic. The tattooist had been an older woman. She'd used needles attached to a wooden stick that she tapped with a mallet, and an ink made from fat, ash, and dammar resin. Other women had held her still. Yes, it had hurt, but she hadn't cried out: It would have brought shame on her family. Afterward they had rubbed the tattoos with a crushed leaf whose sap prevented infection. In her village it was only women who were tattooed, and none of the younger ones had them. The last tattooist in Long Bagun had died many years before.

Getting this information took a horribly long time, and not only because of my timidity. As I said, the old lady wouldn't look at me; she gazed down at the dust or anxiously at her husband, who said nothing. He did what husbands are supposed to do: He stayed by her side; he gave her what protection he could. Once, when Dean asked if he could take a photograph, the old man said that it would not be possible. That was the phrase he used: *Tak boleh jadi.* "It is not possible." I wondered what he felt he had to protect her from and then realized that it was probably the same thing that made his wife refuse to meet my eyes. My gaze was shameful to her; every question I asked was shameful to her; her tattoos were shameful to her. They reminded her of a past that had not only vanished but been disavowed. The only tattooed people she saw on the TV in the village meetinghouse would be the gangsters in Indonesian crime shows. She had heard her shopkeeper call her an *orang hutan*. In her own lifetime she had become primitive. It is a term that may be nostalgic to us but can only be humiliating to the people we use it to describe.

It took us another three days to get back to Samarinda on the public boat. Flipper had booked us into the city's one luxury hotel: All, I guess, was forgiven. We took hot showers and slept like babies in air-conditioned rooms, and the next evening the four of us ate dinner in the bar. Actually, we were five. While he was waiting for us, Flipper had made friends with a guy named Titin. He was lean and stooping, with atrocious teeth that took away your appetite, they were so splayed and stained. Titin said that he worked for the Department of Forestry, but Charlotte made him for secret

police. They have a way of attaching themselves to Westerners, especially in Kalimantan, where the government feels harried by foreign environmentalists. Policemen, secret or otherwise, represent a
booming occupation in Indonesia and I suppose through most of
the Third World: They seem to be one of the things the West has
bequeathed to its former territories, along with polluting industries
and obsolete TV shows. Titin was pleasant enough, but once he
said something that made my blood freeze. He was telling us how
some friends of his on the police force had invited him to an inter-
rogation: "They had this fellow and he would not tell them anything, so the boss is saying to me, 'Titin, maybe you will talk to
this bad man?' And I say, 'Sure! Okay!' And they give this fellow
to me and in ten minutes he is telling *everything!*" He guffawed and
made a horrid twisting gesture.

"Oh. In the States they give guys like you junior detective
badges." I elbowed Flipper to shut up, but Titin laughed some
more. He was crazy about Flipper. He kept buying him gin and
tonics and Flipper kept tossing them down, and I kept trying to
make him stop because I was sure that this orthodontist's nightmare was setting us up for a bust. In Singapore, less than a thousand miles away, they cane foreigners for petty vandalism. What
do they do to subversive aliens in Indonesia?

It gets later and later and Flipper gets drunker and drunker.
He's calling to the waiters in Spanish, which is the only foreign language he knows. *"Mas bebidas, señor. Mas gin y tonicos."* The sound
system starts playing karaoke music. Titin punches in "Storybook
Lover." The lyrics scroll across the screen above the bar, over
blown-up stills of besotted Western couples, big blond barbarians
walking hand in hand against a California sunset. Titin stands and
sings along; his eyes are closed, his head thrown back. His voice is
eerily sweet, with a Mario Lanza vibrato. When the music stops
there are tears in his eyes.

"Now you," he tells Flipper.

Among other things, Flipper is clinically tone deaf. But he fumbles some coins into the jukebox and wobbles to his feet. The song is "Puff the Magic Dragon." "It's the only one I know," he says. He opens his mouth, and sounds come out of it. They are the sounds made by someone being strangled ineptly. Not one note is on key. Not one phrase is on beat. His face is contorted with sincerity. Titin watches, nodding in time to the music. He's smiling, and although I'd like to ban the use of the word *inscrutable* in conjunction with anything Asian, I have to say that Titin's smile is inscrutable. Can he actually enjoy Flipper's smashed violin of a voice? Is he thinking about working on us with forceps and hot wires? Or is he just getting off on watching an *orang barat,* a "Western man" stuffed with beef and bucks and privilege, humiliating himself in a country that other Western men once owned? Does Flipper yowling "Puff the Magic Dragon" make up for having to look at inscrutable Caucasians swapping spit on the big screen every time you want to hear a love song?

I left Borneo two weeks later. Flipper and Dean had already gone their separate ways. I was coming down with a case of sweats and shakes that I thought might be malaria, and after buying my plane ticket I was also broke, since it was a Muslim holiday and even the airport exchange was closed. I was stuck in Banjarmasin for six hours with nothing to eat or drink and no cash to buy it with. And I'm sitting in the waiting room, cradling my throbbing head in my hands, when someone pounds me on the back.

"Hey, Pete! What the heck are you doing in this neck of the woods, you old son of a gun you?"

It's Buddy. He's wearing his Gatorade baseball cap and a violet batik shirt. He's grinning his pie-faced redneck grin. I loathe the sight of him.

"Lord, Lord, ain't it a small world! Last time I saw you we was all chowing down on that *raccoon peen!* What's the matter, not feeling so hot? Got yourself a case of that Montezuma's revenge? Gee, am I glad to see you, fella. Damn, I was lonesome for a friendly face!"

He can't have been all that lonesome. Buddy has his arms around two dainty women in miniskirts. Their lipstick gives them the pout of tropical fish. They giggle in terror at everything Buddy says. "Oh, Pete. I want you to meet some friends of mine. This here is Kartini and this . . . this . . ." He gropes in the air for a name. "This is . . . *Mardiana*. Is that right, sweetheart? Girls, I want you to say hello to my good friend Pete. He's an American like me."

I hate to admit it, but I have been waiting for this moment ever since I first spotted Buddy on the Garuda flight from L.A. Because I've always *known* that every Christian fundamentalist is either a tight-lipped sexual psychopath or a smirking lecher, and any time one of them sets out to convert the dusky heathen, he will sooner or later end up fucking them.

"Delighted to meet you." I shake the women's hands. "Are you with Buddy's church?"

"No use asking, they don't speak English too good. I'll tell you, Pete. I wish I could say these gals is sisters, but you know and I know they's just whores, excuse my language. Like I said, I was *lonesome*. Borneo's a long way from home."

He invited me to have a drink with him, but I had to turn him down. "You a little short?" The look he gave me was almost tender. It took in my arrogance and my godlessness and judged them no more than it judged the swampy stink of my fever. "No problemo. I got plenty of rupiah on me. Heck, let me buy you something. You look like you could use a Co-Cola. Kartini, sweetheart, they got Co-Cola in this airport? You be a good girl and fetch us two, and whatever you want for you and your girlfriend." He shook his head as they skipped off toward the snack bar. "Mmm-mmm-*mmmh!* You ever get yourself a piece of that?"

I couldn't help myself. "I thought you were a *Christian*."

"Well, sure I am!" He wasn't embarrassed at all. "I been giving out Bibles left and right. It's like I told you, Pete. Ain't nobody's saying you got to be perfect to be a Christian. There's only One who's perfect, and I ain't Him."

We wander in our thousands over the face of the earth, the illustrious and the obscure, earning beyond the seas our fame, our money, or only a crust of bread; but it seems to me that for each of us going home must be like going to render an account. We return to face our superiors, our kindred, our friends—those whom we obey, and those whom we love, but even they who have neither, the most free, lonely, irresponsible and bereft of ties—even those for whom home holds no dear face, no familiar voice—even they have to meet the spirit that dwells within the land.

Dinah moved soon after we broke up: Really, she vanished. I never even saw a moving van pull up before her house, though I was practically glued to my front window in those first few weeks, waiting for a glimpse of her, and dreading it. One morning the house was empty, with a boy's tricycle gleaming with rain on its front steps. No one could tell me where she'd gone. But less than a month after I came back from Borneo, I saw her again. I was walking on Greenmount when a bus pulled up in front of me and she was sitting at a rear window, tapping frantically against the glass. I called her name. "It's so great to see you!" I couldn't hear what she said back. She'd gained weight since our last meeting—she always complained about her thrifty Indian genes—but she was still beautiful to me, maybe even more beautiful because for so long she had stood at the epicenter of my remorse. Lake Tenaya is also beautiful and it owes some of its beauty to the story of its name, that romance composed by sentimental killers. I leaped up, and we must have been thinking the same thing because our palms pressed the window at the same moment. There was so much I wanted to tell her, but already the bus was gunning its engine, its doors were hissing shut. I didn't even know her phone number. So I pulled off my shirt, there on that crowded street corner where people do stranger things every day. And I showed Dinah my tattoos, especially the Dragon Dog on my left biceps, the design with which the Iban expressed the cosmic twining of male and female and which I had gotten to protect me from regret, though I cannot swear to its efficacy; I have had regrets since then.

The last word is not said—probably never shall be said. Are not our lives too short for that full utterance which through all our stammerings is of course our only and abiding intention? I have given up expecting those last words, whose ring, if they could only be pronounced, would shake both heaven and earth. There is never time to say our last word. . . . The heaven and the earth must not be shaken.

4

I KEEP THE RED FLAG FLYING

I tremble for my country when I reflect that God is just.

Thomas Jefferson

The high point of my political life occurred in 1972. Richard Nixon was running for his second term as President, and I was a student at one of those colleges that are more like sanatoriums than schools: It was very expensive, the students cultivated a look of translucent tubercular delicacy, and most of us were spending our parents' money learning to be special. It was located just outside of New York City, and Nixon or his handlers had chosen a nearby town for one of his campaign appearances.

So a bunch of us in the Student Revolutionary Union—our party line was a kind of anarcho-narco-Trotskyism: armed struggle, solidarity with all oppressed peoples, and speed—insinuated ourselves into the crowd lining the main street of this quaint Westchester hamlet, with its mock Tudor houses and hedges trimmed as strictly as Bob Haldeman's flat-top. We were smack in the middle of Nixon country. On every side pearl-draped housewives and old-timers in windbreakers waved child-sized American flags. I ducked past a kid who was wearing a button that said MCGOVERN: ACID, AMNESTY AND ABORTION. The Secret Servicemen were bug-eyed in their sunglasses and as silent as reptiles; they had the honed ex-

pectancy of people who've had their unconscious surgically removed, id and superego yanked out like septic adenoids. The only
voice that ever muttered in these guys' heads came out of a gum-
drop-sized speaker wedged in one ear, and when they checked out
a girl in the crowd, they weren't wondering what she'd be like in
the sack, only if she might be another Squeaky Fromme—well, this
was before Squeaky Fromme, but you get the idea.

But maybe the guys they had on duty that day weren't that
good. I was a definite hostile: hair down to mid-back, big hoop ear-
ring and a bulging knapsack that might have held a field-stripped
AK-47. But nobody stopped me. I got right up to the barricade. My
comrades in the Student Revolutionary Union had dispersed, of
course—we followed Mao's dictum that revolutionaries should
swim like invisible fish in the sea of the people—so I had to remember to let five police cars and some limousines roll past until I saw
the one with Richard Nixon sticking out of its open top like something lugged home from a flea market, a cane-backed Adirondack
or faux-Federal dresser, too bulky to be crammed in the back, too
weirdly shaped to fit in the trunk. I don't know, maybe it was a
Nixon *dummy*. The arms were flung out in that tetanoid scarecrow
salute; the smile might have been chiseled in wood. Poor Dick
Nixon: The only expression that ever came naturally to him was
the glower of the eternally unloved. I pulled a brick from my knapsack, I leaped over the sawhorse in front of me. I yelled, "Fuck pig
Nixon! Fuck Amerikka!" And I threw that brick as though I were
Whitey Ford. I may have been a sorry-ass ball player as a kid, but
I made up for it with that pitch, which sailed over the heads of
cops and Secret Servicemen and turned over and over in the sun
like the jawbone in *2001*. I never saw where it landed, because a
moment later dozens of bricks were arcing after it, bricks, rocks,
tin cans, people were yelling, the cops were swinging their night-
sticks at the nearest heads—leftist heads, Republican heads, it
didn't matter—with the wholesale enthusiasm of amateur hunters

on the first day of Muscovy duck season—*whap! whap! whap! whap! whap!* They were small-town cops, after all, and they must have been grateful for some action.

What saved me from skull fracture was somebody tackling me from behind. It knocked the wind out of me, but I managed to squirm onto my back. I expected to find myself staring into a Secret Service Magnum. I was half prepared to be blown away. But the man straddling me was a civilian who looked to be in his seventies. There was dandruff on his shoulders and his face was so swollen with fury I was scared he was going to stroke out on me right there and get me charged with manslaughter. He tried to punch me, but I blocked it. "You filthy hippie! You . . . you . . . communist, get up and fight like a man!"

I was mortified. "Come on, Gramps. Lay off, will you? You're gonna hurt yourself."

The low point of my political life came twenty years later. Let me set the larger scene for you. It's the third term of the presidency of Ronald Wilson Reagan or the first term of the presidency of George Herbert Walker Bush: These two figures, so different in their personal styles (the one vibrating with confidence and grandfatherly powers of reassurance; the other as peevish and tonguetied as the fourth-grader who raises his hand because he wants to use the bathroom, only to find himself called on to recite "I Wandered Lonely As a Cloud"), nevertheless blur together for me, like two kings with the same name. In the previous year the United States has won a painless, ego-goosing war with Iraq, a Prozac war that left the local dictator in power while the Kurds and Shiites who were encouraged to rise against him were massacred under the noses of American troops. Half of the last presidential cabinet is under criminal indictment. It has lately been announced that it will take some 500 billion dollars to salvage the nation's plundered savings and loan institutions. It has lately been confirmed that the past twelve years of tax and social-spending cuts have redistributed additional billions of dollars from the country's poorest tenth to its richest one percent. The American economy is in free-fall.

The President is standing for reelection, and his response to the bad news has been to mount a clamorous offensive against the forces that threaten the American family. In 1992 these include homosexual schoolteachers, the photographs of Robert Mapplethorpe, and Murphy Brown, a character in a television series. He has proposed amending the Constitution in order to protect the American flag, which was burned by somebody in Austin. He has forbidden government employees to utter the word *abortion* during office hours. American politics has steamed into its postmodern phase, the era of what the French theorist Guy Debord calls "the spectacle." The politics of the spectacle much resembles schizophrenia, one of whose occasional symptoms is an inability to distinguish representations from reality. In the same week Congress has passed a resolution condemning a rap song entitled "Cop Killer" while striking down a Washington, D.C., ordinance that would let victims of assault weapons sue the manufacturers, ruling out the possibility that a fifteen-year-old black drug runner whose spine was severed by a round from a Mac-10 might actually collect something from the white men who put it on the market.

This is what's known as history.

Sometime in the course of the aforementioned events I attended a meeting of the New York Tattoo Society. Attending a meeting of the New York Tattoo Society was like attending a meeting of the New York Sidewalk Spitters' Society, since tattooing has been illegal in the city since 1961. The official story is that the craft was banned for hygienic reasons, following a hepatitis epidemic originating in some slovenly waterfront parlor. People inside the industry, however, insist that the true reason for the ordinance was that at around this time a tattoo artist improvidently decorated the underaged son of a police commissioner or city councilman. Tattooists are a conspiratorial bunch, and in this respect they remind me of my old compatriots in the Left, the ones who never got tired of reminding you that the operative word in the phrase "official story" is "story."

The New York Tattoo Society held its meetings once a month at CBGB, the club known as the birthplace of punk. From 1976 to 1981 I had spent four nights a week there, a rough total of six thousand hours, listening to Blondie and Television and the Voidoids and the Ramones, or really, in a state beyond listening, I was so wasted and the music was so loud; it seemed to bypass the auditory nerves and throb directly into the bones of my skull, churning the brain within to gray gruel. I hadn't been back in ten years. Ten years since I'd stood before the squat stage, breathing in a swampy fug of beer and piss and cigarette smoke. Ten years since I'd last hung out with unrepentant lawbreakers. There was the notorious Tommy DeVita, tattooist to New York biker gangs—Hell's Angels, Nomads, he did them all. He'd opened his first shop in 1961, right after the city had made his livelihood illegal, in a calculated gesture of defiance, and he'd actually spent a couple of months in jail for refusing to pay the fine.

There at the bar was Spider Webb, with his graying waist-length hair and baleful shamble, the exaggeratedly casual gait of a man who is about to blindside someone with a pool cue. Many years before Spider Webb had had a show at a SoHo gallery—it was one of the first times tattoos had crashed into the precincts of fine art—in which the principal object on display was a collection of tattooed human fetuses. I remember watching them floating in their tanks, pale, big-headed, and precisely calligraphed, and experiencing a rare tremor of shock. This was before I became an expert at disapproval—I was still too busy courting it from others—but even then I had the distinct sense that what I was looking at was wrong, maybe even wicked. Poor Spider Webb. If only the Christian

Coalition had been around back then, he'd now be as famous as Robert Mapplethorpe.

And everywhere in the room, baring bits of skin for one another's admiration, were svelte gays and lesbians whose heads were shaved like the heads of Egyptian priests. Their arms were embossed with verses from Sappho in Attic Greek or with the biohazard symbol. Their noses, ears, lips, tongues, eyebrows, and nipples were pierced with studs as big as horses' bits. I'm not a Reichian, so I don't believe that sex is inherently revolutionary, but in 1992 the Party of God had succeeded in making it so. And by virtue of their enhancements, these people were declaring themselves erotic dissidents, members of a previously uncharted sex in which flesh coupled with ink and leather and metal. In the age of AIDS, this kind of sex was safer than plain fucking—the S&M contingent at that year's Gay Pride parade had carried a banner that said WE USED TO BE SICK, NOW WE'RE SAFE—but it was also wilder, more stringent. It insisted that any part of the body could be turned into a locus of pleasure. I met a guy that night who had so much hardware in his ears that the lobes hung down like loops of taffy and you could have stuck your thumbs through the holes. Which is what he liked to have done to him. "I love it when somebody finger-fucks my earlobes," he shuddered. "It's so totally transgressive." It occurred to me that fucking the holes punched in somebody's earlobes had probably never made it onto any sodomy statute, anywhere. But, as the critic Louise Kransniewicz once noted, "Nothing breaks down social, moral, and legal boundaries faster than bodies that are thought to be misbehaving."

I was attending the New York Tattoo Society bash as Slam's date. This counted as a coup, like snagging the Homecoming Queen for the big dance. People knew Slam. She had credibility. And if my own tattoos felt like paltry things (among the New York Tattoo Society's membership four tattoos counted as nothing), Slam's body work—the tattoos that covered her arms and legs, the labret in her lower lip, the clit and nipple studs that anchored her in a state of perpetual sexual alertness—more than compensated. Actually, I was attending this event as Slam's exhibit. She wanted to enter me, or a piece she'd done on me, in the tattoo contest that would be held at the end of the evening. There were several categories: Best Color, Best Black Work, Best Traditional, Best Tribal. Slam wanted to enter me in Best Original Tattoo.

The piece she was thinking of was barely an hour old. My right arm was still stinging from it, but in a distant, almost vicarious way, since the pain was pleasantly inhibited by my brain's stash of natural opiates. I was almost high enough to enjoy the prospect of going up on the stage where Patti Smith had once conquered me with her rapturous, heartbroken groan and parading my new ink before the cream of New York's needleworkers. Slam thought we had a chance of winning.

"Oh, this is sweet," she'd kept saying as she pecked away at me with her Zeus tattoo gun. "This is so fucking sweet. You should see how I'm doing the shading."

The tattoo Slam had given me was a drawing of a wrench placed diagonally between two gears. She'd rendered the spanner with punctilious thoroughness, down to the highlights on its chrome-plated shaft, while leaving the gears black silhouettes, and she'd unified the composition by framing wrench and gears with a red triangle that sat athwart my deltoid. The design was a bow to Russian Constructivism, the last unfettered breath drawn by revolutionary art before Stalin strangled it with the noose of Socialist Realism. And I had chosen it because it was 1992 and America was in the hands of assholes. Well, let's not say "assholes," don't want to sound like a crank. Let's call them "the Great Ones," as did the fourteenth-century Lollards, who refused to labor for them, or "the Persistence," a word that is almost an antonym for "the Resistance." Let's give them the faces one saw on television in those years, though behind those faces there were always other faces, more numerous but less identifiable: The Pat Robertsons and Jesse Helmses were only point men, easy to hate, easy to wipe from sight simply by changing channels, but they represented constituencies that couldn't be erased. I hated them all; there were thousands of people I hated in those years, millions: the bankers and the arms dealers and the lumber barons, the fag-bashing preachers, the judges and the lobbyists, and the lawyers, let's not forget the lawyers. So many people to hate, with the delirious bitterness of absolute impotence. And as I added my name to the list of contest entrants and waited, fiercely chain-smoking, to be called onstage, I kept imagining the look on those bastards' faces when they saw the emblem of sabotage on my right arm, which might happen if someone photographed my ink for *Outlaw Biker Tattoo* and a copy of that magazine somehow found its way into a congressional mailbox or onto the coffee table of a corporate waiting room. Maybe then.

There's a story—it may be apocryphal—that in the late 1930s the American Communist Party instructed some of its members to go underground. It may have had something to do with Stalin's impending pact with Hitler. It may have been the party's way of preparing for a new phase of the class struggle. But a number of loyal communists stopped attending meetings, severed old associations, started families, bought small businesses, burrowed into the crevices of bourgeois life.

At first they must have seen what they were doing as a masquerade. Picture yourself as one of these shadow cadres, sitting on your front stoop on a Friday evening after a week of running a tool-and-die press or slicing cold cuts at a corner deli. And now you're sharing some Rheingolds with the neighbors, who are fans of Father Coughlin. You've got the kitchen window open so you can follow the Dodgers game on the radio. And this is your existence. But when you say, "How about them Bums?" a voice is whispering in your head, and the voice is full of triumph. Because what it's saying is: *Nobody suspects.*

For these agents-in-place life became a theater of the innocuous. Every gesture was calculated to lull. Of course, some of them had real things to conceal: Think of Julius and Ethel Rosenberg, spying industriously away in the Bronx. But thousands of others were actors without a subtext: They had no mission except the masquerade itself; they had no agenda except to seem. To seem until some coded summons called them back into the light. *Arise ye prisoners of starvation. Arise ye wretched of the earth.* Ten years pass, fifteen, a world war and then a cold one. McCarthy's spade plunges into the earth and digs up their comrades. It cuts them in two, tosses them onto the trash heap of history. Those who escape burrow deeper. They sign no petitions; they skip the vigil for the Rosenbergs. Maybe they're afraid, but maybe they're already beginning to forget. Because after a while *seeming* becomes *being*. By the time the sixties arrive and the entire country is writhing with hope and discontent, those buried cadres have gone too far underground to resurface. And when they turn on their televisions and see college kids torching their draft cards, Black Panthers marching in the streets like the Red Army outside the Winter Palace in 1917, they mutter, "Look at those bums!"

When I first heard this story many years ago, I immediately thought of my father. He'd been a Socialist in Austria in the 1930s. He used to make it sound like he'd belonged to a rowdy fraternity. "Sure we marched. For the workers. Against the Nazis. We marched and we went to the opera and we got laid. That's the whole story." But the stories your parents tell you are never whole. And I wonder whether my father's socialism was really just a phase that he outgrew along with the cheap leather jackets and soft caps of the Viennese proletariat. Just recently I learned that when my father was trying to leave Austria after the Anschluss, he was standing in line at a government office, waiting for a passport, and the woman ahead of him saw his name on a list. You know what sort of list. The first thing the Germans did, in each country whose door they kicked down, was make a list. They hadn't yet gotten around to netting Jews wholesale, like trash fish, so my father was just cited as a communist. And when he heard that his name was there, on the Germans' list, he bolted from the line and ran for his life.

He ended up leaving Austria on a Nansen passport. The Nansen passport is named after the Arctic explorer Fridtjof Nansen, who considered himself a citizen of the world long before the term became a cliché. And he took this designation so seriously that he had a passport made for other like-minded people, as well as for those who had been forced into global citizenship simply because no country would have them—or because those that would had suddenly ceased to exist. The Nansen passport was recognized by the League of Nations, and it became the salvation of thousands of refugees in Europe between the wars. As far as I know, no such document exists today. Which is a pity. Because the fastest-growing population of this century may be the population of the stateless, and they would probably be happy to possess a piece of paper that let them cross from one country to another, and even more pleased to see themselves identified as Citizens of the World instead of citizens of nowhere.

My father didn't talk much about this part of his past, and I suppose there were reasons for him not to. Among other things, when he'd escaped Austria he'd left his parents behind and in due time they died as he would have died if he'd stayed. The first inkling I had that he wasn't an unthinking passenger on the American gravy train was during the Cuban missile crisis, when I asked, "Why can't we just bomb those Russians?" I was nine years old and terrified by news bulletins. Every plane that growled over our apartment building was carrying the end of the world. "Because they are people," he said. "Sure, they do terrible things. They got a terrible government that puts people in camps like Hitler's. Maybe they want to bomb us, I wouldn't put it past that bastard Khrushchev. But you don't bomb people because they believe different than you. You cannot even hate them."

I don't know if my father hated the Vietnamese, but he was put out a few years later when I began to march against America's practice of bombing them. "This is war! What does a twelve-year-old *pisher* like you know about war?"

"I know this one is wrong."

"How do you know what is right or wrong? You think you know more than the President?"

I think I answered that it wasn't hard to know more than a Texas cracker who liked flashing his surgery scars. I was big on ad hominem attacks then, little guessing that a day would come when I'd think of Lyndon Johnson with nostalgia. Actually, my father looked sort of like Lyndon Johnson's Jewish cousin. He had the same assertive nose and bellpull ears.

"You think you know more than anybody!" he fumed. "But you don't. You don't know *bupkis,* my friend. I just pray I live long enough you should find that out. How little you know."

Of course, all fathers say this to their sons, but when my father said it to me, his voice was thick with malice. It was as though there was nothing he'd relish more than the sight of me crushed and humbled by my ignorance. But looking back thirty years later, I think statements like this might have been part of my father's cover. In 1965 Americans were still swaddled in the woolly blanket of anticommunism. Which meant that any *real* communist would have had to huddle down there with his countrymen, even though it was as hot as hell and the smell was enough to make him sick. He would have had to fake enthusiasm for his government's global agenda. Would have had to feign loyalty to the President who kept pouring arms and money and bombs and blood into a war that even at that early date was looking more and more like a bottomless pit, so that the man who conducted it was in the same position as a small-town adulterer draining his bank account to pay off the slutty file clerk he'd banged after the office Christmas party three years ago and had kept on banging, banging and paying in loveless motel rooms with a view of the service road to Route 70, shackled by desire and dread and regret that bound him tighter with every payment he made and every lie he told. And this hidden communist who might have been my father would have had to pretend to be indignant when his son began to ask the questions he couldn't.

Wouldn't he?

The mystery is what turned me against the Vietnam war in the first place. Only a year before this I'd been debating it in my sixth-grade class and I'd reeled off the same arguments that sounded so specious coming from fifty-year-old State Department flaks. Not to mention that war was cool. What eleven-year-old boy wouldn't want to blow up an entire country in his own B-57? But something changed in me and I can't say that it was my conscience or my mind, since I didn't think much about anything at that age beyond the next model airplane I wanted to buy. Maybe I just liked the girls I saw at the few demonstrations that made it onto television in 1965, that ironed hair, those orphans' mascara-larded eyes.

But suddenly I had crossed over and was going to marches and stuffing envelopes at Mobilization Committee headquarters. And once I crossed, I acquired the information that justified my crossing. (Twenty years after the war's end, it shouldn't be necessary to remind people that the Vietnamese were fighting off invaders long before Americans helicoptered into their rice paddies. Nor that it was we who canceled the plebiscite that in all likelihood would have brought Ho Chi Minh into power in 1956. This, after all, is what's known as history.) On my first day folding flyers a cheerful, unkempt woman who might have been one of my friends' bohemian moms ruffled my hair and called out, "Will you look at this terrific kid! He comes here straight from class—you aren't cutting school today, are you, sweetheart?—to do his bit for peace. Don't anybody tell me that kids today are apathetic, I don't want to hear it!" It was only years later that I saw her again at a writing seminar and found out she was Grace Paley. In my parents' house, where tears were shed when I balked at doing my homework, being a good kid meant doing what you were told. Now this nice apple-cheeked lady who unbeknownst to me was also a saint of American literature was calling me a good kid for doing what I *believed*.

This is probably why I wasn't scared out of my pants two years later, when I was hauled in by the police for putting up stickers in the Union Square subway station. I think they were announcements for the first big march on the Pentagon. One moment I was supervising a bunch of fourteen- to sixteen-year-olds, with all the giddy officiousness of a kid who's been given his first taste of power, and the next I feel a hand on my shoulder and am staring up at two gloating transit policemen. One of them has Johnny Ottinger by a skinny arm, and he looks as if he's about to cry.

"What do you think you're doing, kid?"

A year later, brazen with amphetamines and campus riots, I would have told him, "What does it look like I'm doing, pig?" Maybe I would've just slumped to the floor and dared them to brutalize me in front of rush-hour traffic. But I was only fourteen, which is not that far from the days when you're filling in the blue uniform of a coloring-book cop above a caption that reads "The Policeman Is Our Friend." So instead I say, "No harm intended, Officer. We're just exercising our First Amendment right to free speech here."

Now it's the cop who gapes. "First Amendment?" He turns to his partner. "You ever hear of a First Amendment, Frank?"

The second cop grins. "Oh yeah, yeah. I know that thing. It's on the books. Only it says 'free speech.' And you ain't speaking, kid, are you? No. What you're doing is defacing city property, which is a class B misdemeanor. You're gonna have to come with us."

At this point I want to burst into tears myself because a class B misdemeanor sounds like a terrible thing: My father yells at me if I dare bring home a report card with a B+. But I'm amazingly restrained. "All right, Officer. But these kids were just doing what I told them to. I take complete responsibility. Could you please release them?"

But the two cops herd us down a corridor and through an unmarked door, a big steel door thick enough to muffle the sound of blows and screams, into a windowless cubicle with some folding chairs and a big gray interrogator's desk with yet another cop sitting behind it. "Picked up these little pricks on a 433."

"What are they, writing 'fuck' on the walls?"

I point at Laurie Wickes, who is the object of my despairing fat boy's crush. "If you don't mind, Officer, there's a young lady here."

Cop one snaps, "Look, Junior. Don't you fucking tell me there's a fucking young lady here! You think I'm fucking blind?"

"Looks like we got more than one young lady here. Will you check out the hair on these guys." The cop at the desk rises and yanks Bruce Heyman's mane. "Hey, Junior, what's your old man say when you come home with hair down to your ass? Poor guy probably asks himself, Do I got a son or a daughter?"

He jerks once more and Bruce's head bends back, baring a vulnerable knoll of Adam's apple mossy with teenaged beard. We all quiver silently. But he just shoves Bruce down into a chair and loses interest in him. He picks up one of our stickers: " 'Stop the War Machine.' What are you, communists or what?"

"No, sir," I pipe. "We're not communists. We just want to stop the killing of American boys and Vietnamese children. Do you know how many Americans have been killed in Vietnam? Do you know they're dying in a war that hasn't even been *declared?* Do you—"

Cop one yells, "Hey, douchebag, skip the lecture, okay? I didn't take you into custody so's I could listen to commie propaganda. Jesus, I ought to give you a fat lip!"

"Don't provoke him, kid. He doesn't like to be provoked."

Johnny punches my arm. "You asshole. You're going to get us killed!"

"I'm sorry, Officer."

Cop one grumbles, "You ought to be sorry. You're the sorriest fucking bunch of losers I ever seen. If this is what they're teaching you in school, no wonder my kid can't fucking read." He writes something in his citation book.

"So are we under arrest?" Laurie asks. She sounds hopeful. In later years I notice that it's always the movement's women who are eager to get thrown in jail.

"If you're going to arrest us, we'll need to call our attorneys," I say. "I believe we're entitled to a phone call."

Cop three slams his hand down on the desk. "Will you get a load of this douchebag here!" He laughs in disgust. "What are you, kid, some kind of Jew Philadelphia lawyer?"

"My father's a lawyer," Bruce says. "We could call him."

Maybe it was mentioning Bruce's father that got us released, with a written warning to desist from political agitation "on or about the property of the New York Transit Authority." But I should have been smarter than to mention my near-arrest to mine.

"Are you crazy! What are you doing getting yourself in trouble with police? What kind of *shmendrick* are you? You have any idea what could have happened?"

"They could have beaten the shit out of me. They wanted to."

"They should have beaten you! It would have served you right."

"Served me right? All I was doing was putting up some stickers and they dragged me into their cell and called me a 'Jew Philadelphia lawyer.' Doesn't that *bother* you?"

"They were doing their job."

"So were the guards at Auschwitz, Dad. I believe that's what they told the judges at Nuremberg."

He slaps me then and I have nothing more to contribute for the duration of our interview. It is all I can do not to cry. "Don't you talk to me about Auschwitz. You ain't got a right to say that word. Auschwitz! A policeman raises his voice to you and calls you a name, and you're crying Auschwitz. Well, don't you come crying to me. Where I grew up, the police didn't just call us names. You want to go around aggravating your government, you better expect to suffer a little. You'll be lucky if they let you into college."

Beyond the astonishment of the slap—my father was always threatening to hit me, but he rarely did—what I remember is the tears in his eyes. Maybe the lie they tell you is really true: *This hurts me more than it hurts you.* Maybe the mere mention of his mother's death place was what did it. To most Americans, a people disappointed by life but unmaimed by history, Auschwitz is just a talisman, the relic of a church nobody prays at. Auschwitz is what Newt Gingrich says he stands in the way of. But to other people, the ones who were not passed over, Auschwitz isn't a sign of anything. It's a name that breaks bones. Maybe my father cried—well, *crying* is too strong a word—but maybe his eyes got wet because he sensed *why* I felt compelled to share my run-in with New York's finest. Because I wanted him to know that I spat on his values and pissed on his authority: that even my future, inasmuch as it was something he worried about (he worried about it horribly), meant nothing to me, I'd wad up all my chances and throw them in the gutter for the sheer pleasure of hurting him. That's it. I just wanted to hurt him, the way all teenaged boys want to hurt their fathers: *Take that, asshole! This is for whatever.*

Of all the explanations for the upheavals of the 1960s and early '70s, the one I hate most is the one that reduces it to a generation's Oedipal tantrum. Oh, blame the riots on communist agitators, blame them on the panic of privileged young men who saw Vietnam descending on them like a spiked portcullis. But give us, give *me,* more credit than to accuse us of merely abreacting. By the decade's end, the war's dirty secret was out: Anyone who knew how to turn on a television had seen the little girl on fire and the bloated corpses strewn in the ditches of My Lai. And at the same time we were getting almost daily evidence of how useless the throat-clearing demurrals of sit-ins and petitions were against the entrenched violence of the Persistence. First Martin Luther King was killed, then Bobby Kennedy. At the Chicago convention of 1968 the Democrats handed the nomination to a candidate who proclaimed a politics of joy while dissenters were clubbed bloody in the street outside. And the Republicans gave us a President who commissioned feasibility studies for concentration camps and whose Attorney General announced, "This country is going so far to the right, you aren't going to recognize it."

So in May of 1970, I think it was, I went down to Washington with twenty to a hundred thousand other people, depending on whose estimate you're going to believe, to overthrow the government: "the fascist government," we always called it, as though there was another government somewhere else, a good one, a Platonic republic waiting to be called into reality through the appropriate magic. (Some of us vested our hopes in real states, China, Cuba, Vietnam, but history kept betraying us. In the end, our leftism remained a kind of eschatology: Our kingdom was not of this earth.) Overthrowing the present regime wasn't the march's official aim, but there were those of us who believed that we could just stroll into Washington waving some NLF flags and take over. I remember the pre-march planning session at the New York headquarters of the Revolutionary Youth Movement (which within the year would fission, like some rock band plagued with hypertrophied egos and "artistic differences," and disgorge the Weather Underground). Someone asked, "What if they fire on us?" It couldn't have been me. I would have been too scared of sounding timid, *progressive.* This was about the worst thing you could be called if you belonged to the Revolutionary Youth Movement. The coordinators assured us that if the pigs were stupid enough to fire on us, the resulting bloodbath would cause the fascist government to collapse on the spot. This kind of answer is consoling only to those blessed with a long view of history.

I try to take comfort from it the next afternoon at around the time I'm charging toward the Department of Justice building. I'm charging because the crowd in front of me and behind me and around me is charging. Also I'm loaded on a cocktail of hash and speed that I ingested on the bus down; so, I imagine, is a sizable percentage of my fellow travelers. These are the years in which the Left is just *awash* in substances. Behind us thousands and thousands of other demonstrators are registering their disgust with the national bloodletting responsibly, by marching through the streets of Washington at a pace that would be appropriate for a funeral (which in a sense this is). But *responsible* is another one of those words we snicker at. The farther left I travel, the more words I find that have been declared off-limits, to be uttered only in scornful italics. Which may be why most of us in the action group have jettisoned words altogether. We yell or yodel that blood-chilling falsetto cry that was made so popular by the Arab women in *The Battle of Algiers* (you couldn't call yourself a leftist that year unless you'd seen *The Battle of Algiers*). There are few things more exhilarating than being part of a large mass that's moving at great speed and making a lot of preverbal noise. You feel you could do anything.

But just as we foam up the wide stone staircase of Justice, a phalanx of infantry appears at the summit: God knows where they were hiding. They're wearing helmets and gas masks that make them look like a cross between elephants and ants, and they've got M-16s. And as we thunder haplessly toward them, they raise their rifles with a crisp *clack* and they aim at us. As though some invisible leash has been yanked taut, everyone just stops. Some people in front of me fall backward and almost carry me down. "What do we do?" someone cries. "Charge the motherfuckers! Take 'em down!" "No way! Come on, Lucy. We're going back to the bus. Now!" "You fucking pussy!" "Who are you calling a pussy?" "Join us! You have nothing to lose but your chains!" "Sit! Sit! Everybody sit!" "Two, four, six, eight! Organize and smash the state!" A contingent from the Revolutionary Union begins singing the old Communist Party hymn, the one with the same tune as "O Christmas Tree": "Though cowards flinch and traitors sneer, we'll keep the red flag flying here." It's like some absurd replay of the story of Babel. One moment we were storming heaven, the next we've been broken into so many disputatious atoms of private language. We are milling on the steps, waving our fists for the news cameras, RYMers denouncing Yippies, Yippies cursing Progressive Laborites, when astonishing numbers of riot police come to drag us away. We grapple with them halfheartedly, shoving, squirming, then going down. The whole time the soldiers watch us through the lenses of their prehistoric gas masks. They never lower their guns.

In a similar demonstration a few days later, four students at Kent State University were shot dead by National Guardsmen. "What do you think, Dad?" I ask my father as we watch the coverage on TV. (This time I've had the sense to say nothing of my arrest or the smelly night I spent in the D.C. jail with a thousand other politicals for company. We totally outnumbered the legitimate criminals, so nobody bothered us, and we were released the next day on ten dollars' bail apiece. When I got home my mother asked me if I'd had a nice time on my sleep-over.) "You think Nixon was right? That those kids were bums?"

My father doesn't look away from the screen. "They were stupid. Tell me, what did they think they were doing, trying to burn down their school? The school their parents paid good money for?"

In retrospect I sympathize with his indignation. He lives with my stepmother in a two-room apartment in a residential hotel; its carpet is the greenish-gray of an old man's oldest suit. His own suits he buys at discount, and when we eat out he orders off the prix fixe menu. All this so that, a year or two in the future, he will be able to send me to a college that offers a major in puppetry.

"They weren't trying to burn down the school! Only the ROTC building. Where they train the soldiers."

A dead boy's parents are talking to the cameras. Their voices are flat, devoid of indignation or even any sense of unfairness. They might be talking about a natural catastrophe. My father sighs and taps ash off his cigar. "Then they should have burned it down sooner."

Why do I cling to this remark twenty-five years later? Why do I deconstruct it so anxiously? *Then they should have burned it down sooner.* Who did he mean by "they"? When was "sooner"? Don't tell me that it was just casual irony. That wasn't my old man's style. I tell myself that maybe that one time he was speaking from the heart of his belief. That everything else was just cover, a spiel to lull the men on the other end of the microphone in the base-boards, the informants in the next apartment. I remember the look on my father's face when I baited him, the way his forehead burned and his jowls shook, and I wonder if these were not signs of repressed rage but of suppressed laughter. "Listen to this *boy-chik,*" I imagine him chuckling. "A little Nechaev. Fifteen years old and he's going to liquidate the reactionaries." I picture the two of us sitting in his living room beneath posters of Lenin and Trotsky that have somehow magically replaced the Utrillo reproductions on the walls. The bookshelves burst with spines of Kropotkin, Marighella, Ho Chi Minh. "You think you had it bad, *shmeggege?* There was no TV cameras on the Ringstrasse. And those Brown-shirt bastards, you think they worried about who they shot? They would kill us all. Who told you you can make a revolution by sitting down like old *bubbes* with sore feet? What happened to your revolutionary praxis? Ach, theory, theory, I don't want to hear from your theories. True revolutionary theory comes from revolutionary praxis!"

But my father never blew his cover. He never even told me whom he voted for in 1980. I hate to say so, but I suspect it was Reagan, though he must have held his nose as he tripped the little lever, which so reminds me of the one beside the electric chair. My father despised Ronald Reagan. "That cowboy," he'd grumble whenever he saw the President's jovial turtle's face. "He's not even a real cowboy. He's a *movie* cowboy, is what he is. I never liked him, not even in that picture everybody says was so great. What was it? *True Gip*?"

"I think you mean *True Grit*. It had John Wayne in it."

"Wayne, Reagan. All the same. Stinking cowboys. Billions he wants to spend on his spaceships, and our own people go hungry. They can't even find nurses what speak decent English. This morning I ask the girl to kindly empty my bedpan, I don't like smelling my own waste, and she says, 'No speak.' "

"You want me to find another nurse?"

"No. I already found. If I was counting on you, I'd be up to my eyeballs in shit." He pushed the button that was supposed to make his hospital bed fold up into a comfy chaise longue, but the motor was broken and I had to pull him upright myself, tugging him from behind as you are advised to tug a drowning person. My father had just had his spleen removed. "Just like this country."

"Well, if you hate him so much, why did you vote for him?"

"It's none of your business who I vote for." He swatted at me testily. "Watch how you're yanking me, stupid! You think I'm a sack of potatoes? Who was I supposed to vote for, the other *nebbish* what can't control a bunny rabbit, not to mention the inflation?

Four more years and my savings won't be worth nothing. When I'm gone you'll be using the money for toilet paper. Just like in '29."

I must have argued that he wasn't going anywhere.

"When are you going to grow up? You're not a child anymore. And I ain't going to be here forever. Take a look at me, won't you? For once in your life, you got to be realistic. Sometimes you got to vote for your bankbook."

That was the last political discussion my father and I ever had. A few months later he was dead, as dead as Emma Goldman and Carlo Tresca, as dead as Karl Leibnitz and Rosa Luxemburg, as dead as Che, as dead as Martin Luther King, as dead as Abbie Hoffman and Allard Lowenstein, who was killed by a former pro-tégé who walked into his office one day with a revolver, goaded to murder by the voices in his head. He was a lot deader than Ronald Reagan, who was almost exactly my father's age and had been a Progressive Democrat until he saw the light—shining, I suppose, from a bulb manufactured by General Electric. I know why right-ists tend to be durable types: Kings always outlive the peasantry. But why do leftists die before their time? Not the dinosaurs of the Politburos—they live forever—but the stormers of barricades, the organizers of factory workers, the seekers after a justice so per-fect that even the atheists among them came to resemble those medieval Christians who wandered through Europe, trying to has-ten the millennium by lashing themselves with nettles and slaugh-tering the local burghers. Are they exhausted by the years they spend hacking at the bulwarks of what is? Are they so dumb that they just dart into the traffic of history, to be run down by the first eight-wheeler that comes along? Or are they so enamored of losing that dying comes naturally to them?

I sometimes think that the politics of the last forty years can be charted entirely according to trends in drug use. Think of it. The 1950s: Eisenhower and Miltown, the director of the CIA engineering coups from his paneled den, then unwinding with a scotch and water and a yellow pill while the country plays quietly in the rec room. "Shhh, not so loud, honey. Daddy's had a hard day." The 1960s began with a President who owed much of his youthful vigor to the speed his doctor fired into his butt cheeks; there was a nice interval when everyone was getting goofy on grass and acid, but the decade crested in a mass amphetamine psychosis that lasted into the seventies: the irate hairsplitting of SDS kids hunkering down for three-day self-criticism sessions where they denounced one another as running dogs for siding with the wrong vanguard class; the dank-lipped paranoia of Richard Nixon with his enemies list as long as a New York phone book. The 1970s? Quaaludes and Gerald Ford, a President who is remembered chiefly for bumping into things. And "Just Say No" aside, the metabolism of the 1980s was *based* on cocaine: cocaine snorted off of Cartier salvers in Wall Street corner suites, inducing an alchemical euphoria that transmuted the paper shares of debt-rotten companies that manufactured nothing that anyone anywhere had ever wanted into purest gold. Cocaine, with its migraine aura of abundance and invincibility. Cocaine, which gives you—"you" being, say, a young policy gunslinger for the Heritage Foundation—the most brilliant idea you've ever had, an idea so brilliant that it erases every idea you had before but lasts only until the next line, at which point it, too, is zapped into obsolescence, nonexistence, really, by an idea that's even more brilliant. "This is *it!*" you yell, smacking your forehead so hard that leftover grains of coke sprinkle from your nostrils; you siphon them thriftily back up. "A tax cut. Can't lose with a tax cut." You reward yourself with another toot. "No! Cut *spending*. Welfare, Jesus! Legal Aid. The E.P. fucking A. All fat." Another line. "No, I got it. It's defense. Increase the sucker. Ten, twenty, hell, thirty percent! Walking tall, America." Sniff, sniff. Your septum burns. Your head swivels like Linda Blair's. "No, no. Here we go, here we go. The goddamned deficit.

A balanced-budget amendment, that's the ticket. Yesss! You are cooking today, my friend! You are one smart son of a bitch!"

And in the late 1980s, cocaine begat crack, a pharmaceutical lumpfish caviar for the lumpenproletariat, who could now get high as a lord on a two-dollar rock. Unlike cocaine, crack never enjoyed a vogue among the powerful (you can just picture George Bush exclaiming, "Jesus-Peezus! Where's a white man supposed to *get* that stuff?"), but it permeated the zeitgeist as surely as though its fumes were drifting up from the projects where Uzi-toting dealers scythed down entire street corners to cap one rival, drifting into the air ducts of the White House and the Capitol, the National Rifle Association and the Christian Coalition, this is potent shit we're talking about, one nugget is supposed to be all it takes to create addiction, and the mere rumor of crack was enough to inflame the limbic system of the body politic, infecting it with that snapping, gnawing, blood-simple crack meanness that makes people just want to *git* somebody: Git the niggers on welfare; git the Jew liberals; git the faggots and git the dykes; git the flag-burners and the porn "artists" who soak our Lord in piss; git those aliens who're creeping over our borders and stealing our jobs and sneaking their alien brats into our schools; git the unwed mothers and the women who don't want to be unwed mothers, bitches think they can just abort a white man's baby, we'll show 'em. Git 'em. Git 'em all.

The only reason I didn't succumb to this progression may be that in the 1970s I got into heroin, and heroin narrows one's interests to heroin and the means of getting it. Heroin turned me into a sour know-it-all, nodding out over *The New York Times* on a cigarette-pocked mattress and having discussions like this:

"Fucking Reagan."

"Yeah, that asshole."

"Nicaragua. Bogus."

"What a scam."

"There's Jesse Jackson."

"He's an asshole, too."

"Yeah, you're right. He is. You think Suicide's open?"

Reagan was still President when I got straight, but for a while I scarcely noticed. I was too busy trying to repair my own damage to worry about America's. I was learning to keep promises and work regular hours. I was balancing my checkbook. I was paying off debts. I was operating under the assumption that everything I'd ever believed was wrong and was prepared to discover that that included my politics.

Only once in those first few years did I actually go to a demonstration; it was the first time I'd been in Washington since the mid-seventies. The immediate pretext was abortion rights, which was under especially heavy fire then, but there were also people marching in favor of public housing and decent schools and affordable health care, things that had once been taken so much for granted—and in most of the developed world still are—that the idea of having to demonstrate for them was almost surreal, like having to demonstrate for air. But the whole march took place in an umbra of neglect. There were no news cameras in sight. We couldn't have gotten ourselves arrested if we'd tried. And it soon became clear to me that the demonstration's value was purely commemorative, like that of a religious pilgrimage to Lourdes or Santiago, someplace where miracles had occurred two thousand years ago. We were making a nostalgic grand tour of the sites where the Resistance once had tilted against the Persistence and almost unseated it, and in the end failed. There was the bloated white tit of the Capitol, bursting with milk for those who know how to suck on it and dry as a stone for everyone else; there was the Department of Justice, whose employees were now too busy investigating the last Attorney General to pay attention to our law-abiding ranks; there was the White House, whose stammering patrician occupant was trying to reinvent himself as America's next-door neighbor, a nice

guy who'd lend you his John Deere if he weren't using it to invade
Panama. And there was us, thirty thousand–odd neatly dressed
and mostly middle-class women and men, sitting on the sweet-
scented lawns that were maintained with our tax dollars, politely
listening to speeches in which no one cried out for class warfare or
the overthrow of the state and no one called anyone a pig.

At the time I'm writing of I was also a home owner, since I'd
bought one a year or so after I'd gotten clean, when the fact of
having any money at all seemed so dangerously tempting that I felt
I'd better sink it into real estate before I sank it back into my arm.
The place I bought was a small brick row house about half a mile
from Babe Ruth Stadium and a quarter mile from the Johns Hopkins campus. The neighborhood was inside city limits, but with its
wide front porches and climbing rosebushes it felt suburban, and it
was one of the few integrated areas in Baltimore. My block had
African-American families living on it, and gay and lesbian couples
and college faculty of all colors and a houseful of cheery, undissi-
pated rock musicians who played Tex-Mex polkas on their front
porch on Sunday afternoons. I was living a dream of community,
going to my neighbors' yard sales, borrowing their gardening
tools, chatting with them over the backyard fence as I climbed a
ladder to repoint the brick around my bathroom window. Who'd
have thought I'd ever repoint a brick? Who'd have thought I'd
ever have neighbors who would want to talk to me?

But in the late 1980s, things changed. Let me fill in the larger
picture for you. The stock market deflated with a gaseous hiss, followed shortly by the real-estate market. The financial institutions
that had invested in them teetered like gutted tenements while the
people they had loaned fortunes to during the boom years scurried
off with the last looted bits of copper pipe. Factories shut their
gates, emitting a flood of workers whose skills were suddenly obsolete and whom no one would bother to retrain. The federal gov-

ernment cut back its spending on cities, which in turn cut back their spending on schools and social services and hospitals and police. Crack came, and guns, not just the old pedestrian Saturday-night specials that took out one or two people at a time, but a generation of designer weapons that could turn any ambitious teenager into a spree-killer and that seemed to mirror the decade's preoccupation with brand names: Glocks and Uzis and Mac-10s, the Beamers and Rolexes and Versaces of the inner city.

This is what's known as history.

A house on my block was broken into, and then another. A Hopkins kid was jumped on his way back from the Laundromat. A neighbor was raped at knifepoint. For Sale signs sprang up along the street like late weeds. Late one August night I turned onto my street and my car's headlights picked out a crowd of teenaged boys who were walking toward me with the languid menace of mercenaries on their way home from a sack. Well, menace was something I read into their loose-kneed gait, as I read it into their baseball bats and the broken auto glass that littered the asphalt behind them. It was what I read into the way they stayed in the street even as I pulled hesitantly forward, debating whether to ease into a parking space or reverse or just grind down on the accelerator. Would they scatter, I wondered, or would I have to plow into them?

What saved me was a pair of squad cars that appeared at the other end of the block, their dome lights slowly turning. They rolled forward without stopping, sending blue spokes of light gliding across the windows on either side as they herded the boys before them. A siren squawked. A voice cracked from a loudspeaker. The crowd reached my car and parted around it. A boy said something to the others and they all laughed, the drowsy laughter of summer nights, and suddenly they were no scarier than any group of teenagers out past their curfew. I was mortified at my fear. But just then someone smacked a baseball bat against my rear fender, casually enough that an onlooker might take it for an accident but hard enough, I found out later, to crack a parking light. "Fucker," I growled, but I said it under my breath. The police cars trailed the intruders as far as the corner and then stopped. A policeman got out and walked over with that diffident cop waddle. He was black, like the kids. As far as I could tell, I was the only white person out there. "You all right?"

"Yeah. Thanks a lot." I gazed at the retreating crowd and at the trail of glass they'd left behind. My voice shook like an old man's. "Look at those bums. Just look at them!"

I left Baltimore a while later, but I still have that house. It's worth barely half what I bought it for.

My father was born to property: My grandfather owned a paper mill near Kiev. By all accounts, the old man was a benign employer but a domestic terror, a pious bully who'd lost a leg in a streetcar accident and used to thrash my father with his wooden one when he disobeyed him. But then the Revolution came, and the Civil War. The Bolsheviks seized the mill. The family fled to Austria, the children huddling in the bed of a straw-heaped wagon. It's a story out of a fairy tale: the prince dethroned, pursued by enemies, disguising himself in the rags of his humblest subjects.

But in fairy tales the banishment is always temporary; the prince is always restored. Rarely does he come to identify with the usurpers. But this is what happened to my father, who as a young man marched through the streets of Red Vienna with a red flag cracking above his head in the October wind. I imagine my grandfather waiting for him in their refugee flat, an old man made feeble by his fortunes' downfall. He sits in a chair by the coal stove, his aching stump propped on a stool, the wooden leg leaning against the wall like an umbrella drying after a rainstorm. He frets to himself in Yiddish. What does the boy think he's doing, carousing with Bolshevik rabble? Already he's forgotten what they went through? What they took away? But when my father comes home from the rally, flushed and a little drunk, his lip cut where a Nazi punched him, the old man says nothing.

As much as I like to picture my father as a lifelong revolutionary, nursing his convictions faithfully in the land of exile, I have to accept the likelihood that his socialism was just an interregnum, that over time he bought into the ideology of the Great Ones. I can think of two reasons why this might have happened. In one scenario my father's radicalism was an Oedipal stratagem, a way of dethroning—even of symbolically killing—the despot who once had terrorized him with a wooden leg that was also (you don't have to be Freud to see this) a monstrous wooden phallus. But by the time they got to Vienna, the tyrant was already dethroned. And not too far in the future he would be killed without a drop of symbolism (the Nazis didn't believe in symbolism, or at least not in deconstructing it: One of the first things they did when they came to power was outlaw Freud's loathsome Jewish science), locked into the killing box of the Vienna ghetto, where malnutrition and typhus took him a few weeks before he would have been sent to die with his wife at Auschwitz. I wouldn't be surprised to learn that my father renounced socialism on the day he got the news of his father's death.

But there's also the prosaic fact that socialism is a strenuous ideology. Socialism requires a belief in the goodness of human nature and the benignity of history, which Marx thought would sweep mankind to a godless heaven if we just helped it along. Socialism requires adherents with energy and leisure, students or the unemployed, who can march and canvass and seize the means of production and distribution. But when my father came to America he was thirty years old and he was tired. He wanted to earn a living, to start a family. He wanted to forget. And even if he'd still believed, there just wouldn't have been time. As Hannah Arendt noted, "The transformation of the family man from a responsible member of society, interested in all public affairs, to a 'bourgeois' concerned only with his private existence and knowing no civic virtue, is an international modern phenomenon."

Is this what's happening to me? Every day I see myself becoming more like my father—not the one I dreamed of, but the one I knew—a tired man scowling over the morning paper. I fret about property values. I grouse over my taxes. I stomp past the dreadlocked white kids who panhandle on Avenue A, my spine thrumming with indignation. Not long ago, when one of them tried to hit me up for a buck, I muttered, "Get a job, junior." And the kid must have heard me because he hollered, "I'll take yours!" Most days I walk around in a swoon of self-pity. I have so little, I tell myself: a small apartment, a house no one will take off my hands, a freelance job writing jacket copy for a publisher that could fire me at any moment, ship my non-job off to Mexico (well, not Mexico, there aren't likely to be too many English copywriters there, but some Anglophone developing nation, Nigeria or Belize). I have so little, and they all want to take it away.

To be a member of the American middle class today is to live between fear and hate. It is to suspect that we belong to an endangered species, whose privileges are being taken away by forces beyond our comprehension. It is, all too often, to resent the people who have less than we do, and to blame them for the waning of our way of life. One peculiarity of the American class system—apart from the fiction that it doesn't exist—is that it teaches us to admire those who are situated higher up on its rickety ladder and to despise those who cling to the rungs below. Above us, the nation's till is being emptied. Above us, those who already have are helping themselves to more. Above us, a new language of dispossession is being invented ("downsizing," "rightsizing," "outsourcing"), a language that will be used to classify us. But we are always looking down, in fear and hate, muttering about welfare queens and unwed mothers and ignoring the sound of sawing that we half hear overhead.

We are distracted so easily.

How do you remain focused? How do you keep the enemy in your sights when the enemy is your own fear and greed and self-pity disguised as a set of political convictions? Socialism may have failed because it was too Platonic, presupposing a spotless core of virtue in every citizen. But fascism is pure de Sade, even if American fascists have gone to such vast lengths to deny their ideology's sexual content and repackage its cruelty as right-minded Biblical wrath. Well, we all want to murder somebody: the only question is whom, and how close do we come to actually pulling the trigger? All through 1992 I bought newspapers for the childish satisfaction of drawing crosshairs on the heads of John Sununu and Dan Quayle. I even painted a T-shirt with the slogan "SHOOT QUAYLE FIRST," which might have made me rich if I'd mass-produced it. I slandered the President on call-in radio, accusing him of starting the war with Iraq over the hidden relics of Jesus, some of which were squirreled away in Baghdad and others in the sealed vaults of the Skull and Bones Club. I hoped that someone on the Christian right might actually believe this.

And don't forget my tattoo. I was so proud the night I went to CBGB. Later that same year the Party of God would call for a religious war at its Presidential convention. Here, arrayed before the fact, were the infidels against whom that war would be declared. Amid the smoke and popping flashbulbs, a three-hundred-pound biker with a bracelet of swastikas tattooed on his biceps chatted amicably with a guy whose hairless cranium was emblazoned in Gothic script with the words "WE ARE ALL HIV-POSITIVE." Up onstage a woman known as Pulsating Paula was baring the fancy Japanese work on her left breast, and the breast along with it. The tattoo contest's emcee had once been the object of a city-wide manhunt after he'd videotaped the police riot in Tompkins Square Park and smuggled the evidence to the TV news. Here they all were, the heathen, the outcasts, the transgressors, and myself among them. I was with my people.

But who *were* my people? At one point I found myself standing behind Tommy DaVita and another tattooist, and I couldn't help eavesdropping on their conversation. And what I heard was "Manhattan? Yeah, you get more walk-in business in Manhattan, St. Mark's, Tompkins Square, I'm not going to argue with you. But the rents, man. The rents! You're going to have to bump your hourly a good twenty percent to make that kind of change."

The guy who liked to have his earlobes fucked—the one who'd once engaged in such heavy edge play that one of his pierced nipples had torn in half, necessitating an emergency visit to a piercer who stitched it up as neat as a pin for a tenth of what a plastic surgeon would have charged—*he* turned out to be a bond trader. The proudest moment in his life was when he'd helped arrange the buyout of RJR Nabisco. I asked him if he'd had his hardware in—I pointed gingerly at his ears—when he closed the deal, and he gave me a pitying look. "Oh, no, dear. It would be like coming into the office without a tie. You just wouldn't."

The truth is tattooists are craftspeople and small-business owners, and they tend to be conservative. Even Slam bitches about the junkies who panhandle on her front stoop. The truth is that, no matter what Pat Buchanan may say, there is no such thing as deviance anymore. Or rather, deviance is just another spectacle, to be trotted out whenever the Great Ones want to distract the *polis* from the looting of the national patrimony. It's no accident that deviance became a threat at exactly the time that communism ceased to be one, as though the Iron Curtain fell only to reveal a chorus line of muff-divers and sissies, all of them, naturally, tattooed, and all of them coming for *you*. The truth, the most painful truth of all, is that in the 1990s deviance is a marketing strategy: It's what sells

CK fragrance, whose ads feature wasted, tattooed models who might as well have needles dangling from their arms. And so hipped are we to the rules of the game that only the smallest, most susceptible percentage of us will end up with junk habits or whip marks; the rest of us will end up with our own personal bottles of CK, the fragrance that lets you Just Be.

By the time I was called to go onstage, I wanted to skip the contest, to just go home and nurse my arm and gorge on Chinese take-out. But Slam was fussing over me with a spray bottle and a tube of antiseptic, trying to re-create that fresh-from-the-needle shine that makes even a bad piece look as tasty as a slab of fresh-baked pie. But this piece wasn't bad at all and the last thing I wanted was to disappoint her. So I climbed up, the third person to slouch before the panel of grizzled, seen-everything tattooists and their geeky young protégés, who all looked like Trekkies, and a gorgeous woman editor from *Skin and Ink*. Maybe she'd be impressed enough to go home with me.

I wanted to say something, the way movie people do when they collect their Oscars. I could have urged the crowd to vote. That's what rock stars have taken to doing: "Vote, dudes, and go easy in the mosh pit." I could have told everyone to vote Revolutionary Social Democrat, though no such party exists and the idea is a contradiction in terms. (I once told some investigators from the Defense Intelligence Agency that the only country I'd consider spying for was Sweden, and I suspect that this was enough to make them tear up my dossier, assuming I ever had one.) I could have mobilized them in a project that my friend Rob and I once dreamed up when we were imagining the one thing that might actually shake the foundations of power: A Day Without Buying. A day when millions and millions of Americans, all over the country, refused to take part in the remorseless daisy chain of consumption that turns everything, *everything,* into a commodity—the consumer included. I could imagine getting them, the entire audience at CBGB, to chant the slogan Rob and I had made up: "DON'T BUY ANYTHING [*clap*]. DON'T BUY ANYTHING [*clap clap*]. DON'T BUY ANY-THING."

Or maybe I could have gotten them to sing the old, sweet song that once meant so much to so many before it was spoiled by what happened to communism, the hopeful faith that created a theocracy as deadly as any imagined by Jerry Falwell or the Ayatollah Khomeini. The song that can be hummed by anyone who ever celebrated Christmas:

> *Then raise the scarlet standard high!*
> *Within its shade we'll live or die.*
> *Though cowards flinch and traitors sneer*
> *We'll keep the red flag flying here.*

But I never had to decide. Slam's beautiful tattoo only came in second in that night's contest, I hope through no fault of mine. The winner was a guy whose forearm was tattooed so that the skin seemed to have been peeled back, disclosing an intricate metal skeleton bristling with wire and cable and hose. A tattoo that makes its wearer look like an android was a brand-new idea at the time, but it caught on quickly, and by now thousands of people have one. They're everywhere.

5

I DO THE RIGHT THING

> Amazing how the world keeps on offering new opportunities for betrayal.
>
> *John Banville*, ATHENA

The Kafka story "In the Penal Colony" is set—presciently, since Kafka wrote it in 1914—in a concentration camp where the principal instrument of punishment is a machine called the "Harrow." It sounds like a tattoo gun designed by the Marquis de Sade. A prisoner is strapped onto a bed padded with cotton wool. A gag is wedged in his mouth. And then the Harrow is lowered onto him. It's equipped with two sets of needles, and as it descends these begin to vibrate. One set of needles pierces the victim's skin hundreds of times per second; the other scours the incisions clean with jets of water. What emerges, etched in the penitent's flesh, outlined in pearls of blood that an instant later are sluiced away, is the name of the crime for which he is being punished. A visitor to the colony asks if the man they're about to inscribe in this manner knows what his sentence is. And this is his answer: "There would be no point in telling him. He'll learn it on his body."

I think I was unconsciously referring to this story a few years back, when I paid Slam to tattoo an angel on my left shoulder blade. I don't mean one of those swooning pre-Raphaelite androgynes you see in every New Age bookstore, reassuring us that the universe is a loving place with a winged nanny for every one of us. This was the Archangel Michael, copied from an old design that was once common in Egypt and the Holy Land. It's a stern, hieratic figure with the suggestion of a scowl on its face. I suppose this is appropriate for the messenger who drove Adam and Eve from Paradise and is said to bar its gate to this day. In one hand the Archangel bears a sword; in the other, a set of scales: to menace and to weigh. He is stubby-winged, rooted in place, a defensive player from the moment of the Fall. All in all, I think the image was a good choice, since I conceived the tattoo as a mark of penance. When Slam began working on me that day, she warned that it might hurt more than usual, the shoulder blade being a bony place. I didn't want her thinking I was any stranger than I thought she already thought I was. Otherwise I would have said, "That's okay. I want it to hurt."

I could have gotten something more representational. In the prison camps of the former Soviet Union tattoos constitute a language in which every image is a "word" whose meaning may be mysterious to outsiders but is immediately apparent to other convicts. Gamblers wear a suit of cards, murderers a skull pierced by a dagger or a bolt of lightning. Each additional sentence is denoted by the dome of a cathedral: Lifers have entire heavenly cities inked on their backs. Sex offenders, for some reason, are tattooed with flies' eyes on their noses, cheeks, or upper lips. In photographs these look like the lesions of a corrupting skin disease. Maybe I should have gotten a syringe—I used to want a syringe—or a heart with a hole at its center. But the scowling Archangel seemed less literal, an all-purpose signifier of trespass. It is the sentence I wear on my body.

I am a sick man. . . . I am a wicked man. Legally, I have been guilty of petty larceny, the use and sale of narcotics and controlled substances, fraud, sodomy, and assault, which technically includes yelling "I'll kill you, you motherfucker!" as I have done more often than I can count. If I were a Catholic, I would have to confess to sloth, gluttony, anger, lust, avarice, envy, and pride. (During my active addiction I once tried to confess at St. Patrick's Cathedral: I was so addled with dope and guilt and grandiosity that my nice neighborhood church on Avenue B wasn't good enough for me. But I nodded out in a pew while waiting for a free priest.) As far as the Ten Commandments go, I have broken all but the ones against murder and bearing false witness, and that's only because I never could stand a snitch. In the abstract none of this bothers me that much. It's only where people are concerned that I feel remorse, whose sting is so much like the sting of a tattoo needle trawling the skin above the heart.

Specifically, there were three people whom I'd used badly and had to make some restitution to: my mother, my father, and a woman named Catherine, whom I'd lived with for three years back when my principal interest was making myself stupid. At the time I became ready to atone, one of them was dead, another had disappeared, and the third and I were on terms of such brittle formality that we might have belonged to some imperial court in Asia where every rank speaks a different language. Each of these people preyed on me. Or, really, it was the memory of my behavior toward them that preyed on me. Memory is supposed to fade with time, but the memory of my unkindnesses grew sharper with each year that passed until it no longer seemed like memory at all. It had become my present. It had the present's awful open-endedness. I had wronged these people and I was wronging them still, slamming the same doors, saying the same words and seeing them register in the sudden stillness of a face over and over and over, only I had become conscious enough to recognize the wrong for what it was even as I remained powerless to stop it.

It's fashionable for people to see themselves as their parents' victims and I suppose we are, inasmuch as they condemned us to live in the first place. I used to say that all I'd ever wanted from my mother and father was love, that want that justifies everything, that the cruelties I came to inflict on them later on were only a response to some original denial. But I have no memory of my parents denying me anything. What I remember is their offering me everything and me refusing, resisting love with all the blind tenacity with which most people are assumed to seek it.

My parents' love was a despairing kind: It was the love of people who've lost so much that they can't care for anything without waiting for it to be taken away. There were reasons for this. By the time he was thirty, my father had fled three different countries and lost both parents in the Holocaust. At the time I was born, my mother's mother was dying of cancer. They had learned the Buddhist lesson that life is suffering without acquiring the detachment that goes with it. Maybe that kind of detachment is beyond the reach of Westerners. My parents remained attached. When I took my first steps, they held their breath: All they saw was that I could now fall down stairs and walk off curbs into the path of speeding trucks.

Maybe they saw clearly. From the very first I was running away. "You wouldn't walk," my mother used to tell me, in the tone of fond complaint that parents use when they talk about your childhood, when you might have been a nuisance or a worry but hadn't yet become a heartache. "You had to run. I don't know why. I'd take you to the park and put you down in the sandbox, and a minute later I'd look up and you'd be running away as fast as your little legs could carry you. And I had to run after you. Do you know what it was like, running after a two-year-old in my high heels? It was no picnic, I can tell you. And when I picked you up, oh, the tantrums you had!"

The fact that I had tantrums is corroborated by a man I once met who grew up in my old neighborhood in Manhattan and who, as a very little boy, used to watch me in awe as I howled and thrashed: "You were lying on the ground. I don't think anyone could have picked you up, you were kicking so hard. And your face wasn't blue, it was *black*. The grown-ups just stood there while you kicked and screamed and slobbered and threw up fistfuls of dirt. I'd never realized that a kid could do that—paralyze a bunch of grown-ups by making a lot of noise. Right then and there you became my hero. When you were finished, I walked up to you and said, 'Do that again.' "

When I got too old for tantrums, there was language. Both of my parents were relatively recent immigrants—my father from Russia via Austria and France, my mother from Finland—and very early I intuited that English was a place they couldn't follow me. I sought out its roughest terrain. I crawled into its narrowest crevices. And then I peered out at those big, slow-moving foreigners thumping overhead and hollered, "Come and get me, coppers!"

I'm seven years old and watching *Huckleberry Hound* on TV, and my father announces that it's time for bed. "Why is it time for bed?" I whine.

"Are you getting smart with me?" In his voice there is a warning pulse like the sound of an engine shifting gears. When my father yells, the glass coffee table in our living room vibrates. And maybe I am trying to forestall his rage and maybe I just want to end the suspense of waiting for it to crash over me, but I say, "Oh, Daddy, why do you have to be so intransigent?" My father falls silent. And even at that age I can tell he doesn't know the word. *I* don't know the word, either, not really. It's just something that I picked up in *Time,* which I read because I'm a hair too bright for *Highlights,* and have thrown out the way you'll throw any old piece of junk at someone who's big and mad and bearing down on you like a cartoon bull—a pot, a fire poker, a sofa cushion, an alarm clock that starts ringing frantically when it hits the wall. My father stays silent, but he moves toward me.

"Don't be like that, Anatole," my mother cries. "Didn't you hear him?"

"Sure I heard him! I heard him contradict me! Who does this lit-tle *pisher* think he is, contradicting his own father?"

"But didn't you hear what he said? He said—what was that word you said, darling?"

"Intransigent."

She kisses me. Back then she wore a bright red lipstick that set off the blackness of her hair. In photographs she looks like Ava Gardner, though without Gardner's wild, unnerving gaze. " 'In-transigent.' Listen to him! Didn't I tell you? I told you he's gifted."

"Sure he's gifted. I've been saying he's gifted for years. Does that mean he gets to contradict me?"

"Of course not. Don't contradict your father, darling," my mother says, but she's mocking him even as she says it. And al-ready a complicity has sprung up between us and a gulf formed between the two of them. Well, maybe not "formed." My parents were old enough to trash their marriage on their own, a job they finished five years later. But let's say that the fault line between my mother and father widened another quarter-inch. Let's say that I was using language not only to deflect my father's anger but to win my mother away from him, which is no more, after all, than any little boy wants. But how many boys actually pull it off, and then turn their moms into accomplices in their fathers' humilia-tion? Even then I was learning how to play them against each other.

At the age of nine I stayed home from school one day to watch my dad on television. He was a guest on Joe Franklin's *Memory Lane,* an afternoon talk show whose guests ran to has-been charac-ter actors, never-was lounge singers, and people like my father, who just wanted to plug their businesses. For my father, this meant displaying glossy photographs of his catering hall's Viennese table and explaining that those luscious-looking éclairs were made *com-pletely without dairy,* "with a rabbi in the kitchen so you know you're getting kosher." What I heard was "vit a rebbi in de keetchin so you noh you're gettink kosher." It might have been Boris Badenov saying "Moose end Skvirril." For the first time I realized that my father had an accent, the accent of cartoon spies, an accent in which *w*'s were *v*'s and *v*'s *f*'s and every vowel seemed to issue not from a mouth, but from a snot-clogged nose.

When my father came home I said nothing. But from then on, I began to mimic him. I mimicked him to my mother, I mimicked him to my friends, especially as a teenager, when recounting one of his desperate stabs at discipline—the way he reacted to my getting busted for drugs and kicked out of junior high by hauling me from the principal's office to the nearest barbershop for a crew cut that made me look like a fat-faced Young Pioneer from a Minsk *kolkhoz;* the time he phoned me at a friend's house (how on earth did he track me down?) when I stayed out past one A.M. on a weeknight and bellowed, "You do that again and I'll kill you! *I'll keel you!*" I'd growl and reduce a room to sobs of dopey laughter, as I reduced him. Once, I mimicked my father to his face. We were fighting, the way we fought all through my adolescence, and he said something, I don't remember what exactly except that it struck me as a quintessential expression of his belligerent stupidity, a stupidity I would have called "peasantlike" if I hadn't been a lover of the working people. Whatever it was, I repeated it, word for word, in my version of his voice. He stared at me for a long time. Then he said, "Very funny. How did I ever get such a smart kid?" I imitate my father to this day, lowering my voice and constricting my throat to produce those sounds that are as unmistakably foreign as a cardboard suitcase held shut with twine, and I tell myself that I do it out of love. But I never imitated him to his face again.

Not that I didn't imitate my mother, too, though her accent was harder to get: Finland has no Boris Badenov. But from very early I could do her plaintive delicacy, the yearning quality that made her seem light—fragile—even after she ballooned from comfort-eating and cortisone shots. My mother had an expressive voice: She could croon, she could simper, and even in her seventies she still had the giggle of a naughty child who knows she will never be punished. But I have few memories of my mother speaking in those years. Mostly she *called*. "Peterle," she'd call from her bedroom. "Come sit with me a little, I'm lonely." "Bring me my pills, the green ones. I've got such pain with my back." "Peterle, phone your father and tell him I've got to go to the hospital. Tell him it's serious."

My mother's voice made me cringe in a different way than my father's did: If his sometimes made me fear for my safety, my mother's made me fear for her life. And if my father's accent drenched me with social embarrassment, the embarrassment felt by Pip in *Great Expectations* when his benefactor turns out to be an escaped convict, my mother's voice inspired a shame that was deeper and more secret. It may have been the shame of having a mother who was always at death's door but never died (which at least would have made people feel sorry for me). It may have been the shame I felt at being so afraid for her, because every time she came home from the doctor I expected her to tell me that this time she had something fatal, and every time she left for the hospital I was sure she'd never come back. It may have been shame at the intimacy that formed around her sickness, like a cocoon forming around a caterpillar, the afternoons spent sitting at her bedside when I came home from school, holding her hand and listening to her tell her rosary of hurts: her back, her lungs, her legs, the doctors who never returned her phone calls, the husband who never came home. It was all hurt, with only one bead of pleasure, and the pleasure was me. It was a shame that couldn't be joked away. I never imitated my mother to my friends.

Sometimes I mimicked her to my father, especially after he left and I was anxious to win him as an ally. I'd collapse theatrically onto the convertible in his residential hotel room and place a hand against my brow. "Those doctors," I'd moan. "None of them cares.

Not one. They say, 'Call me in the morning.' But what if something happens at night? Can you tell me? Do I have to make an appointment to get sick?" My father would chuckle, "Ach, that's your
mother, all right. I don't envy you, you got to put up with that.
Maybe now you understand what I had to go through all those
years."

But mostly I imitated my mother to her face. Whatever qualms
I had about injuring a parent didn't seem to operate when it came
to her. Perhaps because she already seemed so injured. "Why must
you dress like that?" she stammered when I came home wearing a
pair of bell-bottoms made from scraps of American flags and engi-
neer's boots that I'd spray-painted gold, so that they looked like
the plated footwear of a baby Hell's Angel. "You have to make
yourself so ugly? You can't see what it does to me?" Her voice
started trembling. "You're stabbing a knife in my heart!" I don't
know which of us was closer to crying: my mom, who really
thought I was dressing to spite her rather than impress some
eleventh-grade girl who wouldn't have gone out with me even if I
had managed to replicate the outfit Brian Jones wore on the sleeve
of *Beggars Banquet,* or me, because even at fifteen or sixteen, I
couldn't hurt my mother without feeling pain—her pain or my own
ghostly approximation of it—lance through me, as though after all
those years outside her belly I was still wired into her nervous
system.

But I wouldn't cry, no more than I would have said, "You're
right, I *do* look ugly," and calmly changed into blue jeans. I just
stared at her, transfixed with shock and horror and rage, the kind
of rage that doesn't make you yell but hiss, as though your vocal
cords had become too swollen with its poison to produce any
other sound. When I finally opened my mouth, what came out
was a wobbly falsetto: *"You're stabbing a knife in my heart! You're stabbing a knife in my heart!* OH, I WISH!"

The thing to do next would have been to stomp into my room

and slam the door behind me. Instead I kept watching my mother. Was I that sadistic or just paralyzed? Ross Carlson, who murdered his parents and then tried to pass himself off as a multiple personality, claimed that he remembered watching someone else—an alternate, presumably—fire the gun. My dissociation was milder: I knew that it was I who'd spoken, but I was stunned by what I'd said and how I'd said it. It was as though I'd found myself in a circle of Dante's hell, where the sin of filial ingratitude took the form of a great black bird that had burst from my mouth and now flapped crazily around the room, terrorizing both of us. My mother pointed at me. "You talk like that? To your own mother?"

I vomited up another bird. " 'To your own mother?' Who do you think I'm talking to? There's nobody else here."

"How did you get to be so vicious? What did I do to you? Will you tell me?" Her voice broke. "Oh, I can't take it! I'm not well. You know I'm not well. You're making me—oh, I can't! I can't!" She began to sob, cupping her face in her hands. And I was still young enough, I guess, that I began to sob myself. "I'm sorry, Mom! I didn't mean it. Oh, don't cry. Please don't cry." I came over to her and held her. Not the way I'd held her when I was little, when I used to fling my arms around her in a wild attempt to make her safe, but stiffly, as though she were explosive. I had reached the point where I hated touching her. "I'm sorry, Ma. I'm so sorry."

I was always saying I'm sorry: to my mother, to my father, to many others. *I'm sorry I said that. I'm sorry I hurt you. I'm sorry I ate that piece of Nesselrode pie. I'm sorry I forgot your birthday. I'm sorry I lied to you. I'm sorry I took that thirty dollars. I'm sorry I fucked your best friend. She was a lousy lay.* In the years I'm writing about I said "I'm sorry" so many times that the phrase lost its standard English meaning and metamorphosed into its virtual opposite. Every time I said "I'm sorry," what I was really saying was "Can I screw you again?"

By the time I was in my late twenties, I no longer cried when my

mother did, maybe because I heard her cry only over the telephone: I rarely saw her. There was one time she'd gone into the
hospital again—it was her back or a spot on her lungs that she was
afraid was cancer—and I didn't visit. Mostly, it was sheer laziness
on my part, but the laziness engendered guilt, which was never
that far from me, anyway, and that in turn folded into resentment.
The origami of repression never ceases to fascinate me, the way in
which a few deft pleats will morph one feeling into another, so that
you start out with a plain square of fear, perhaps, and end up with
an intricate, cornute swan of righteous fury. It happens so quickly.
The night my mother called me from her hospital room, I'd barely
had time to recognize her voice before I was seething at her.

"Is that really you?" She was trying to sound breezy.

"Of course it's me. Who else would it be?"

"Well, I wouldn't know. I've forgotten what you sound like."

"I guess I should have called more," I said, but I said it through
clenched teeth.

"How should I know how often you're supposed to call? Most
sons *visit* their mothers when they're in the hospital. That's what I
always thought, but what do I know? I don't understand you
at all."

"Maybe you need to try harder."

"I've been trying for fourteen years! Fourteen years I've been
trying to understand what changed you from a sweet little boy to
whatever it is you are now! What are you now, anyway? Can you
tell me?"

"I'm a man, Mother—"

"*Man?* A man goes three weeks without visiting his mother
when she's lying in the hospital?"

"—a man who's got a lot more important things to do than come
fluttering up to your goddamned bedside every day just because
you decided you needed a rest cure!"

"You think I'm here for a rest? If you'd been coming here, or even calling me once in a while on the telephone like a human being, you'd know I'm not here for a rest. Do you have any idea what kind of pain I'm having? This time it's serious, Peter. I'm not joking. Just yesterday Dr. Grassheim said he was worried for my life!"

"Well, that must have made you happy."

She emitted a little grunt, as though she'd been punched in the stomach. "Och, I can't believe you! You're wicious. Wicious!" Excitement made her turn her *v*'s into *w*'s: It was the only identifiable feature of her accent. "I never thought I'd say this about my own son, but that's what you are! My friends come to visit me—thank God at least I've got them—and they ask me, 'Where's Peter?' And you should hear me. I *lie* to them. I say, 'Oh, Peter was just here.' But I can't look them in the eyes, I don't want to see they're feeling sorry for me—" And here her voice broke, which was what I'd been dreading all along.

I snapped, "Don't tell me you didn't look, Ma. You've got more mileage out of having a shitty son than anyone I've ever heard of. I'll tell you what: I won't come visit for another two weeks. That way you'll have them *really* feeling sorry for you!"

But my mother's weeping cut me short. I remember having the sensation that I wasn't listening, but *watching* her through the kinked tunnel of the telephone line. I could see her as though I were looking down from the ceiling: She was curled up on a bed in a beige room, wearing one of the fussy nightgowns that I used to pack for her when I was a kid because even ill she was a fastidious person who would no more go to the hospital without a few changes of nightclothing than she would go shopping without dabbing on some lipstick, pausing before the hallway mirror to trace her lips, then popping them together as though blowing a kiss at her reflection: *There, not so bad!* But now I saw her without lipstick, her hair uncombed, the nightgown slipping from her heaving shoulders. It seemed to go on forever. She said, "What kind of person are you to treat me like this? You're an animal. That's what you are, an animal!"

I snarled at her, a sound I've made only a few times in my life. "OKAY, I'M AN ANIMAL! I'M AN ANIMAL! I ADMIT IT. AT LEAST THAT'S BETTER THAN BEING A VEGETABLE LIKE YOU!"

I slammed the phone down. Then I took it off the hook. Then I did a shot of liquid methedrine from the bottle I kept in the refrigerator next to the milk. I'd been shooting speed at least twice a day for months. Sometimes I'd take a vial to work with me and sneak little swigs in the bathroom: my pick-me-ups. One day my coworkers had thrown a birthday party for me, which made me so anxious that I dashed into the john fifteen minutes into the festivities only to discover that the vial had leaked and that the lining of my sport coat was sopping with liquid speed, about half a week's salary's worth. So of course I whisked off the jacket and began sucking with all my might, not caring if my mouth was full of lint or if the door was bolted or if someone came in and found me: I would have explained that I was trying to get out a spot.

I have to be careful not to use the drugs as an excuse. I would have been the same unfilial prick without them, maybe a more controlled unfilial prick. But the speed partly explains what I did next, that and the fact that I'd broken up with my girlfriend a few months before, and had been dumped by another woman afterward, and gotten rejection slips from three different literary magazines within the previous week. I was in a bad way all around. I sat hunched on the edge of my bed with the blinds drawn, jerking a mixture of blood and speed into the big vein in my left forearm. Every time I pushed down on the syringe's plunger I felt my heart thrash like a hooked trout. I remember I had a Lou Reed record playing very loudly—at least it seemed very loud to me, though I doubt it actually was since I was petrified of drawing the attention of my neighbors. And at one point I found myself listening to the words Lou was singing: "You're just cheap, cheap, cheap, cheap uptown dirt, cheap, cheap, cheap, cheap uptown dirt." And I was certain he was singing to me, or maybe God was, delivering His judgment upon me in Reed's baleful *sprechstimme*.

A while later I wrote the words "I'm sorry" on a postcard and placed it on my nightstand. Then I took thirty Fiorinals that a doctor had prescribed me for migraines—I had migraines constantly when I was doing speed but somehow never connected one with the other—and flushed the pills down with a bottle of cheap wine. Before I passed out I also tried slashing my wrists, but I was too timid to cut very deeply. I could spend hours methodically puncturing my arms and spraying the bloody residue all over the bathroom walls, but I couldn't cut my wrists.

If I'd been serious about killing myself, I suppose I would have gotten a better wine. I came to the next morning in a lava field of dried vomit and blood. Two of my coworkers were pounding on the door. They told me later that they'd called when I didn't show up at the office and I'd actually picked up the phone and mumbled, "Lemme alone. I'm dying." Once I realized that I was still here I was humiliated. (You know that expression "I wouldn't be caught dead"? Well, I had been.) "I fine," I moaned. "S'jussa flu." But they wouldn't leave. I made Carlos and Deborah wait outside until I'd managed to crawl into some clothes, but my fingers were too numb to negotiate the buttons: I stumbled to the door holding my pants up with one hand and at once pitched forward into Carlos's arms, then apologized for my vomity breath. I apologized for the state of my clothing, as poor Deborah buttoned me up and guided my arm into a shirtsleeve that I'd somehow forgotten about. I apologized for my soiled comforter, which I tried to stuff into the hall incinerator. I apologized for wasting their time, and the company's, and the admitting nurse's at the hospital, and for all I know the time of the doctors who pumped my stomach, though by then I was out again and remember nothing more of that day except for lying on my reeling bed some hours later, groaning, "I just hope I haven't done any lasting brain damage."

In time I even apologized to my mother, though I told her nothing about the aftermath of our phone conversation. And she, of course, forgave me.

There's a difference between apologizing and atoning, as anyone who's spent any time at criminal sentencings can attest. Nine times out of ten the condemned person says, "I'm sorry, Your Honor," as he stands before the bench. I've seen men say it with tears rolling down their cheeks. But nine times out of ten the prisoner is a repeat offender, and the next words out of his mouth are likely to be an excuse. The word *apology,* after all, comes from a Greek root that means "to justify." There's a story in the Talmud that after Cain murdered Abel, God rebuked him and Cain flew into a rage. "Wait a second!" he cries. "Who planted the Evil Inclination in my heart? If I killed my brother, it's Your fault!" I don't know what God is supposed to have answered. But we know what He did: *And the Lord set a mark upon Cain, lest any finding him should kill him.* People often think of Cain's mark as a punishment, but it was also a token of divine protection, a warning that anyone who fucked with Cain would have to answer to God, Who reserves vengeance for Himself.

We can see Cain's mark as the first tattoo. From the very beginning tattoos were associated with wrongdoing. Cain, of course, was marked against his will, as were the inmates of Kafka's penal colony. The tattooist Hanky Panky once told me that authorities in medieval Japan would etch a line on the face of a first-time offender. If they caught him doing the same thing again, they'd etch a second line nearby. The third time they caught him, they'd connect the two strokes with a third, forming the character for "dog." In those times and places punishment was a public event, a spectacle enacted on the criminal body. God's mark on Cain or the word *dog* inscribed on a felon's cheek were messages from the judges to the judged, from those who made the law to those who suffered it. And not only to the condemned, but to everyone who saw them. The message was: "Your body belongs to us. We can do this to you, too."

What distinguishes kind and usual punishment from the cruel and unusual variety is that its locus is not the body but the mind or soul contained within it. Modern punishment is invisible, which may be the reason that so many people find it unsatisfying. (Those upright sadists who call for a revival of caning may not be the sadists we think they are. They're just frustrated; they want to see that "justice" is still working. Who can trust something that is inflicted only on gray matter behind gray walls? We want a justice that leaves scars.) The odd thing is that when the authorities stopped tattooing prisoners, the prisoners started tattooing themselves, as though unconsciously reenacting the cruelties their keepers had abandoned. Jailhouse tattoos are often advertisements of their wearers' criminality: the jaunty skull on the breast of a Russian hit man, the gory dagger that announces "This is one bad motherfucker." Prisons are miniature warrior societies, and their members tattoo themselves for the same reasons that the Iban and the Maori did. But jailhouse tattoos are also signs of defiance. They announce that some part of the wearer, if only a few square inches of skin, is still his own, colonized but unconquered.

But I'm also struck by the other tats you see on convicts, the ones that recall the life outside, the life that was cut short or thrown away in the moment that someone hot-wired a car or fired a gun at a checkout clerk in a 7-Eleven. Alongside those daggers there are hearts with "MOTHER" inked beneath them in a feminine script. There are portraits of sweethearts whose names might be forgotten if they weren't written on the skin. Of course those tattoos are kitschy. But their kitschiness fades into insignificance when you see them juxtaposed with the iconography of captivity and death and realize that the men who have them may never see mothers or sweethearts again (or see them only for a half hour every weekend, while sitting on opposite sides of a counter beneath the bland gaze of guards who tap their wrists when the time is up). As its name suggests, a penitentiary is supposed to be an institution for penance, but it is more likely to be a place where men who were hard to begin with are made harder, like lumps of coal pressed into diamonds. In penitentiaries there is no room for longing or remorse: Crying in public can get you killed. So those maudlin tattoos, which suggest nothing so much as the pictures on old greeting cards, may in fact be a secret language. They express sentiments that cannot be put into words or even recognized, because to recognize them would reverse the hardening that has kept you alive, might turn the diamond back to coal or, further, to the soft, decaying matter that preceded it; those feelings might turn you back into shit: *I loved her. I miss you. I did wrong.*

The only thing I learned from my suicide attempt was to alternate speed with heroin, which was more addictive, physiologically, but less deranging. Once I was doing dope regularly, I was no longer cruel to my mother, at least not consciously. I scarcely knew she existed. Heroin banished other people from the landscape. It turned them into accessories or inconveniences, and the inconveniences could be shrugged off with another bag. In time heroin led me to Catherine. It's a commonplace that you can predict the outcome of a relationship from the circumstances of its beginning. When I met Catherine I was expecting to get into a threesome with her roommate and another woman I was seeing then, and we spent our first evening together copping.

I showed up at their loft, a gray, sepulchral space that might once have been a ballroom and that had plaster sifting from its ceiling and feral cats scuttling through the rubble underfoot. My two prospective partners were sitting on a bed in the center of the room. They were in their underwear, which was expensive looking but yellowed, like Miss Havisham's wedding gown. "Oh, goody!" The woman I knew clapped. It was an ironic clap; she was one of those people who does everything ironically. "We can start. Why don't you take off your clothes and let Madeleine get a load of your dick?"

They looked at me as though I were a plumber who'd shown up hours late for an emergency call. I felt my dick shrink down to a two-inch stub, a thing you might call "The Little Fellow" if you were in a joshing mood. "Don't you have anything, Ronnie?" I asked.

The roommate arched an eyebrow. "He's into toys?"

"No, no. Dope. Don't you have any dope?"

"Shit, keep your voice down!" She gestured at the leprous walls and whispered, "They're monitoring us."

"Well, do you have any?"

"No," Madeleine said loudly. She was very tall, with a tropical abundance of curly black hair. "We don't have any . . . TAPES in the house. We haven't been able to buy any new MUSIC lately. If you want to LISTEN to some TAPES, you'll have to buy them yourself. There's a STORE on Tenth and D. Maybe Catherine can go with you and buy some TAPES for us. Catherine!"

The woman who came in was small, with poreless milky skin and short brown hair so fine it was like the down on a baby chick. Her jeans and white T-shirt made her look incongruously wholesome. "What?" She seemed simultaneously annoyed and cowed.

"Our *friend* here is going to go out to buy some TAPES. I was thinking maybe you could go with him and get us some, too."

"I'm reading."

"Well, I'm sure that'll hold for an hour. I believe you owe us fifty dollars."

"*I know.*" She flung on a jacket and stalked out the door, slamming it so that its four locks rattled.

"Don't mind her," Madeleine said. "She gets peevish." She might have been talking about a poor relation she'd taken in as a charity case in exchange for light cleaning and laundering. "Just make sure she gets five."

Catherine was waiting for me when I came downstairs, hugging herself against the cold and glaring with such malice that I immediately began apologizing. "I'm sorry. I didn't mean to drag you out. What were you reading?"

"*Ethan Frome*. You wouldn't have heard of it."

"I've heard of it. Go back and read if you want. I can cop for you. Oh. Is it okay to say that, or are they listening down here, too?"

"Oh, Madeleine's so paranoid. Actually, she's not even really paranoid, she just likes to *sound* paranoid. She thinks it's dramatic. The way she thinks it's cool to do threesomes." She was the second person that evening who'd looked at me as though I were hired help. I wanted to tell her that the threesome wasn't my idea, but that would only have proven her right.

This was probably why I didn't mind waiting forty minutes to cop and why afterward I made no effort to whiz back to the loft for a night of strenuous, many-orificed boffing. I told Catherine, "There's a club near here. We can get off in the bathroom. You can tell me all about *Ethan Frome*." For the life of me I can't remember the plot, but it must have been interesting because we didn't get back until five A.M.–Madeleine and Ronnie were snoring in each other's arms–and when I said, "I guess I'd better get home," Catherine answered, "You don't have to." Sometime later I heard footsteps nearby, and then Ronnie's voice: "Oooh, is he eating her pussy? I want to watch. The bastard wouldn't eat mine."

I wonder if there's something odd about that. I don't mean what Ronnie said; it was typical of her. But Catherine's words: not "Stay," but "You don't have to," as though her taking me into her bed was just politeness. Did she feel she owed it to me after I'd missed a threesome and spent hours listening to her impressions of *Ethan Frome* while we hunched greedily over our little bags of comfort on the swampy floor of a unisex toilet? Did I make love with her because I wanted to or because I didn't want to seem ungrateful? Maybe I just wanted to prove that I still liked sex, even though I *had* passed on the orgy, the prospect of which, if you want to know the truth, had scared the bejesus out of me.

What puzzles me even more is why we became whatever it was we became to each other: lovers, cohabitants for a while, fiancés almost, and then, or simultaneously, jailers, tormentors, and disappointments. Aside from not knowing what Catherine ever saw in me, I can't call up the feeling I then identified as love. What I called love in those days was partly loneliness and partly the corkscrew of sex boring through my indifference, and partly a sense of recognition. What I recognized in Catherine was the tone of her voice when Madeleine summoned her from *Ethan Frome,* the way she scowled when I joined her outside her building. It had something to do with the way she'd refuse to answer the phone no matter how long it rang but instead would sit stiffly, eyes closed, as though each ring were the pulse of a miserable headache. Something was owed her. Something had been denied her. Something had been asked of her that should never have been asked, that no one had any business asking for. It was her sense of grievance, and it was exactly like mine.

I must have thought that loving Catherine meant restoring whatever it was she'd been cheated of. And I suppose I thought that if she loved me, she'd consent to be made happy. Neither of these things happened. The discontent we shared was the kind that can't be banished by other people. But I didn't know that then. I didn't even recognize my own unhappiness as something other than the need for more—more vodka, more clubs, more dope, more sex. If you'd asked me how I proposed to make Catherine happy, I would have told you, "Well, I make her come."

And it was true that in the instant after orgasm her face became as smooth as a blackboard that's been wiped down with a damp sponge. But moments later the handwriting of pain would inscribe itself once more across her forehead and I'd watch hopelessly, arms throbbing, as she frowned up past me at the ceiling. "What's wrong?" I'd ask her. "Tell me, baby. Do you want me to go down on you?" I'd try to open her legs and she'd clamp them together, then yank the covers over herself. "Didn't you come? You didn't come." "I came," she'd say. "Will you just lay off me?" "What do you want me to do?" Once she answered, "You don't get it. You can't *do* anything. For a smart guy, you're so fucking dumb."

I paid her back by sleeping with another woman whose face stayed smooth for a whole half hour after she came. This made me so grateful that I told Michaela I loved her. I didn't tell her about Catherine. For a few months I skulked back and forth between their apartments, keeping the monitor on my answering machine turned down, trying to remember which lies I'd told, and to whom, stoking myself with alkaloids and holding my guilt at bay until the night I felt it lapping around my chin and confessed, first to Michaela, and a few hours later to Catherine, and waited for one of them to rescue me from my confusion.

Michaela was pretty calm; she told me to leave and never call her again.

Catherine tried to stab me.

"You bastard! You said you loved me." We were lying on the floor, fully clothed, and Catherine was holding a kitchen knife that she'd grabbed from the counter. Moments before she'd been using it to slice an apple. Her face was flushed and wet.

"I meant it."

"You don't mean anything! You're such a fucking liar." She rolled on top of me and held the knife against my chest. I didn't try to stop her. "I should cut your heart out." It got very quiet. I could hear the drumming of Catherine's blood, but my own seemed to have stopped, not from fear—I wasn't afraid at all—but out of *anticipation,* the kind you'd feel watching an especially engrossing movie. What I felt, I think, was aesthetic wonder at the chaos I'd managed to generate around me.

"Go ahead," I said. "Just do it. Get it the fuck over with. I don't care."

She cut me then, very lightly, a thin slit down my sternum that only drew a little blood. "You don't mean that, either." She clambered off me and dropped the knife in the sink. "You'd get yourself killed because you thought it sounded good. And get me sent up for life. I'm supposed to be getting my master's degree, I don't have time for this shit."

"So what are you going to do?"

"Do? What am I *supposed* to do? You want me to leave you? Is that what you want? Just say so and I will."

"Don't leave." I was limp with shame—I'd never asked anyone not to leave me—and at the same time hugely relieved. At that moment I suppose I chose Catherine, just as she'd chosen me by picking up a sharp instrument instead of being as sensible as Michaela. She'd convinced me that she loved me. I was like poor crazy Krazy Kat, who sighed "L'il ainjil" every time Ignatz beaned her with another brick.

I mean to be absolutely unflinching, but the urge to exonerate myself is too strong. I have to say I tried. I stopped fucking other women. I moved Catherine in with me, though the truth is I needed help with the rent. I cooked her dinners that would have been delicious if the heroin hadn't made me so sluggish. Most nights she'd get cranky with hunger and shoulder me from the stove where I was staring dimly at a vat of boiling spaghetti and fry herself some popcorn. Its smell still brings back the old queasiness. When she was sick from dope or, more frequently, from booze, I'd hold the bowl for her while she puked and wipe her face with a damp towel. One night she got depressed and wondered loudly why she didn't have a life like other women's, with a home and a husband and kids, and her misery so unnerved me that I ended up proposing to her.

I was still regretting this when I learned that my father had cancer. I hadn't seen much of him in the past two years: He was suspicious of Catherine and Catherine was terrified of him, of his Russian sentiment and Viennese sarcasm, and I had too much to hide from him to be comfortable the times we'd visit him. He told me his diagnosis on December 30, and I promised I'd come out to see him on New Year's Day. On New Year's Eve Catherine and I celebrated with a bundle of dope and a quarter-ounce of coke and a fifth of vodka, and in the morning she was too hungover to get out of bed. "But he's dying," I said. I was feeling sick myself, but I'd done a speedball for altruistic reasons and was almost chipper, in a twitchy way. "Oh God, do you really need me there?" she groaned. "Your father doesn't like me. He never did." I didn't ask her a second time. I took the bus out to New Jersey and spent the day lying to my father, who said nothing about his illness but insisted on showing me where his bankbooks were hidden. Then I took the bus back to the Port Authority, where I made a phone call to a woman I'd been flirting with in a way I thought was playful but suddenly turned out to be serious, because within a week I was sleeping with her and in another month I was moving out of my old apartment, while Catherine watched to make sure I didn't steal anything. One of the last things I said to her was, "This never would've happened if you'd just come out to Jersey with me."

The last time I spoke with her, the last time until I got better, I called her late one night after I'd come back from visiting my father at the hospital. The moment she recognized my voice she was skeptical. "What is it, Peter? Don't tell me you want to come back. I'm not in the mood to be played with."

"I'm not playing with you. I wasn't calling for that."

"Why are you calling, then?"

"You sound bitter."

"It's a little hard for me to sound overjoyed. You're not exactly a font of happy memories."

"I'm not happy, either."

"So that's why you called me? To let me know how miserable you are? Please don't try to get into a suffering contest with me, Peter. I'm going to win hands-down."

"No," I said. "I know you will." I was on the verge of telling her that no one could ever compete with her suffering, she had the event sewn up: The wounding impulse was so strong in me. But this time I stopped myself. "Look, I'm sorry. I just called to say I'm sorry. I'm not asking you to take me back; I'd probably do the same thing again. I'd fuck up. I always have. And I'm so, so sorry." I hung up before she could answer.

When people asked me why Catherine and I had broken up, I'd tell them it had to do with my father, the implication being that I was too busy attending him on his deathbed to worry about something as fluffy as a relationship. Dying, my father made a good excuse. It was true I saw him almost every day those months he was in the hospital, being ransacked of one failing organ after another. I'd leave work and go downtown to cop and get off in whatever apartment I happened to be staying in, then take two subways uptown and show up in his room a little before visiting hours ended. If he was awake, he'd grunt, "So you came. I didn't think you would," and I'd say something about working late. "Sure, you got to work. You think you're the only one? I had to work late, too, when you were little. You don't remember."

"No, I do." I wanted to tell him that I used to fall asleep waiting for the click of his key in the lock, but it was easier just to nod and pretend to be present.

"Your mother was always angry with me. She didn't understand. You understood. You never complained. You were a good boy then, I got to say. But your mother, no. Always she complained." The room sighed and gurgled around him. "You want to know why I left your mother—well, I didn't really leave her, your mother was the one who wanted the divorce, don't ever let her tell you any different. But the reason I did what I did was your mother wouldn't stop complaining. I couldn't live with that. It wasn't you. You know that, *shmeggege*. I just couldn't take it. You're tired."

My eyes snapped open and I gaped at him, scared he'd ask me to roll up my shirtsleeves or let him inspect my pupils. But he only said, "Go home and sleep. You're working too hard." And I left gratefully, almost invigorated. It would be hours more before I went to sleep.

I said Kaddish for a year after my father died. It was one of the few religious obligations I remembered from my years of Hebrew school. No matter how many times I recited the prayer, I could never do so by heart. Every morning I had to refer to the card they'd given me at the funeral home, reading aloud from an English transliteration. I had the idea that it would be sacrilegious to chant while high, so I'd postpone my wake-up shot until I'd sprinted through the thing, nose dripping, bones throbbing, at a clip that would have done credit to an auctioneer. *Yis-ga-dal v'yis-ka-dash sh'may ra-bo*. That's all I can remember. I lost the card years ago.

One is also supposed to recite a prayer for the dead on the Day of Atonement, though not the Kaddish. People who have lost a parent within the year are instructed to leave the synagogue during the memorial, lest the recollection of recent loss prove too bitter. The paradox of Judaism is that it is an essentially kindly religion dedicated to a ferocious, or at least capricious, God. In Leviticus He unscrolls a daunting list of mortal crimes: death for insulting one's father or mother; death for adultery; death for sodomy; for bestiality and incest, death; for sorcery, death by stoning; for marrying a mother and her daughter, death by burning. Yet in the same book, He offers a way out: "On the tenth day of this seventh month there shall be a day of atonement: it shall be a holy convocation unto you; and ye shall afflict your souls, and offer an offering made by fire unto the Lord. And ye shall do no work in that same day: for it is a day of atonement, to make an atonement for you before the Lord your God."

It is said that on Rosh Hashonah God passes judgment on all living things, decreeing which is to live and which to die. Yet for ten days He suspends sentence. During those ten days, which culminate on Yom Kippur, justice hangs over us like the sword of a reluctant executioner. He is anxious to reverse His judgment, perhaps even desperate. All He asks is that we do the right thing and atone for our transgressions. In Biblical times the process was magical and simple. The tribes gathered before the temple altar. The high priest brought forward two goats and sacrificed one of them to the Lord. Then he shrived the community of its collective sins and passed these into the second goat, "the scapegoat," which was flung over the edge of a cliff as an offering to the demon Azazel. For all its savagery, the ritual must have been comforting. When the last bleat had faded in the desert air, the multitudes shouted for joy. They had been cleansed. The strip of cloth that hung from the temple gate was white for purity. Catholics must feel something similar when they leave the confessional. Someone with a direct pipeline to the Almighty has told them, *Te absolvo.*

Later on everything became more problematic. Communal pollution gave way to individual guilt. Atonement gave way to repentance, which entails the transformation of the soul. And souls, as we know, are stubborn and mysterious; they are the moral equivalent of the unconscious, which has resisted ninety years of psychoanalytic battering. Confessing your sins is relatively simple, even if you have to account for fifty-six categories of them and beat your breast for each one; even if you have to lash yourself forty strokes with a whip, as used to be common among the Orthodox. But it's another matter to renounce sin in your heart and remove it from your thoughts and call out to Him who knows all hidden things to witness that you will never return to that sin again. Which seems to be what is required.

And, according to the Talmud, true penance is not just a squaring of accounts between human beings and the Almighty. One also has to "appease"—that's the word the elders used—the people one has sinned against. I hadn't read the Talmud at the time I came to, which is the only way I can describe what happened to me about a year after my father's death, but I must have absorbed this idea by osmosis. Where God was concerned, I felt no guilt. I didn't believe in Him, or believed in Him only inasmuch as I blamed Him for making me someone who, given a choice between right and wrong, would always choose the wrong, and if He had seen fit to haul me before His throne back then and rebuke me for my shortcomings, I probably would have answered Him the same way Cain is supposed to have: "You started it." But I was afflicted by the thought of the people I had claimed to love and had instead injured, and I was eager to appease them.

But how do you appease the dead? What point is there in winning the forgiveness of someone who has already forgiven you too often? How can you honestly tell the ones you hurt that you will never hurt them again? I'm grateful I had these doubts, because they kept me from doing what I at first wanted to: from racing to my father's grave, from telephoning my mother at three in the morning, from tracking Catherine down to wherever she'd removed herself (she'd left New York about a year after I'd left her, and such was my inverted self-regard that the only reason I could imagine for her doing this was that I'd managed to poison the entire city for her), and saying the thing I'd always said: "I'm sorry, I'm sorry, I'm sorry."

But this time really *meaning* it.

So I waited, and took an accounting of my wrongs, and tried to banish the evil inclination from my thoughts and renounce it in my heart. I can't tell you how I went about this. Beside the rank meat of transgression, reform is as dull as institutional oatmeal. We don't want to hear about the square john who never pilfers from the petty cash, or the good son who obeys his parents, or the schmuck who, given a free pass at cheating on his wife with a beautiful and very drunk woman who fixes him with an addled gaze and breathes "Don't I know you?" at such close quarters that he can almost taste the nectary inside of her mouth, murmurs, "No, I'm afraid I don't think so," and edges away. We want to hear about fucking and sucking, howling sirens and broken glass, patricidal duke-fests in the rec room, adultery and tears. Read your Genesis. How do Adam and Eve spend their time before they raid the forbidden orchard? The book is silent, as though even its authors found rectitude too boring to waste words on. Human history only begins with the Fall, the barred garden with a forbidding angel at its gate.

I found Catherine some years later. It wasn't that hard—it had just been more convenient for me to believe it would be. The first thing she said when she recognized my voice on the phone was, "I thought you'd be dead by now." I didn't ask her if this was a fear or a wish. I thought it best to assume good intentions all around. We met at a coffee shop in the neighborhood both of us had abandoned five years before, like fighters leaving a ring in which they've beaten the shit out of each other without either being declared the winner. She still had something of the gamine about her, although she was wearing a suit and a sedate string of pearls. Her short hair now looked more professional than waiflike. Once I'd run my fingers through it, tugged it when making love, but I recalled this only in an academic way, as you do when you run into someone at an airport and remember the job where you both worked years before, a crummy job in a field neither of you ended up staying in: It's just the reason your lives intersected for a while.

"What are we doing here?" she asked me.

"There are some things I need to say to you in person."

"*What* things? Why do you have to be so mysterious? I had to lie to my boyfriend to come into the city. I hope you appreciate that."

"You didn't have to lie to him."

"Oh, excuse me. I didn't realize you disapproved of lying."

"Look, if you're going to be sarcastic, we can—" I pressed my fingers against my eyelids. "Sorry. I'm feeling defensive." She nodded. I couldn't tell if she was agreeing with me or encouraging me to say more. "I get defensive when I'm in the wrong. And when it comes to you I am. Wrong, I mean. I wronged you."

Inside me a furtive other self was waiting for her to say, "No you didn't" or "Not that badly." One of the pitfalls of atoning to a live person is that it can easily become an attempt to erase the past, to win not just forgiveness but forgetfulness. We want to awaken from our sins as from a bad dream, in a bed whose sheets have never been stained with blood and semen.

Catherine said, "Yes. Yes, you did."

"Well, we agree, then. I don't know what to say. I didn't treat you well. I loved you and I should have given you everything. But I had no idea what you needed from me. Not a clue. I couldn't hear you when you told me, and even if I had heard you, I doubt I could have given it. I was *cheap* with you."

"You were wasted."

"Yeah, that, too. That's what absorbed all my interest. There wasn't much left over for you." I spoke more quickly, glancing at her warily and then staring down at the tabletop, as though a menu of my transgressions were written on the place mat. "You have to know it was nothing about you that made me that way. It

was all me. You just happened to be there. I lied to you. I was un-
faithful to you—don't laugh. Please, this is serious to me. A few
times I stole from you. I don't know how much I took, but I can
pay you back if you don't find the idea insulting. I know I can't
pay back the other. I can't undo it. I wish I could, but I don't know
how. Did I say something funny?"

Catherine was laughing again. I suddenly wondered if she'd
been drinking. "Oh, you're sweet. I always said you were basically
a sweet guy with a few major problems." She took my hand in
both of hers. "Peter, didn't you realize I was fucking around on
you, too?"

"What?"

"I was. Maybe not as much as you did, in the beginning, but afterwards, yeah. At least three different times."

"No! You're just saying that."

"I thought it was obvious."

"Not to me, it wasn't."

"Jesus, you were out of it. I can't believe you're still alive."

"*Three* times? When? Who with? No, don't tell me, I don't want
to know. Three *times?* Or with three different guys?" Amid the in-
terstation hiss and crackle of incredulity, various psychic commen-
tators were clamoring to put their spin on things: "What are *you*
apologizing for, schmucko? You oughta deck the bitch!" "Look at
you, for God's sake! Look how fucked up you were! You *drove* her
to this!" It was all I could do not to listen to them, or at least not
take them any more seriously than I would Rush Limbaugh. The
airwaves inside your head are unfortunately free, and open to any
content that cares to broadcast on them.

"Thanks for telling me," I said. "It doesn't change anything. I
was still wrong. You still deserved better."

She smiled at me then, a smile unlike any I'd ever seen when we
were harrying each other in our succession of cheap apartments

whose rent we could never pay on time. It was, I think, the smile of a particular kind of comradeship, the kind that occurs among people who may not even like one another all that much but have together endured an ordeal on the order of being held hostage by Hezbollah. "Thank *you*. We both did. But you were who you were and I was who I was and, honestly, we were both a mess. How could it have been any different?"

Making atonement to my father took longer. We had been connected for thirty-one years—more, if you counted the fact that he was still resident inside me, reproachful even after death. I drove up to his grave site on the day after Yom Kippur. The next day was his birthday. At least that's when we would have celebrated it, since he'd been born under the old Julian calendar and we'd always used the Jewish holiday as a point of reckoning. New Jersey is an ugly place to drive through, but the cemetery had sweet green grass and the light fanned through its pine boughs and cast a grate of shadow on my father's stone. Once I saw a robin hop between the graves. I sat there and told my father everything I could think of, all my wrongs against him, and placed three small stones on the edge of his monument. Then I drove into the city.

But I still felt incomplete. This may just be what you have to expect from a conversation with a dead person. They rarely rise from their tombs to let you know you're forgiven. So the next day I made an appointment with Slam and showed her a picture of the tattoo I had in mind. At first she disapproved. "It's so crude. There's no detail." But the design, after all, was from the early Middle Ages. Some say that crusaders used to get the tattoo of the Archangel Michael to commemorate a journey to the Holy Land. Another story has it that the device was worn by Egyptian Copts, as a sign to their Moslem rulers that they, too, were people of the Book: The tattoo was a kind of pass that spared them the treatment that was generally meted out to other infidels. Slam squinted at me through the smoke of her *kretek*. "Well, which reason are you getting it for?"

"Both, I think. Yeah, both. Also, it's for my dad."

"For your *dad?* You know me, I'll do anything, but shame on you, Peter! I mean it. Your father was Jewish! He'll turn over in his grave!"

"No," I said. "I don't think so. I was just there."

She rolled her eyes and began tracing the design onto a piece of treated paper, then transferred the drawing onto my shoulder blade. "Let's just get this thing on the road, then. You're the one who's going to go to hell."

"I need to do something first. Promise you won't laugh at me." I'd brought some objects along with me: A photo of my father, looking snappy in the tuxedo he used to wear for work and which, if I recall correctly, he'd had on the day he appeared on *Memory Lane.* Another photo of him in his sickness, his skeleton jaggedly declaring itself beneath his clothing, his eyes beseeching. There was a photo of me as a child of three, racing down a hallway on chubby legs. I placed them on a table and then added a *yahrzeit* candle in its little shot glass and a small earthen pot of sage. "I'm aiming for kind of an ecumenical, multiculti experience," I told Slam and then hated myself for joking. I turned my back to her. I lit the candle and then the sage, and passed the vessel back and forth before the photos. The studio filled with the smell of burning desert.

I addressed my father's pictures: "When I was a little boy you loved me, and you wanted me to be safe. But I wouldn't let you. I was afraid, I was scared all the time, but I wouldn't admit it, and I blamed you for making me that way, and I fought you. I put myself in danger. That was my way of hurting you. And I told myself that I was brave and you were a coward. And I told myself that I knew everything and you knew nothing. And I let you know it over and over. Forgive me. I want to tell you that I'm a man now, and that I'm safe. I'm as safe as you wanted me to be. And what I'm doing now I do with love, and in remembrance of you."

"Okay," I said and turned around. "I'm ready."

"Jesus," Slam said. She wiped her eyes and smeared kohl halfway down her cheeks. "You spoiled my makeup. I never work without makeup. That was very moving. I take back what I said before."

I winced as the needle hit me. "This will hurt more than the others. You've got no meat there."

About an hour or so into the tattoo, when I'd gotten used to the drilling, I said, "I should've brought a cake, too. Today's my father's birthday. Two days after Yom Kippur."

Slam turned off the needle's motor and sprayed my shoulder with Hibiclens. "Yom Kippur was yesterday."

"No, it was two days ago."

"Did you go to temple?" Her voice had that scolding tone again.

"No, I didn't go to temple. I haven't in fifteen years."

"Well, there's a synagogue down the block from me, and I want to tell you it was doing stand-up business all of yesterday. And when I asked one of the guys outside what the deal was, he told me it was Yom Kippur. And he looked like *he* knew what he was talking about."

"Oh," I said. "Shit." My father's voice burst from me like the Alien, like a dybbuk that emerges only when you do something especially derelict or stupid. "Typical. *Teepikul*. The *shmendrick* don't even know when Yom Kippur is!"

Hardest of all was the penance to my mother. A single interview wouldn't do, and I didn't think she'd appreciate a tattoo. When I first made an accounting of my wrongs to her, she wept, which made me so uncomfortable that I wanted to leave right then and never come back. My mother's sadness frightened me: It was something I couldn't take away, no more than I could take away her sickness when I was little, and I have never been able to tolerate the evidence of my powerlessness. Part of my penance was to endure her sorrow, or really just witness it without flinching. A year ago her best friend died suddenly of a heart attack, and I was the first person my mother called. "I feel so bad," she told me. "You know how I talked about Liesel. I always complained about her. I couldn't help it. She just gets on my nerves. You see? I said 'get.' I can't believe she's gone. And still I talk badly about her!"

"You loved her, Mom. That's what you do with people you love. You complain about them."

"I don't complain about you."

"Are you sure?"

She laughed, that charming, sheepish, gleeful laugh. "Okay, yes, I complain. But you know I love you. Do you complain about me?"

"Oh, all the time. Who else do I have to complain about? I'm going to get worked up over strangers?"

We celebrated that Rosh Hashanah together; it was only the second time we'd done this in twenty years. My mother still lived in the same big Upper West Side apartment that I grew up in, the one my father left when I was twelve. It was familiar without being comfortable. I suppose it was haunted for me, but the ghosts in it were all my own, a host of selves that I wished were dead but had only managed to discard, and that just barely. In the shadows of the gloomy living room, in the closets of my old bedroom, I sensed them waiting for me. The ghosts seemed wistful. Or was it I who was wistful for them? Their presence was why I always tried to get my mother to go out when I came to see her, to a restaurant or a movie, any place but that oversized apartment with its draped windows and the closets in which lifetimes of evidence collected dust. But her health had been frail the last few years, and she left the house less and less.

We were sitting in the kitchen when I became aware that something was squeaking intermittently in a corner. It might have been an unbalanced load in the washing machine. But the washer was turned off when I checked it. On the floor nearby, though, I found a glue trap with a small gray body caught in it, splayed helplessly on its side. The mouse craned its head and squeaked, not at me (I don't think it could see me), but out of a general reflex of despairing terror. There was a cracker crumb a half inch from its nose: That was the source of its whole problem.

"What is it?" my mother asked.

"Be calm. I think you've got a mouse."

"Oh God, where?"

"By the washing machine. It got stuck."

"NO! Oy, don't tell me such things, I can't take it!" She was half laughing and half crying. "Is it dead?"

"No, but the poor thing's going to starve to death if we don't—"

"Call the super! No, I can't, I'm fighting with him, you don't know the name he called me yesterday. What am I going to do?"

"Go to your room and lie down for ten minutes. You're just going to get upset, you stay here. I'm going to try and set it free."

"Not inside! Please not—"

"Go to your room, Ma. Please!"

She left and I placed the trap beside the flowerpots on the grate outside the kitchen window. I thought of just leaving it there, but that seemed too cruel. Whoever first called glue traps "humane" ought to be shot for abuse of dumb animals and the English language. I tugged gently on the mouse's abdomen and it swiveled its head and snapped at me with little Chiclet incisors. I was scared I might accidentally tear it apart. I tried curling the cardboard underneath it, hoping that the bugger would slide off, but that didn't do any good, either. No matter what I tried, it kept squeaking at the same tragic interval, as monotonously as someone chanting.

From time to time my mother would call from her bedroom, "Is it gone?" and I'd say, "Just a few more minutes." At last I took an ice cube from the freezer and rubbed it over the mouse's fur, which was soon soaked. I stroked its head to keep it calm, feeling the little ridge of its brainless skull. Suddenly its feet were loose. It began scrabbling at the cardboard, but its flanks and tail were still glued down. "Hold still, for Christ's sake." I opened a bottle of vegetable oil and sprinkled the mouse with it. Its feet flailed more violently, its sides heaved, and suddenly it was free, though pitifully matted and beslimed, and an instant later it skittered between the grill-work and down the wall, where it disappeared from sight.

"It's okay," I called. "You can come out now. All clear."

My mother appeared in the doorway. She was wheezing a little from her emphysema. "Thank God," she sighed. "Now wash your hands and we can eat. But wash them *good*."

Was this enough? Is my slate clean? There is a story—Kafka might almost have written it—of a pious Jew who once went to see his rabbi. Before he entered the house, he thought he might receive the customary forty stripes of the whip so that the holy man would find no defect in him. At that moment the rabbi opened the door and asked him, "What is the reason why the sages of blessed memory only lashed themselves thirty-nine times, though it is written in the Torah, 'Forty stripes he may give him'?" The rabbi went on: "When a man commits a transgression and is flogged he may think that if he receives a full forty stripes he will have wiped away his iniquity. That is why the sages of blessed memory took one from the forty: that the sinner might know that he had not yet received all his punishment. That nothing was ever wiped away."

6

I KISS HER GOOD-BYE

It seemed to me that all the devilment, and meanness, and shiftlessness, and no-account stuff in my life had been pressed out and washed off, and I was ready to start out with her again clean, and do like she said, have a new life.

James M. Cain, THE POSTMAN ALWAYS RINGS TWICE

I've never been tattooed with anybody's name. I doubt I ever will be. It would seem like a way of tempting fate, which is most dangerous when it appears tame, though maybe what I'm really thinking of is my own character. The closest I ever came was getting a copy of a girlfriend's tattoo. I got it less out of hope than out of pessimism, for the same reason I break my neck looking for souvenirs when I'm leaving a place I love and suspect I won't be visiting again. I got it not because I thought that Tara and I would stay together but because I knew we wouldn't, couldn't probably. Well, who ever knows what could or couldn't be? Who knows when fate is only the euphemism for a bad character?

With a few changes, we could have been enacting the opening scene from a noir thriller of the 1940s: the sailor and his girl on the night before he ships out for the Pacific. She's played by Gloria Grahame or Susan Hayward, seemingly cast against type—who ever heard of one of those gals playing an ingenue?—he by some juvenile you've never heard of before or since, a boy with a face as vulnerable as an isolated prairie farmhouse. It's San Diego, a seaside amusement park on a warm night. A ferris wheel's lights climbing through the sky, a crowd of sailors in ice-cream whites, girls in filmy dresses that flutter in the salt breeze. A distant calliope, the hiss of waves. The camera follows the couple into the tattoo parlor. The proprietor wears a sleeveless undershirt that displays arms covered with years of needlework, whole menageries and armadas.

"What'll it be, kid?"

Sailor boy, scared but trying to sound nonchalant: "Oh, give me the usual. An anchor or a battleship. What the hell do I care as long as you put 'Mona' underneath it?" He indicates his girlfriend with a jerk of his thumb. "That's her."

She, laughing: "Oh, Nick, you shouldn't!"

Close-up: Nick and Mona facing each other in profile, so close that we keep waiting for them to kiss. The camera cuts back and forth between their faces but always returns to that establishing shot with its postponed promise of erotic merger.

Nick: "Don't say what I should or shouldn't be doing, baby. There are no shoulds in this crazy world anymore. I shouldn't be apart from you. You shouldn't be apart from me. But a couple of hours from now I'm going to be on a tin can heading halfway across the ocean."

Mona: "But you'll come back, Nick. You've got to come back! I don't know what—"

Nick places a finger on her lips: "All I know is that I'm crazy about you, get it? And wherever I'm going, whatever happens to me, I want to take a part of you with me. Something that no one can take away. Even if it's just your name. I want to be able to look at it on those long nights belowdecks, or when I'm standing watch under the stars not knowing if a torpedo with my name on it is coming for me, boring through all that dark water. I want to see your name on me and know you'll be waiting when I come home."

Mona: "I will, Nicky. I promise. No matter what. I'll be there."

Only then do they kiss. But instead of the pro forma fade-out, the last shot is a close-up of the finished tattoo on his right biceps, an anchor with a chain wrapped around it and the name "MONA" written underneath in a finicky Palmer script.

They don't make movies like that anymore.

The truth is I was almost twenty years older than that kid, and I wasn't going to war, and the tattoo I got was a simple arrangement of black stick figures that people assume are trees or barbed wire or Nordic runes, though it is none of these. I had it inked on my right wrist, which is where Tara had hers, on a hot September afternoon in a studio off of Tompkins Square Park. Through the open windows you could hear the shouts and thuds of a basketball game in the court below and the hollow slap of congas. The place had an altar in its foyer, a folding aluminum table bearing a potted cactus that had been stuck full of tattoo needles—I think they must have been used—and a yellowed dog skull that someone had decorated with feathers. Tara sat beside me through the whole process, as cheerful as though we were picking out engagement rings. She was protective of me and she kept telling the tattooist to go easy with the needle, and I think it pissed him off since he ended up doing the opposite and leaving me with a thick black biscuit of scab that peeled painfully and unevenly, taking off a good deal of the pigment underneath. Many of the figures came out blotched and prematurely faded. It was a bad tattoo. I had to have it retouched later. But you know what tattooists say: "If you don't have at least one fucked-up piece on you, you ain't serious."

Given a choice, I'd have gone to Slam. She had the taste and imagination that make for a great tattooist, and by that time I thought of her as my friend. But Slam had fallen in love with a big, dreadlocked woman named Roxy, and they were moving to a lesbian commune in Santa Fe. So I had no choice but to go to the place on Tompkins Square, where the tattooist was a guy named

Gareth, whom I knew slightly from the New York Tattoo Society circuit. He had a shaved head that was shaped exactly like a light-bulb and tribals by the English master Alex Binnie on his fore-arms, and he went at me as though I were a cheap color TV he was engraving with his Social Security number in case somebody tried to rip it off.

"You're going too deep," Tara complained some ten minutes into the session. "He shouldn't be bleeding that much."

Gareth grunted, "Some people are bleeders."

"I don't usually bleed." I said it as mildly as I could. I didn't want to alienate the guy.

"Maybe it's your attitude." He gazed into my eyes the way certain therapists are wont to do, as though he meant to batter me to death with empathy. "I mean it. You're fighting it. You're tensing up. You're doing it right this minute. You tense up, it dilates the capillaries and shit, pumps all your blood to the surface. You need to chill."

"How's he supposed to chill if you're hurting him?"

"I'm not hurting him. Am I hurting you?" He didn't look at me. "Look, sweetheart. I've been in this business for ten years, you know what I'm saying? I've done work for fashion models and a very well known actor with his own soap and three guys in D Generation. And not one of them has ever complained about me hurting them. Your *boyfriend* isn't complaining about me hurting him. So it looks like you're the one who's got the problem. No offense, babes, but maybe you should look at that."

I could see the retort quivering in Tara's throat. She resembled a pretty pit bull, small and deep-chested, with a broad, blunt nose and a powerful jaw that would have been ugly if it had been a shade wider. When I'd first met her she'd had a stricken quiet about her; it was one of the reasons I hadn't found her attractive. But over the past year she'd remembered that God had given her a mouth. She would argue with anybody. She had more or less argued me into going out with her. "I'm okay, sweetie," I said. "Really. It's just blood."

"You sure? I don't want him hurting you. You don't know what this means to me."

Most women I've known would have preferred a ring, but Tara and I were at that point in the affair when small gestures count for a lot. She watched raptly while a runny mirror image of her tattoo appeared on my wrist and afterward swung my hand in hers as we walked through those acrid East Village streets that excited her with their overflowing storefronts of vintage seventies dresses with S&M zippers and used CDs and cheap jewelry. Actually, I *did* buy her a ring at one of these places, a steel band incised with little black spades and diamonds, like something a gambler would wear. "Just don't over-interpret this," I warned her.

"What do you mean?" She didn't sound suspicious, she just wanted to know what I meant, but I was mortified.

"I'm sorry. It was a bad joke. It means nothing."

Baltimore was where we'd first gotten to know each other, but we hadn't become lovers till later, after my move. She'd driven up a few days before in her used Honda, with twelve changes of clothing in the trunk. And just being together in New York that weekend had the feel of a tryst stolen in a town where everyone is in transit, sailors shipping out for Subic, whores following the fleet, no one rooted, no one committed to anything but boardwalk days and nights of panting, valedictory sex, which we dove into later while fire engines whooped outside my windows, clutching and gnawing as greedily as children, as wholly inside and around each other as we could get through our layers of spermicidally dusted latex. Once I whispered, "Lick my tattoo. I want to feel your tongue against it."

She eased away from me in the dark. I could hear sheets crackle like cellophane. "I can't do that, baby. You know I can't. It's not safe."

• • •

Speaking of ports and sailors, what happens next in that movie is that Nick sails out for Truk or Bougainville and about a year later his ship goes down. Zeroes shrieking across the firmament, pillars of oily smoke, the night sea a broken mirror with flames glaring in every shard. Almost everyone on board is drowned. The kid makes it out alive but badly maimed. Just how badly is left to your imagination, since this is a film from the days before directors and special-effects technicians succumbed to the pornographic compulsion to show *everything*. The next thing we know he's lying in a navy hospital bed, mummified in gauze whose whiteness is an ironic echo of the uniform he wore earlier. An offscreen voice: "We did our best, but even his own mother wouldn't recognize him now." When the bandages finally come off, he looks exactly like John Garfield, John Garfield or Robert Ryan, handsome in a crooked way, but no charm boy. His is a *traveled* face, an odometer that measures how close its owner came to dying.

Back Stateside Nick tries to get in touch with his girl, but when he knocks at her door, a stranger answers. "Oh, Mona moved out months ago. I don't know where she lives these days, but maybe you can find her at Corrente's. You know Corrente's? It's a club down in La Jolla." Corrente's has a discreet bouncer at the door and banquettes like submarine grottoes. It's a place where you can pack a gun if you're a regular, but where showing it will get you blackballed or worse. Mona comes in wearing an expensive, low-cut number and enough diamonds to give an insurance adjuster nightmares. Gone is the skittish ingenue of the opening scene. The actress, Susan or Gloria or whoever, has shucked off her innocence the way she might shuck off a tight girdle. If Nick's experience is gouged into his face, Mona's is recorded in her eyes and in the avidity of her breathing. With each breath her breasts rise and her nostrils dilate as though she were trying to inhale the entire room.

Nick strikes up a conversation with her at the bar. "Excuse me, I don't mean to sound like I'm throwing you a line, but don't I know you?"

Mona: "Not unless you're a regular."

Nick: "These days I'm not a regular anywhere. I thought I might have seen you a couple times around—" He mentions the place where they grew up. "You ever been there?"

Mona: "Yeah, once." She looks at him sharply, but his face is unrecognizable. A perfect stranger's.

Nick: "What were you doing there?"

Mona: "Being dumb. I left when I wised up. I never went back."

Nick: "You're a little young to have memories, aren't you?"

Mona: "Mister, I've got memories in every town in this crummy state."

They are two dry sticks rubbing together on a bed of sawdust, and the sawdust is soaked in gasoline. A man comes up behind them, places proprietary hands on their shoulders. "Friend of yours, Mona?" Picture the top-heavy bulk and sharkish good cheer of the young Jack Carson.

Mona: "No, Ray. He's just a guy from—. You know, my hometown."

Ray: "He's a long way from home. What's the matter, did he get lost?"

Nick: "I was just telling your lady friend that it's been a while since I've been back. I was wondering if she'd heard anything about the old crowd."

Ray: "This isn't my 'lady friend,' pal. This is my wife. Mrs. Ray Corrente. Or didn't she tell you that?"

"Sure, I told him," Mona says. Too quickly. "But we might as well make it official. This is my husband, Ray Corrente. He's the owner of this establishment. And this is—"

Nick: "Dillon. Alex Dillon. I'm pleased to meet you."

●   ●   ●

In most noir films men and women are fatally matched. He is a wounded loner who's picked up his cynicism on breadlines and in foxholes. His greed is the kind that comes from standing too long in the cold watching big shots ride past in limousines; his callousness is what kept him from going crazy after he wiped his buddy's brains off his fatigues. These things are the scar tissue that has formed around the ragged hole at his center: the hole made by history. The woman was born bad. The films posit no other origin or explanation. Evil goes with her sex; it lies at the root of her attractiveness, as though her cunt secreted a poison that makes a man kill for another taste before it kills him, too. In *Double Indemnity* Phyllis Dietrichson describes herself as "rotten to the heart." The story of *Double Indemnity* or *The Postman Always Rings Twice,* of *Criss Cross* or *The File on Thelma Jordan,* is the story of a marriage made in hell, of an evil woman homing in on a weak man and making him her accomplice in crimes that neither of them could commit alone. He needs her to give him ruthlessness; she needs him to pull the trigger.

On the surface this seems like a remarkably fair arrangement, especially when you consider the general state of marriage in the early postwar years. The noir couple eerily anticipates the democratic partnerships we strive for in the 1990s: "Honey, can you come here and help me a minute? I need to haul this body out of the Lexis." "Oh, all right. But only if you promise to help me write that blackmail letter afterwards. I'm having some trouble with the voice." But the equality is only superficial. As bad as Walter Neff is, in the end he remains Phyllis Dietrichson's patsy, weak where she is strong, merely venal where she is rampantly malign. The sexual politics of these films is a throwback to the politics of Genesis, where a woman initiates the sin that will banish us from Paradise while Adam, that poor sap, just goes along for the ride. In noir, feminine evil is a virus that invades a passive male host and replicates itself inside him. The ordinary logic of reproduction is inverted: She impregnates him with her rottenness, and often childbirth is fatal to them both.

A feminist critique sees noir as propaganda that broadcasts a coded warning of the dangers of unchecked female autonomy and power. According to such a reading, it's no accident that most of these films were made between the mid-1940s and the mid-1950s: The war was over, millions of soldiers were coming home, and the women who had occupied their jobs during the emergency now had to be coaxed off the assembly line and back into the kitchen. What better vehicle than a cinema that portrayed independent women as ruthless predators and the men who fall for them as moral eunuchs? But there's another interpretation that occurs to me, one in which noir expresses wishes as well as fears. In real life—in real life as it was lived forty years ago—the masculine paradigm was powerful, even sadistic. But power has its burdens and every sadist at times falls prey to guilt. Inwardly, he shudders at his slave's cries. And he secretly wonders what it would be like if the scenario were reversed: if he were the one to be hurt, abased, plunged into a terrifying, blissful passivity that is so much like the passivity of the cradle. In noir films those repressed speculations became concrete, allowing the domineering American man to discover, however vicariously, the pleasure of surrendering his dominance, of submitting to a woman who was not just his match but his superior. His mistress.

Have I ever met a woman who was my match? I mean in that slit-eyed, drive-ninety-miles-an-hour-to-the-edge-of-the-cliff-with-a-cigarette-burning-between-your-teeth-and-a-box-of-nitro-at-your-feet sense? When I was with Catherine, her sullenness unnerved me so much that I'd do anything to appease it: answer her phone calls; pick up her clothing from the dry cleaner's; go out on freezing Sunday mornings to cop Valium for her cramps. We had a routine we practiced whenever we were out visiting. One of us would keep the hosts occupied in the living room while the other foraged through the bathroom medicine cabinet for likely mood-alterants. Once we were lucky enough to get a dinner invitation from a friend whose mother had just died miserably of bone cancer. All through dinner I practically hugged myself, picturing the look on Catherine's face when we got home and I presented her with a handful of Dilaudids. "Oh, honey, you shouldn't have! You've made me the happiest gal in the whole wide world."

I think of Dinah, who so overpowered me with fear and yearning that I'm reminded of a novel I once read in which a woman tells a man she loves him and he asks her how much and she answers, "Enough to let you cut me open and fuck my heart." How do you protect yourself when you are willing to let your lover slit you open like a fish? When you are ready to issue her an open invitation? I know all about the gay leather scene and have been to clubs where potentates of commerce paid good money to be trussed like smaller cousins of the marbled carcasses that were hanging in the packinghouses down the block and thrashed with buggy whips while they squirmed in hog-tied rapture. But my own masochism scares the shit out of me. Somewhere in the back of my mind it is written, "Real men don't wear ball-gags." And when Dinah asked me why I left her I said, "Don't you see? Because I'd do anything for you."

I once knew a woman I'll call Pauline who liked to be whipped when we made love (though "making love" seems a misnomer for what we were doing), and I found myself getting into it, falling dreamily into a sexual wind tunnel whose suction tore us into so many flailing parts, an arm, a hand, a braided leather quirt, a reddening, welted ass, sweat flying like shrapnel, cries that might have been hers or mine, "No!" or "More!" I stopped seeing her when she told me she wanted me to beat her—I mean with my fists. Her response was to start stalking me. I thought it was a gentlemanly breakup, as breakups go, but no sooner had Pauline left my house than she was calling me. Every thirty seconds. I'd pick up the phone—out of the moronic reflex that tells me that I *must* because the person on the other end may be dying or offering me a Publishers' Clearing House check for ten million dollars—and I'd hear a voice on the other end, a voice I used to love. Sometimes it said, "Oh, come on, Peter! What's so bad about a little edge play? You want to. You know you want to." Sometimes it said, "How can you do this to me? HOW CAN YOU DO THIS TO ME? Don't you know I *love* you?" And once, at around two o'clock in the morning, it whispered, "Call your friends and say good-bye to them. Say good-bye to them forever."

I had my number changed, but for months afterward she kept following me. She'd be posted across the street when I left my house in the morning, a perfectly ordinary-looking woman who had the power to strike terror into my heart. On bright days her wire-framed glasses threw the sunlight back in blinding darts, as though she were about to vaporize me with her stare. She'd glide up behind me at a street fair, an untouched ice-cream cone dripping down her fingers. For a long time, neither of us said anything to the other: I was too scared, and what could Pauline say that would top "Say good-bye to them forever"? I finally lost it one day at my neighborhood smoke shop when I felt something feather the hairs on my neck and turned to see her standing behind me, gazing at me with the blandness of the truly crazy. "Will you give it a break?" I snapped. My voice quivered. "What do you want from me?"

"I want you to suffer." She said it the way someone else might say "I want a pack of Mores."

I'm sorry to say that I started crying. The cashier gawked at me. The other customers gawked at me. "WELL, I AM SUFFERING! LOOK AT ME, FOR CHRIST'S SAKE!"

Pauline was suddenly solicitous. "You look awful, sweetheart. You haven't been eating. You must have lost twenty pounds."

"Well, whose fault is that?" I sobbed. "Huh? How am I supposed to eat with you skulking after me all the time!"

"Well, you've got to cut that out. There's no need for you to be so dramatic. I mean it, sweetheart, you're going to make yourself sick."

She walked out without buying anything, favoring the cashier with a cheery wave. It was the last time I ever saw her. It was also the last time I went into that smoke shop.

But these stories are exceptions. I tell them mostly because it gives me the chance to feel sorry for myself. The fact is I've usually been the top in my relationships, even in the ones whose sado-masochistic architecture was hidden beneath all sorts of Victorian gingerbread. What made me the top wasn't my aptitude with a belt or my ability to say the cruelest thing at the most vulnerable moment, all those things I tried so hard to give up and finally did, only to discover that my nature was still the same. S&M is not so much about pain as it is about power, and in sexual relationships power resides with the one who is willing to leave.

Back when I was a bad boy, I walked because there was always someone to walk *to,* someone I was boffing, or flirting with, or just fantasizing about, a woman-shaped future that made it possible for me to turn my back on the present. I used to arrange it that way, like a crook who never pulls a bank job until he's rented a safe house in another city, with a Magnum and a roll of C-notes stashed beneath the floorboards. But after I became merely a troubled man, with rampaging scruples in place of a rampant prick, I left because it was what I knew how to do (think of Lauren Bacall's famous line in *To Have and Have Not:* "You know how to leave, don't you? All you have to do is open the door and walk"). I left because I had gotten used to being alone. And I left because whatever I felt afterward—the loss, the guilt, the unrequited straining toward a vanished other in a bed as vast as a desert—was still preferable to what I felt each day I remained with a woman I had stopped loving or still loved but no longer trusted or loved so much that I no longer trusted myself not to yield to her completely, not to become her chump, her patsy, her stooge, her pussy-whipped gunsel (a word that originally meant "sissy" but that Dashiell Hammett fobbed off on his readers as a synonym for hit man), the abject bottom kneeling at her feet, hands cuffed behind him, tongue extended, with his eyes raised to catch the flicker of permission that must occur before he can begin to adore her boot.

Actually, when I try to imagine just what that submission would amount to, what comes bubbling up is the last scene in *A Hell of a Woman,* where Jim Thompson's schitzed-out narrator allows his wife to castrate him: "You deceived me, she said. You're no different from the rest, Fred. And you'll have to pay like the rest. . . . You won't feel a thing, and when you wake up it will all be over. There'll be nothing more to worry about. Won't that be wonderful, Fred, don't you want me to, darling. I nodded and she began unfastening and fumbling and then, then, she lowered the shears. She began to use the shears, and then she was smiling again and letting me see. There, she said, that's much better, isn't it?"

Back to my movie. Let's call it *Riptide* or *The Undertow* or, my personal favorite, *The Mark,* which has the further advantage of being a double entendre. Nick/Alex knows he should stay away from Mona. We could throw in a scene where Nick pays a visit to the one person who knows his true identity, an old buddy who's now a police lieutenant: "Sure, everybody knows Ray Corrente," he says. "A little gambling, a little graft, a little hijacking. And maybe a little murder. People who get on Corrente's bad side suddenly turn accident-prone. Don't go looking for accidents, Nick. You're supposed to be dead already. Give her up."

But Nick can't get Mona out of his mind: "I couldn't forget the night—it seemed so long ago and not so long ago at all—when we held hands in a tattoo parlor on the midway and I promised to come back to her and she promised to be waiting when I did." We hear him in voice-over as he dresses in his rented room, like a teenager dressing for his prom date. The camera cuts to a close-up of the tattoo. "How could I forget her, when her name was right there on my skin? I couldn't look at my arm without seeing it. I was wrapped around her the way that chain was wrapped around that anchor. And even then I knew I couldn't get loose. I didn't want to get loose. Not even if she took me straight to the bottom."

He drives back out to Corrente's, waits in the sun-baked parking lot until he sees Mona pull up. He greets her.

Mona (warily): "What're you doing back here? You get lost again?"

Nick: "Maybe I'm looking for someone to find me."

Mona: "We're not in the habit of picking up strays around here, Mr. Dillon. My husband takes them straight to the pound."

Nick: "What if one of them bites him?"

Mona: "He bites back. Nobody bites as hard as Ray."

Nick: "Actually, Mrs. Corrente—" He's about to tell her who he is, but just then a third car pulls into the lot and Mona starts in alarm. The man who gets out is just a stranger, but the raw spectacle of her fear turns Nick's anger to pity. "Let's get out of here," she says. He follows her down some stairs that lead to a marina at the foot of the bluff. Pleasure boats bob against the pilings.

Nick: "Actually, I was going to ask your husband for a job. Maybe he could use another bartender. I've been having a run of hard luck since I got back from Iwo. A Purple Heart doesn't cut any ice with the personnel boys."

Mona: "You poor kid. It must be rough. Don't you have any family who can help you? A girl?"

Nick: "My folks passed away a while ago. I had a girl before I enlisted. But it looks like she changed her mind about me."

Mona: "Maybe she had it changed for her."

Nick: "What's that supposed to mean?"

Mona: "I mean maybe she just didn't have a choice." She speaks more quickly, although her voice never gets any louder. She's explaining herself, not so much to the stranger standing beside her as to the man she betrayed. "Let me tell you something. I loved a boy once. Sweet kid, just out of college. He thought the sun rose and set on me, and I guess I thought the world of him, too. But we were young. You know how it is when you're young. And foolish." Her face softens. Her eyes go as dreamy as an opium-eater's. The camera pans over her shoulder to the jetty, where waves shatter amid gusts of spray. "You think love is something solid, that it lasts forever, just like those rocks out there. You know how that song goes. You think it's something you can count on." Cut back to Mona's face in the instant that it sets into its familiar brittleness. "But love isn't anybody's rock. You know what love is? Love is a ship moored in a harbor. It looks solid. On a calm day you can barely feel the deck roll under your feet. But sooner or later that ship will sail. It raises anchor and it doesn't come back. And if you're not on board when it leaves, well, you're just out of luck."

Nick: "What happened to the boy?"

Mona: "The boy? He went off to war, the way boys do. And then one day I heard that his ship had gone down. I guess it was a different kind of ship."

Nick: "Maybe he made it out."

Mona: "Maybe he did, but how would I know? I never heard from him."

Nick: "Maybe something happened to him, something bad. Maybe he was afraid to write you. Maybe—"

Mona (angry): "Who's telling this story, anyway? I told you, I never heard from him again! Maybe he died, maybe he just forgot about me. What does it matter? *That ship has sailed.* And I had to find another one. A girl can't afford to be left ashore when all the ships have gone."

•   •   •

After Pauline, I was celibate for close to three years. I think it took that long for my balls to peep back out of my inguinal cavity, where they'd scurried in sheer terror while she was stalking me. I swore I wouldn't even go on a date unless the prospect could pass one of those multiple-choice exams you find in *Cosmopolitan:* "When my partner hurts my feelings, I (a) Confront him assertively and calmly, (b) Sulk silently, (c) Pretend nothing happened, (d) Sneak into the homes of his friends and family and slit their throats." But I also felt that Pauline had been my just punishment, the thunderbolt God had sent my way as belated payback for a decade and a half of prickery with the opposite sex. I could just see Him peering down from His throne and muttering, "The schmuck wants to play rough? *I'll* give him someone to play rough with!" And I was pretty sure that my penance wasn't over, that one way or another I was supposed to stay alone for a while and savor the bad taste my past relationships had left in my mouth.

Here are the benefits of being alone and celibate:

You can read all night and no one will nag you to turn off the light.

You can go off to Borneo on the spur of the moment without anyone wanting to know when you'll be back.

You can prepare meals so disgusting you'd be ashamed to eat them in company: Grill a slice of bologna till it curls up at the edges; fill the cup with baked beans; then top with a slice of Kraft American cheese and broil till melted. Serve with dill pickle and sliced tomato.

You can fart to your heart's content without having to say "Excuse me," though you may grow so accustomed to this that you find yourself doing it in public places—on the line at your savings bank, for instance—and getting nasty looks from strangers.

You can entertain religious delusions.

You can spend your fury at the world by playing Einsturzende Neubauten and Nine Inch Nails at bone-splintering volumes and dancing along, vaulting and twitching and torquing as though electrocuted while shouting the lyrics you've improvised because you can't make out the real ones: "I gave you no permission!/I give you no remission!/Newt Gingrich, burn in Hell/Jesse Helms, burn in Hell/Larry Wildmon, burn in Hell/I'll know where to find you when I come callin'/In the row next to Hitler and old Joe Stalin."

You can fall asleep with a stack of books next to you on the bed, and if you're a heavy sleeper, you won't even wake when you knock them to the floor.

You may come to know freedom from the tyranny of your penis, which thus dethroned becomes only a benign little tube for the expulsion of urine.

In time you will know yourself so thoroughly that you finally realize what all those people had against you.

You will pray wholeheartedly to be changed. "Make me good," you'll call at night, down on your knees in a bedroom that is used only for sleeping, that smells of nothing but your cigarettes and the dust baking beneath the radiator. "Please, God, just make me good."

On bad nights you can scoop up your cats and cuddle them shamelessly, even kissing them on the nose, though they usually dislike this and will try to shove you away with their paws. If worse comes to worst, you can press your face against their bodies and weep copiously into their fur.

I hadn't reached the cat-weeping stage when I met Tara. She was a friend of friends in Baltimore, a quiet, sulky punk girl who cut her hair with nail scissors and dyed it an arctic blond that didn't go with her dark complexion. She hadn't been clean all that long. In warm weather you could see the tracks on her arms, only partly hidden by a slipshod tribal tattoo that looked like splashed-on paint. Once she complimented me on the piece on my collarbone, and because I couldn't very well say the same about her arm job, I pointed to the tattoo on her wrist. "That's interesting. Where'd you get it?"

"From Kylie at Dragon Moon. You know Kylie? I bet you can't guess what they are."

"I don't know. Runes?"

"No, silly!" It was such an odd, ingenuous thing for her to say. She smiled hugely, baring small crooked teeth. "They're *people*. Dancing people! See their arms?" And it's true that if you looked closely at Tara's tattoo—if you look closely at my copy of it—you'll see a line of stick figures with their arms lifted above knobby heads. They might be dancers, the kind you used to see at Grateful Dead concerts, swaying with the boneless languor of sea anemones. But they might also be people who've been reunited with their loved ones after a long parting, flinging up their arms in the prelude to an embrace so fierce, so greedy, that it could be an act of violence.

It was the most we ever said to each other. As I said, I didn't find Tara attractive. She was a good twelve or thirteen years younger than me, and she had a jealous boyfriend. He was an ex–dope smuggler who now made his living as a bail bondsman. There was a story going around that he paid some of his clients to follow Tara and rough up any guy who tried to get too close to her. At about the time I was moving back to New York, she came up to me at a party and said, "You're a writer, aren't you?" I said yes.

"I am, too," she said. "I mean, I want to be."

"That's nice." I could imagine the kind of things she wrote, poems with titles like "I Piss on Your Values" and "Yes, I Have Tattoos."

"I was wondering," Tara said. She stared down at her shoes. "I mean, if I ever sent you something, some writing, I mean, would you read it? And tell me if it's any good?"

And like a schmuck, I said, "Sure."

A month later I got a package from her in New York. I opened it with dread. It was a short story; the title was "All Tomorrow's Parties," the same as the old Velvet Underground song. It began: "The first thing I did when I got back from Myron's was inspect myself for damage. Well, actually, it wasn't the *first* thing; the first thing I did was to get off in the bathroom, with my coat still on, one sleeve rolled up above my forearm. But that scarcely counted. There was a big purple bruise on my right thigh, the color of crushed grapes, and some welts on my ass from where he'd used the coat hanger. But all in all, Myron had been decent to me. He was a freak, but a trustworthy freak. He always announced what he was going to do before he did it. 'I'm gonna wail away at that little ass of yours,' he'd warn me. 'That's it, I promise. Just your ass, and maybe your thighs. Is it okay if I do your thighs?' 'That's fine, honey,' I'd tell him. 'Just stay away from my face.' "

The power of Tara's writing came from its utter lack of special pleading, from the author's refusal to ask for sympathy for the "I" who told the story. This is very hard to do. Anyone who writes in the first person is in a sense writing an autobiography, from sheer habit if nothing else. You may be a white woman doctoral candidate in your twenties and your narrator may be a Chinese male dentist in his sixties and everything that happens may be the purest fabrication, but just by using that "I," that black hole of English grammar, you are automatically re-creating all the stories you ever told about yourself: You are telling them all over again. And why do you tell these stories, why did you ever tell them, if not to sell yourself? You want your readers to understand you, to admire you, to pity you, to absolve you. You want them to love you. And, of course, the moment you give in to this self-aggrandizing impulse your writing goes down the toilet. But to resist it is like swimming the Hellespont while holding your breath. Byron is supposed to have swum the Hellespont, clubfoot and all, but even he admitted that "I have all my life been trying to make someone love me."

I wrote Tara back and told her that she'd done something

heroic. I scribbled red exclamation points next to the phrases I liked, and I gave her some suggestions that might make the story a little better. The one thing I didn't do was ask her the question that is asked so often of anyone who writes that it has to be counted among the Seven Stupid Questions of the World: Did this really happen to you? You can write a story in which the narrator pedals up to Mars on a Schwinn three-speed and people will still ask, "Did this really happen to you?"

The next story Tara sent me was also written in the first person. The narrator was an ex-prostitute, newly sober after years of addiction. Now she's living with an older guy who's scooped her up out of detox. He's a criminal lawyer who's only a hair less shady than his clients, and he's fanatically jealous. Wherever this girl goes, she's followed by some lowlife he's sprung from the city jail: He's got an entire fleet of purse-snatchers and B&E men and thick-booted biker crank dealers he's paying to dog her around town and terrorize any guy who comes near her. In the course of the story she goes from paranoia to fury to an odd sense of comfort. "When I was a kid," she remembers, "I used to have trouble sleeping. There were too many sounds coming from my parents' room. Every cry pierced the walls between us; every fall made the floorboards shake. I used to watch the shadows the trees cast on my bedroom wall. In winter, leafless, their shapes were scary, like so many grasping claws. I turned them into guardians: giant grandmothers bending over my bed, death to anyone who tried to hurt me. In time, whatever thing you feared most becomes the safest thing of all." She'd attached a short note to the story: "I had to book kind of suddenly from Walt's, for reasons I can't go into right now, so please use this postbox number if you write back. I don't think Walt will try to get in touch with you—he probably doesn't even remember us talking—but if he does, do me a favor and say you haven't heard from me. Thanks a mil. Love ya."

By this time I was weeping into my cats on a regular basis. Mov-

ing back to New York after all those years had done it to me. In
Baltimore, solitude had been a protective mechanism, like those
sterile, climate-controlled bubbles in which they seal people with
no immune systems. In New York my aloneness became the plate-
glass window of a shop whose merchandise made me dizzy with
want, a shop I would never be allowed to enter. In these circumstances it was easy for me to become fixated. I had a friend who
was spending hundreds of bucks each month on a phone-sex line
because he'd fallen in love with one of the—do you call them oper-
ators or prostitutes? I was more high-minded. It wasn't enough for
someone to talk dirty to me: She had to talk dirty with class. In
Tara's stories I got the bloody meat of sex, sex with bruises and
coat hangers and crumpled ten-dollar bills, and the pristine Wedg-
wood of literature, or at least something that was trying to be literature, stringent and pitiless in its control. It had the same appeal as
S&M, where Dionysiac abandon turns into Apollonian discipline
and then back into an abandon that is wilder still because no one
writhes more fiercely than someone in a straitjacket, and the hoars-
est cries are those that issue from the mouths of the gagged.

I had enough sense not to look Tara up when I went down to
Baltimore, which I did pretty often in those days. But one evening
I ran into her by accident, in the back room of a coffee shop on the
waterfront. I ducked in to smoke a cigarette, and she was sitting at
a table with another woman, playing cards. She'd let her hair grow
back to its natural dark brown and wore it slicked back, so that her
head had the shapely sleekness of a seal's. She'd lost some of the
weight people put on in their first months off drugs, when sugar is
the only white powder they can still use with impunity. I was
about to leave without saying anything, but just then Tara looked
up. Her face burst into the same reckless smile I remembered from
before.

"What are you doing here?"

"I'm on the Nostalgia Tour."

She didn't ask me why I hadn't looked her up. But she must have sensed my awkwardness and it made her awkward, too, talkative the way people get when they are trying to keep from saying what they mean and say everything else instead. Without my asking, she started telling me a baroque story about Walt: She'd left him; he'd tried to get her back, pleading, threatening, finally offering her some coke he'd scored from one of his retainers, only Tara had turned it down and he'd ended up doing it himself and swan-diving back into his habit and losing everything, business, license, Mazda, home, friends, he'd sold his dentures for a couple bags, it was pathetic. I didn't want to hear any of it. I didn't want to hear her gloating about her escape and her boyfriend's ruin, even if he was a prick, which of course he was; I preferred to think of Tara as a stoic victim instead of a human being with a capacity for spite and smugness and petty sadism. I didn't want to know where her stories came from. And I didn't want to look at her broad unfurrowed forehead, at her smoke-colored eyelids, at her wide mouth with its lazy hammock of underlip, at the perfect, white-topped breasts that made me glance away whenever she leaned forward, because I wanted to kiss them: I wanted to kiss every part of her. I realized it only now and realizing it made me sick with anger and shame. I'd prided myself on the notion that I was acting as this girl's mentor out of pure good faith, and here was my dick again, as insolent and unbanishable as Freddy Krueger in the *Nightmare on Elm Street* movies. I could practically hear it sneering in my pants: "Didja miss me?"

"I've got to go," I said. "I've got a ride waiting."

"No, don't." I almost shuddered when she touched my sleeve. "Listen, would it be okay if I came up to visit you sometime? I've never been to New York."

"I don't know. Let's talk about it later." Her face fell. For the hundred thousandth time in my life, I tried to unhurt someone's feelings, even though ninety-nine thousand of such attempts have only led to worse hurts down the line: "Look, it's just my apartment's only one room. You're a very attractive woman and I wouldn't want to be tempted to abuse your friendship. You may not have any problem with the man-woman thing. But I do."

Let's get back to *The Mark*. Mona puts in a good word and Corrente hires the man he knows as Dillon as a bartender. One night a customer tries some rough stuff, a gun is pulled. A long moment in which the gunman, a skittish hophead, holds Corrente in his sights, his finger flirting with the trigger. At the last moment Alex disarms him. Before Corrente and his boys can inflict punishment, the police burst in. Afterward Corrente tells Nick: "You handled yourself good back there, Dillon. I had you wrong, all wrong. Tell you the truth, I thought you were playing Mona. You know Mona. She's a good kid, but she's a sucker for anybody with a hard-luck story. She can't judge a guy's character. I can. You didn't lose your head. I can use a guy who doesn't lose his head."

When Nick closes up for the night, his lieutenant pal is waiting for him in the parking lot. Once more he tries to warn Nick away: "You think you can get Mona back? You think you wait long enough, she's going to leave the guy who buys her diamonds? You think even if she does, Corrente's going to let her go?"

Nick: "Leave me alone. I don't know what I think."

Lieutenant: "That's your whole problem, Nick. You don't ever know what you think."

He drives back to his rooming house. Someone is standing on the porch. Nick's headlights sweep over her, then click off. It's Mona. She's wearing a trenchcoat belted at the waist. Her eyes are slitted, her skin feverish under the moon. "I hear you were a hero tonight," she says when he steps up to her. "Ray's practically in love with you."

Nick: "Too bad I'm not interested."

Mona: "I didn't think you were. That's why I was surprised. Would it shock you if I told you I was disappointed?"

Nick: "I don't shock that easy. Unfortunately, I was working for your husband. The guy pays me a decent salary, I figured the least I could do was keep him from getting shot up."

Mona: "It could have been so simple. Just one squeeze on a trigger and it would've been all over. Isn't that what you do? Squeeze it?"

Nick (sardonic): "Am I to understand that you and Mr. Corrente are having marital trouble?"

Mona: "I'm the only one who's got trouble." She flings the trenchcoat open. There's a black bruise on her upper right arm, exactly where Nick has his tattoo. "*He* did this to me, Alex. Ray did. Sometimes he uses a belt, but tonight it was just his fists. All in all, I think I prefer the belt. At least that way I don't have to feel him touch me." It's only when she shudders that Nick embraces her. She draws him closer and they kiss.

Nick: "I'm crazy about you, Mona."

Mona: "I'm wild for you, too, baby." She hesitates. "I'm just scared."

Nick: "Of Ray?"

Mona: "He'll kill us both if he finds out. But I'm also scared of myself. You don't know me, Alex. There's something wild in me, something selfish and cruel. Why do you think I ended up with a guy like Ray?"

Nick: "You said so yourself. He was the last ship on the dock."

Mona: "Because he's like me. We see something we want and we take it, no matter who gets hurt. Maybe we're both rotten. And you're not." She runs a finger across his eyelids, down the corners of his mouth, in a gesture that's at once erotic and scientific, as though she could read Nick's face the way a fortune-teller would read a palm. Will she suddenly discern the face that lies beneath the one she touches? "No," she says finally. "You're good. A good man. I just worry that I'm not a good woman."

Nick: "You're good enough for me, baby." He kisses her again. When he clutches her bruised arm, she whimpers. "I'm sorry, baby. I didn't mean to hurt you."

Mona: "Go ahead and hurt me. I don't mind being hurt. Not if it's by the right guy. Oh, yes, hold me, Alex. Hold me close. It feels so good just to be held!"

Nick: "I'll hold you as long as you want. I'll hold you all night. Just tell me, Mona. Tell me what you want. I'll do anything you want."

Mona pulls back and gazes up at him. Her lips twitch in what might be a smile or a grimace of resignation. "You know what I want, Alex."

Blackout.

There was a package from Tara in my mailbox a few weeks later: another story, no note attached. It was called "Why Don't You Do Right?" It began: "I never found goodness attractive in a man. It made me think of the johns who showed me pictures of their wives and kids, then came inside me with a guilty sputter. They were the ones who'd ask, 'Why are you doing this, a nice kid like you?' as they mopped the sperm off their matted bellies with a washcloth, always a little pissed that I wasn't doing it for them. I always wanted to answer, 'Because of guys like you.' " I struck out the last sentence with a red pencil.

The story was about a young woman who leaves prostitution and a C-a-day smack habit and decides to become a writer. She meets another writer, older, successful, an ex-junkie like herself, though his addiction seems very far away. Somehow he has learned how to be good: "Good" was the word Tara used. I put a question mark beside it. From the beginning the narrator is slightly in awe of him. He doesn't come on to her and seems oblivious when she flirts with him, which she does out of habit, because for years it has been her livelihood to make men want her, and because her self-esteem is such a spindly thing that she can't imagine him reading her stories unless he does. He agrees to read them anyway. She supposes he is being kind. When she first sends them to him, she is sick with the fear that he'll hate them, that he'll judge the life contained in them. But he likes the stories. He takes their flaws seriously. And he never asks her if they're true. At first she's grateful for this. But over time it makes her angry. It's as though his refusal to peer beneath the polished lid of her fiction were a tactful but personal rejection, a refusal to see *her:* "Sometimes I wanted to write something that would rip through his detachment, something he couldn't answer with a sincere note. I thought of typing it in capitals with double underlining, scrawling it in crayon in letters ragged as a child's: THIS ISN'T JUST A STORY, ASS-HOLE. THIS IS MY HEART I'M GIVING YOU. WHY DON'T YOU STOP TELLING ME HOW ADMIRABLE IT IS? WHY DON'T YOU JUST TAKE IT?"

I'd barely finished reading when my phone rang.

"I'm sorry. I couldn't wait. Did you get it? You must have gotten it by now. Oh. This is Tara."

"I know who it is. Yeah, I got it. I just finished reading it."

"So? What did you think?"

"You were wrong about the guy."

I could hear her breath catch. "Wrong how?"

"He isn't good. Nobody's ever going to buy such romantic bull-shit. He's just scared."

"What would he have to be scared of?"

"Maybe he doesn't know what to do with beautiful young women. Especially ones with talent. Maybe he's scared of wanting someone who would never want him."

"But she does want him. Didn't I make that clear?"

"Then maybe the age difference bothers him. Maybe he doesn't want to be like Woody Allen, slobbering after a nineteen-year-old."

"She's twenty-five. And Woody Allen's an old man."

"Okay, maybe he worries that she's confused. That she's mixing up gratitude with attraction. That she feels an obligation."

"My narrator isn't confused. She knows exactly what she wants."

"What is it she wants?"

She yelled, "Do I have to spell everything out? I want you to love me!"

"Oh God," I groaned. "Not that word. Listen to me, Tara. I'm trying to tell you something about this . . . this *character* you made up. Because I know him better than you do. And what I'm trying to say is that he has a problem with follow-through. He admires you, he desires you, he may even fantasize about how nice it would be to love you. But he has questions about his ability."

"Stop talking about 'he.' This isn't a story anymore. I want you to love me. I want you to try. That's all. I want you to try. Are you so burned out you can't even try?"

"No," I said. "I can try. I can't promise anything else, but I can try."

"You know what I love about you?" Tara said. "Your enthusiasm."

Nick's affair with Mona is doubly furtive: Even as they hide from Ray, Nick must also hide his tattoo from her. There's a scene on the beach at night, down the bluffs from the club, where the lovers are clinching and Mona tries to pull off Nick's shirt. He warns her that he's got an ugly wound he doesn't want her to see, but she persists, half playful, half brutal, eyes glazed with the pleasure of inverted rape. At the last minute he hisses, "Someone's coming!" and plunges half dressed into the surf while Mona flees. When he comes up for air, Ray is standing at the water's edge, pinching his trouser legs so as not to get sand in the cuffs. During the conversation that follows, Nick stays submerged to the shoulders, as coy as Doris Day in a bubble bath while Rock Hudson leers at her from the doorway.

Ray: "Thought I might find you out here. Turn around." Nick hesitates. "What's the matter with you? You act like I'm about to plug you."

Off on the horizon we see a thin strand of lights against the starless sky. "See those lights out there? That's the *Dorada*. 'The Golden Girl.' It's a gambling ship. Belongs to a git named Thurlow, used to do business for the boys in Los Angeles before he went semi-legit. He keeps it moored just outside the three-mile limit. I run their protection."

Nick (still nervous): "What do you protect them from?"

Ray: "Just losers don't know enough to pay their debts on time. It's a cream-puff job. I'm like Thurlow's alarm clock. I tell people when their time is up."

Nick: "Must be good money."

Ray: "Not good enough. You have any idea what the *Dorada* takes in on a good Saturday night? Try half a million. I was thinking you and me might try for a bigger piece of that." The plan is for Ray to work the ship as usual while Nick and some other men wait in a power launch nearby. When the last suckers go ashore, Ray will signal them to board and they'll overpower the crew, clean out the safe, and make off with the weekend's take.

Nick: "Don't you worry about what Thurlow'll do when he realizes you're in on this? You aren't the only muscle he can hire."

Ray: "He ain't *gonna* realize it. You're gonna knock me out."

The camera cuts to Mona. She stands pressed against the cliff, listening. It cuts back to Nick and at that moment, in his eyes, or really in the space *behind* them, we see the thought that trips his conscience like a lead slug dropped on a jeweler's scale. "I've got a better idea. I'm going to shoot you."

Ray holds up his hands: "Hey, down, boy! Don't get carried away. I want to live long enough to spend that half a mil."

Nick: "You'll live, you lug. The gun's going to be filled with blanks. Only Thurlow isn't gonna know that. I shoot, you fall down boom. We give you the heave-ho over the side, you swim out to the launch. Two months later you and Mona'll be ordering room service in the best hotel in Rio."

Ray: "I like the way your mind works, kid. Nobody'll ever suspect me."

Nick: "That's right, Ray. No one ever suspects a dead man."

In the shadows Mona smiles.

I'm afraid I'm too squeamish to say much about the sex. Somewhere beneath the artifice and disguises there's a real woman whom I loved or tried to love, someone who proved so unsettling to me that I had to tell a story about her. Stories are the way we tell the truth and the way we change it into something bearable, encasing the original irritant in the pearly layers of narrative. I've given my irritant another name and another past. I've put words in her mouth. I've done everything I can to hide her. But I'm afraid you might meet her one day—not Tara, but the woman who is her seed or armature—and in spite of all my efforts recognize her. There's still that tattoo, and the likeness is pretty faithful. So don't expect me to tell you about the shape of her breasts or the clasp of her sex or about the way her face looked when I entered her. I mean to keep her decent.

There was the problem of viruses, for which we were both at risk and which I had been tested for and Tara hadn't. Given her history, she thought there was a chance she might be infected. So we took more than the usual precautions and we undressed only to dress again, in all the stretchy gear that science has devised to reconcile our longing for the little death with our dread of the big one. You can fetishize latex all you want, but there are some things that can't be eroticized: the jerking stops and starts that recall nothing so much as learning how to drive a stick shift, the litter of foil packets that crunch beneath you and whose sharp edges prick your skin, the machine oil tang of Nonoxynol-9, the fear of thrusting too hard, of going too deep, of putting your tongue in the wrong place. They turned the bed we shared into a bomb factory: The last thing we could afford to do there was lose ourselves.

"This isn't very good for you, is it?" she asked me once. We'd been lovers for about a month.

"No. It's perfect. You're perfect."

"You're a terrible liar. What kind of junkie did you make?"

"It's just the technology. It's sort of daunting."

"We can do other things. There's nothing I wouldn't do with you."

I knew this was true. Tara was a generous person. But I couldn't forget her stories. And while the past she revealed in them didn't bother me—if I'm honest, I have to say it excited me in a queasy way—I didn't want to take her back there. "You know what I'd like to do?" I told her. "Read to you."

Here are some of the books I read to Tara in the time we were together: *Bleak House, The Third Policeman, Mildred Pierce, Bad Behavior. Bad Behavior* made Tara sick with envy. We'd make love until exhaustion overtook us, and then she'd arrange herself like a cat, coiled half on top of me, her head on my chest, as I read. In this way we'd fall asleep. Often I'd wake with a start to see that the light was still on, her head still pillowed on me, her breath stirring the hairs on my chest. All my life before her I'd fallen asleep with a dizzy sensation of floating. The feeling scared me. I thought that if I surrendered to it fully, I'd actually levitate out the window and drift endlessly up into the night. In Tara I told myself that at last I had an anchor. But the feeling of being anchored can be frightening in its own way: Really, there's not much difference between floating and sinking.

On one of her visits Tara and I went to the Clit Club, where Slam and Roxy had invited us to a combination commitment ceremony and farewell party; they were leaving for New Mexico in another week. It turned out to be more of a performance piece. We got there late and the upstairs room was already hot with bodies. The audience was mostly female: wiry little dykes with stubble cuts and surgical steel septum rings; big, lush lipstick lesbians in spandex dresses. Everybody was tattooed. I found myself childishly eager for a glimpse of another straight couple, but the only one I saw consisted of a woman in a white vinyl cat suit and a huge, unwieldy guy wearing a blindfold, dog collar, and studded leather jockstrap: With his soft, hairless belly and dimpled knees, he looked like a baby afflicted with some freakish accelerated-growth disorder. His mistress led him in on a chain leash, then parked him against a heavy concrete pillar. I watched her thread some monofilament fishing line through his nipple rings and lash him to the column with it. He remained as docile as a well-trained Newfoundland. "Now I'm gonna leave you alone for a while," she cooed. "Are you gonna be good?" He nodded. She slapped him across the cheek, then yanked down his codpiece and slapped his penis so hard I winced in sympathy. "I hope so. I don't want to hear any *reports* about you."

Tara said, "I bet you anything that guy's got a corner office. Every slave I ever met was some kind of executive."

They'd been playing that furious, chattering dance music that makes you want to drop acid, butcher your parents, and write "PIGS" on the wall in their gore. Now the sound was cut. Slam and Roxy walked onto the low stage at the front of the room. The crowd cheered. In the years I'd known her Slam had all but vanished beneath encrustations of tattoos and facial jewelry, but she'd never managed to efface her nature, which was that of a cheerful, hearty big sister from one of the American suburbs' two hundred functional families. "You like me! You *really* like me!" she cried. Gratitude made her tongue-tied. She didn't know how to thank her friends for their kindness or her clients for their loyalty or Roxy for her love, that thing that defies thanks. "And so," she concluded, "Roxy and I worked up this little ceremony to show you what you mean to us, and what we mean to each other, and—aw, shucks, let's just do it."

The lights went down and someone put on a tape of dirgelike organ music. I could feel the low notes vibrate through the floor beneath my feet. A pair of spots formed dusty white cones in the air. Roxy stood in one of them, her broad back to the audience. She was naked to the waist. Beneath the other spot Slam pulled on a pair of surgical gloves, snapping them smartly at the wrist. She stepped out of the light and an instant later reappeared beside her girlfriend, holding a small bottle and a scalpel: The glinting blade seemed oddly decorative, like something you'd see in a jeweler's display case. I watched her daub Roxy's shoulder with an antiseptic, Betadine probably: It left that familiar rusty stain. Then she began to cut. A shudder rolled through me, a wavelike disturbance that might have been revulsion or arousal, the twitch of blood in the microsecond before it plunges toward the groin. The first stroke was a long downward one that took a moment to begin bleeding. The incisions that followed were smaller. Slam's hand moved as swiftly as though she were cross-hatching a charcoal sketch. Roxy never budged. Only her ribs pulsed into relief as she drew in breath. Beside me I heard Tara hiss. "You all right?" I asked. She squeezed my hand but said nothing.

When Slam was done, she rubbed the cuts with ink, then blotted the excess with a piece of gauze before returning to the vacant beam of light. With her back turned to us she undressed, shedding layers of leather and denim and cotton until there was nothing but skin and ink. She had a pair of black snakes—really, they were the suggestions of snakes, the design was so simple—tattooed along her spine, their coils winding between the vertebrae. Roxy joined her. She gathered Slam's hair in one hand and bound it in a chignon. It was the kind of thing a mother might do for her small daughter. When she began to use the scalpel, I could see her breasts bounce. At first I was afraid she didn't know what she was doing, that her hand would shake, leaving only some ragged scars that someone someday might take for the marks of a bizarre accident. But she was careful; she was careful with her lover's body. The design that materialized in blood on Slam's shoulder and then vanished as the blood streamed downward was a perfect trident, the same design Slam had carved into Roxy.

Afterward the two women greeted well-wishers like newlyweds outside a church, bare-breasted and gleaming with sweat.

I'd worried that Tara would be revolted, reminded of razor-wielding pimps who slice their initials in their girls' asses, but she said she'd found the ritual beautiful. I wondered what would happen if Slam and Roxy ever broke up. She slapped my wrist. "Shame on you! The way you think. They're not going to break up. And even if they do, it wouldn't matter. Not really. Not after tonight. For the rest of their lives each of them will be marked with the other. No matter where they go or who they're with, they'll always know there's someone else who's wounded in the same way. Like a twin. You never lose your twin."

The next day I had Tara's stick figures tattooed on my wrist. We sleepwalked home in a gnat-cloud of endorphins, then made risk-less love in the air conditioner's chilly blast. Afterward she said, "I want to please you," and I said, "You already do," but she brushed it aside. "You know what I mean," she said. "You want to hurt me."

I recoiled. "That's bullshit!"

She gazed at me steadily. "You don't have to pretend. I can see it in you. It's how you're wired. People are wired in all sorts of different ways. And I'm saying it's okay. I want you to."

I protested some more, indignantly, coyly, feebly, and finally submitted to my desires. At least I tried. I got as far as handcuffing Tara with the pair I kept in my closet, the way one keeps suits that were outgrown long ago. But I couldn't get her past out of my mind. I kept imagining her in a room that rented by the hour, naked and shivering with the onset of her jones and consenting to be tied and beaten by men who looked as anonymously ugly as all men must when they're stripped of everything but their wants and the power of the money in their wallets. I told myself that it might not have been as horrible as I imagined, no more horrible, maybe, than having to wipe the piss off a stranger's toilet seat in a Red Roof Inn, and certainly better compensated. I told myself I had no way of knowing how much of it had ever really happened. We tried reversing roles: I had her straddle me and twist my nipples, but all it did was hurt. And the words she barked at me might as well have been in Swedish for all the conviction she put in them. Tara wasn't much of an actress.

I broke up with her a few weeks later, this woman who'd wanted nothing more than to give me pleasure. It lasted hours, the two of us weeping and yelling like idiots, faces mushy with grief. "What the fuck is wrong with you?" she cried, over and over. None of my explanations satisfied her. "I'm sorry," I said. "It's just the way I'm wired." I excused myself to the end.

Marked, too, ends in betrayal. The heist goes off as planned. Scenes click past like the numbers on a roulette wheel: the powerboat roaring seaward with its foaming comet's tail, Nick at the helm; the strained wait beneath the moon; the sounds of piano chords, laughter, the clatter of dice and ice cubes drifting across the water. Then we're on board the *Dorada,* following Ray in his white suit. The last boat ferries off the night's last losers. On the deserted deck Ray releases the rope ladder. The three raiders clamber up and vault over the side. Nick presses a gun to Corrente's spine and walks him forward into the glare of the casino. Croupiers freeze at their green baize tables. The man called Thurlow drops his high-ball glass; it bounces on the Persian rug. Nick's voice is quiet: "Give it up." Ray mutters to him: "Make this look good."

"Don't worry, buddy. I will." His finger tightens on the trigger.

Twenty years later Ray's death would have been filmed in slow motion, the camera tracking every jetting platelet and plunging into an exit wound the size of a football. But in *Marked,* as in all true noir, murder is a psychological phenomenon. What matters is not Ray's blood but the look in his eyes as the bullet spins him in a flailing pirouette: It's the look of the con man who finally realizes he's been conned.

After this everything moves faster: money stuffed in a seaman's ditty bag; Ray's body plunging overboard with a detonation of spray. Nick is the first man down the ladder. The moment he sets foot in the launch, he turns and shoots the accomplices who cling helplessly overhead. As he speeds off toward the lights of La Jolla, we hear him in voice-over:

"It was all behind me now, the lying and the killing. That's what I told myself. I told myself we could make a clean start, Mona and me. Love would wash us clean. But sometimes love only makes you dirty, like the water around a sinking ship. When my ship went down near Midway, I came up covered with oil. It was as black as tattoo ink, and I stank of it for days. Sometimes I thought I could still smell it on me. And here's the thing I still can't figure: Was it love for Mona that turned me into a murderer? Or did Mona just show me what I always was: a killer from the beginning?"

The scene dissolves to Mona's bedroom, where Mona paces, a cigarette clamped between her lips. Nick enters.

Mona: "You did it?"

Nick: "Yeah." He avoids her gaze.

Mona: "What about the money?"

He drops the bag at her feet. "Five hundred thousand, like the man said." Their embrace is almost mechanical. "You'd better start packing. The cops'll be onto us pretty quick."

Mona: "What's the rush? Let me get you a drink." They go downstairs to the darkened lounge. Mona steps behind the bar and turns on a light, takes out glasses and a bottle. She reaches into the ice tray. "What'll it be, stranger?"

Nick: "We don't have time for this, baby. I told you, the cops—"

Mona (she is holding a gun): "The cops will find the man who robbed the *Dorada* and murdered my husband. The man who came here meaning to kill me."

Nick: "You've got it all sewn up, don't you, Mona? I guess you were just playing me all along."

Mona: "Don't be a dope, Alex. I hated Ray. And I loved you. I still do. I loved you so much I almost forgot what Nick taught me. Nick was the boy I told you about, remember? You remind me of him sometimes. You've got the same eyes, only yours are meaner. Anyway, Nick taught me always to keep an eye out for the next ship, the one that won't sail off without you. And you want to know something? It turns out the only ship you can ever count on is the one that's just got room enough for you."

Nick: "You and half a million dollars."

Mona: "A girl doesn't want to get lonely."

Nick: "Ever wonder what happened to Nick, baby? The guy who left you stranded? Let me show you."

He starts to pull up his shirtsleeve and Mona fires: Maybe she thought he was reaching for a gun of his own. Nick staggers backward. The look on his face is not shock but bitter amusement, as though he'd expected this all along and was perversely pleased to be proved right. "Don't be scared, baby. I was just trying to show you something." With shaking hands he finishes what he started.

Mona stares at him in horror. "Remember when I got this tattoo? Remember what I told you? I said I wanted to take you with me wherever I went. I guess I did. Or maybe it was the other way around. That tattoo dragged me all the way back to you. I couldn't fight it. And I guess you were telling the truth, too, weren't you, baby? You said you'd be waiting for me. And look, here we are."

He collapses. Mona kneels beside him, cradles his head in her lap as sirens keen in the distance, coming closer. The last shot is a close-up of the tattoo.

What else can I tell you? A few months after we split, Tara met a guy who turned out to be steadier than I was. They're married now, and I hear they're happy. I think of her every time my eye falls on my tattoo. It's the one I see most often: I am looking at it as I write this. After a while its spotty nakedness became unbearable, and I went all the way back to Amsterdam to get it touched up. Aesthetics aside, those stick figures kept me thinking about the question Tara asked me the night I left. I'm still trying to find an answer to it: "What is wrong with you?" I could blame it on my childhood or on Tara's past or on my inability to come to terms with my own cruelty. But these are just stories I tell myself. They are entertaining and even, sometimes, consoling, and mostly true. But it doesn't pay to take your stories too seriously.

I used to like falling in love. I liked the gratitude that went with it, the ridiculous gratitude for the dime-store present and the late-night phone call. Tara used to call me late at night, and for a while it made me happy. You can tell you're falling out of love when the gratitude ceases, when those gifts feel like shameless bribes and the ring on the telephone makes you mutter, "What does she want from me now?" I suppose that falling in love is good for the character and falling out of it harmful. The one makes you trusting, generous, expansive; the other pinched, suspicious, jealous of your prerogatives. Or maybe what happens is that love offers you an exit from the seedy hotel room of self, the room in which you sit alone with your desires, the desires you take neat, like shots of rye. You meet someone, and she calls you away from the narrow bed whose mattress might be stuffed with iron filings, the yellowed linoleum, the single, fly-soiled lightbulb, the windows with their film of soot that give onto nothing but an air shaft. You walk out of the room and you join her in the bright air outside, and if you're lucky you get to stay there with her. But some of us, you know, are agoraphobes. We can't take the raw, unfiltered light, the hurtling distances. They make us anxious. And sooner or later we turn on the one who lured us out, we blame her for overturning our lives, and we go back to the old hotel, where our old room is always waiting for us.

7

I FALL DOWN

If there be no corpse, then the bed or seat to which the deceased had been accustomed should be occupied by the reader, who ought to expound the power of the Truth. Then, summoning the spirit of the deceased, imagine it to be present there listening, and read.

THE TIBETAN BOOK OF THE DEAD

The last time I was in Borneo, in a muddy village on the banks of the Mahakam, I met an elderly Kenyah woman whose hands and feet had been tattooed as a protection against leprosy. In Burma criminals acquired markings called *Pe Say,* "the medicine of invulnerability," which were supposed to make them bulletproof. In the same country beautiful girls were tattooed on their tongues to immunize them against the potions of seducers. Lyle Tuttle, the grand old man of America's needleworkers, claims that those ancient tattoos actually worked, that they somehow made their wearers more resistant to injury and disease and thus should be considered the first medicine. This may be stretching things. But it isn't too hard to see the practice as a precursor to vaccination, a little wound that paradoxically confers immunity.

I've never heard of anyone being tattooed after the fact, as a measure against injuries that have already been incurred. It wouldn't make much sense. But I suppose that's what I was trying to do in April of 1995, when I had an image of the Archangel Michael tattooed on my right shoulder blade, which I had fractured a year before along with several other bones—nine, to be exact: left radius, right ilium, and seven right ribs. It was an astonishing number of parts to break, considering that I broke them while I was stone sober and not operating any heavy equipment. It almost seemed like an accomplishment, worthy of a gold medal in the Special Olympics, and the whole experience helped me understand the grisly boasting you hear in hospitals. "Such a tumor they took out of me! The doctor said it was as big as a plum." "That's nothing, you should pardon me for saying. Mine they said was a *grapefruit.*"

I think of this one-upmanship as the Jewish counterpart of Irish poor-mouthing, a way of reaping triumph from the flinty acreage of bad luck. My mother used to do it all the time and it used to drive me crazy. I'd tell her that I had a head cold and she'd exclaim, "Och, I know how you feel. You should see how I'm suffering with my bronchitis." She wasn't just saying it, either: Even over the telephone, I'd hear her lungs rasping like some satanic Victorian mill. If I pulled a muscle, she'd herniate a disk. I got to the point where I wouldn't tell her when there was something wrong with me: I was too scared of what she might do to trump it. When I was little, my mother was sick—I want to say constantly, but this can't be true, can it?—she was sick often, often enough that my earliest memory of her is in bed. She is wearing one of the housecoats that became her uniform later on, a fluffy red wrapper with cloth-covered snaps. There are pills beside her on the night table, Kleenex, a steaming glass of tea, a glass because my mother was the child of Russians, who had taught her to drink it that way.

And the tea reminds me of the one time I succeeded in out-sicking her. I couldn't have been more than three. My mother was bedridden with kidney stones. "Pain like that you wouldn't believe," she'd wince in recollection. "I cried every time I made wee-wee." She had a nurse attending her—you could hire home care then, even if you weren't rich or dying—and one of this woman's jobs was to serve my mother glass after glass of strong, amber tea, whether to flush the stones out or melt them in her urinary tract like lumps of sugar I don't know. And she was bringing my mother another tray, laden with teapot, glass, sugar, and lemon slices, the day I collided with her as I raced toward the bedroom, clumsy then, as I am now, and reckless with enthusiasm. Scalding water drenched me. My flesh blossomed in wet burns. I wouldn't stop crying. By evening I was running a fever of 106, the temperature at which the brain begins to cook in its bony oven.

The doctor came. I was swabbed with antiseptic jelly, wrapped in gauze, stuffed with aspirin that made my breath smell of oranges and chalk. I shuddered beneath the blankets. My body was a hot cage. As my fever climbed, I flailed at its bars, desperate to be free. Over the next hours I was crushed like earth sinking into water, boiled like water sinking into fire, then scattered like fire sinking into air. The Tibetans call these sensations the three signs of impending death, and to tell the truth, I have no memory of them—or, really, of any of this story, which was told to me so many times that I've come to think of it as my own. I only imagine that I felt something like them, because late that night the doctor told my parents I might die.

My mother said that my father began to rage at her. "He said it was all my fault. He said I was a bad mother! Can you imagine?" Decades later her voice would still tremble. She was one of those people who have a photographic memory of emotion. She might be terrible with names and dates, but when she talked about a trip she'd taken to Italy thirty years before, her face would glow again with the heat of the sun that had risen off the stones of the Via Appia Antica, her mouth would water as though she were still tasting a *panino* she'd eaten in the Piazza Navona, the hard tortoiseshell roll splintering between her teeth, slabs of mozzarella pliant and milky on her tongue. You could see her marveling at her own pluck, a sheltered woman who for twenty years had never taken a step without her husband lighting out for a strange country filled with men who made grabs at every passing female bottom and backed up their Fiats at sixty miles an hour on streets that had been built for donkeys. It was the same way with hurt. Every slight still stung her. Nothing was ever laid to rest. "What kind of husband would say something like that to his own wife? When his child is dying?"

"But I didn't die," I'd remind her gently, the way you shake someone from a bad dream. "I'm right here."

"Well, thank God. Your father thought he knew everything."

But I'm getting away from my tattoo. I had it done in Amsterdam, where I'd been invited to a tattoo convention. It was a nostalgic trip for me, since Amsterdam was where I'd gotten my first tattoo six years before. And part of my reason for going was that I hoped to get another piece from Hanky Panky. Hanky Panky has always struck me as a cross between a respectable craftsman, a Hell's Angel, and one of those Victorian adventurer-raconteurs who used to treat their ennui by touring the fever-ridden badlands of the colonies and then made a living telling others how much they'd suffered there. Now he was an administrator as well. He'd taken to hosting these annual gatherings—tattooists are always swarming to conventions, where they show off for one another and bad-mouth each other's work, and get companionably shit-faced in the hotel bar—and in this capacity he was riding herd over thousands of visiting tattooists and piercers and bikers and S&M aficionados and punks and hollow-cheeked rockers with great fluffy haystacks of Ron Wood hair who, oddly enough, seemed less dated than the kids with the Mohawks, those wistfully sullen relics of a movement that had begun as a radical rejection of nostalgia, only to quickly become nostalgic for itself, nostalgic for its own lost capacity to shock. Nobody is shockable anymore, at least not in Amsterdam. The Dutch have been practicing tolerance for so long that they immediately domesticate every deviation. The big-thighed whores on the Oudezijds Voorburgwal might have been polishing their vitrines with Windex instead of posing in them, and when a guy with foot-long dreadlocks, full arm sleeves, and several pounds of stainless steel in his ears and lips clanked past a local burgher, the look he got was less likely to be indignant than affectionate: "Heh heh, *there's* an odd-looking *jongen,* but it takes all kinds, *toch?*"

There are few jobs more thankless than trying to organize an event that bills itself as a celebration of anarchy, and Hanky Panky was showing the strain. When I found him, he was standing on the floor of the old Amsterdam stock exchange, which was where the convention was going to be held that year, surrounded by people who wanted his attention. A reporter made the mistake of asking him if the visiting *artistes* were going to enjoy themselves more sedately at this convention, now that so many of them were middle-aged.

"WHAT THE FUCK DOES AGE HAVE TO DO WITH ANYTHING?" Hanky Panky bellowed. "You think I come home from my shop and I pour myself a nice little glass of beer and turn on the telly? You have to know the basics. Sex, drugs, and rock 'n' roll. I don't give a fuck if you're now on the Program and are waving your finger in the air, AA or NA, motherfucker, we still get fucked up once in a while!" He ran out of breath and glowered into the crowd, panting like the last man standing at a barroom punch-fest. Just then he spotted me. "You! What do you want?"

"Oh. Uh. Hi, Henk. I'm Peter Trachtenberg. You don't remember me–"

"Sure, I remember you. The fellow from Borneo. How are you?"

"I'm fine. I was wondering if I could get an appointment with you while I'm in town–"

"Appointment! No! No! Sorry, but I can't. I just can't. I'm up to my fucking ears, you see!" He threw up his lavishly illustrated arms in a gesture that encompassed all his assailants. "Look at them, the *klootzacks* won't give me a moment's peace! Why do I let them talk me into this?"

So he hooked me up with a visiting tattooist from California, a spindly, pale-skinned fellow who looked like a young molecular biologist. His name was Freddy, and he specialized in religious work. When I pulled up my shirt to display my stigma, he nodded and then showed me an even bigger one he'd tattooed on the ribs below his heart. The thing was the size of the Grand Canyon and red blood spurted from it exuberantly. If Jesus's wound had been half that big, there wouldn't have been any Passion: The poor guy would've bled to death before he could say, "Why hast thou forsaken me?"

I told Freddy that I wanted an angel, and he just said "Oh," in that studiously neutral tone that operates as a dog whistle of contempt, inaudible to all but those whose self-regard it is meant to wither. "I don't mean *that* kind of angel," I added quickly. I was pathetically anxious for his approval. I turned to display the Archangel Michael on my left scapula, the one I'd gotten as a reminder of a lifetime of bad karma. Freddy inspected it. "Coptic," he said. "Twelfth century if I'm not mistaken. It could be a little darker." I hated him.

My first angel is rampant, a soldierly messenger, alert and calmly menacing. His sword is raised above his head. He brandishes his olive branch like a whip. The angel I wanted Freddy to tattoo on my left shoulder blade would be his mirror image, but he would be falling, falling as though struck by lightning. His sword would be broken. His olive branch would have dropped from his hand. And there would be a look of terror on his face.

Freddy didn't ask me why I wanted this piece. In this he was no different than most tattooists, who in the course of their careers engrave thousands of customers with thousands of images, most of which are the iconic equivalents of "and" and "the." A sheet of flash may have as many as a dozen different eagles on it, differing only in the tilt of the head or the curl of the talons, all of them representing minute variations of designs that date back a century or more. Few tattooists ask a customer why he's chosen one eagle over others. Or why he wants an eagle in the first place. I'd spent enough time in tattoo circles to understand this. But I would have liked Freddy to ask me. I would have liked to feel that my taste in imagery set me apart from his other clients, the college kids with their Tasmanian Devils, the Valley girls with their winsome ensigns of hummingbirds and roses.

But it's hard to stand out at a tattoo convention. On the day I sat down in Freddy's booth I had six tattoos, and all around me on the floor of the Beurs van Berlage there were people who had sixty. There was an elderly Chinese man, blithely strolling in nothing but Birkenstocks and a sort of diaper, whose body and smooth skull were tattooed with a full suit of futuristic armor. There was a guy named Enigma who had turned his person into a living jigsaw puzzle and who later that day had several pieces filled in simultaneously by twenty tattooists from three continents, who labored over him like a conclave of knife-happy surgeons amid a hum of needles and a fog of antiseptic spray. Of course, people *looked* at me. I was sitting half naked in the middle of a tattoo convention, with an artist of distinction working on my shoulder blade. But they weren't looking at *me*. The professionals were looking at the design, wondering if it was worth stealing. The others, I figured, were studying my body, the body that was imposed on me by God or nature and whose muteness I have been rebelling against all my life. And they were not impressed. They were clinically cataloging its deficiencies: the sagging posture, the Olive Oyl arms, the pods of fat on my fuselage. It was a disaster of a body, not to mention an injured one. My cracked ribs still ached when I lay on my right side, and if I slammed down too hard while doing sit-ups, I felt the bones in my pelvis and shoulder twang like tuning forks.

But pain, of course, is another way in which the body becomes remarkable. It is often the route chosen by those who feel unloved, or unworthy of love. Pain is what we settle for when we believe that pleasure is beyond us. And I don't think it's just coincidence that my chain of injuries began the day after I broke up with Tara, who'd wanted nothing but the chance to give me what I wanted, a prospect so frightening that I had no choice but to leave her. It was October, late afternoon, when the city sky turns as blue as a gas flame. I was Rollerblading down Fifth Avenue with a bag of groceries hitched over my arm. This was my standard way of getting around during the warmer months, and I no longer bothered wearing wrist guards. I'm gliding down the right lane between the curb and the southbound traffic. I feel as close to graceful as I ever have since I stopped using drugs. And suddenly Tara's face floats up before me with all the vividness of grief. It's her face in the moment before I told her that I had to stop seeing her, expectant but still unperturbed: The forehead is childishly broad and high; the lips are slightly parted. It might almost be a hallucination, it's that clear. But it's only my heart sighing up its final image of her, the woman I used to stroke and kiss and talk to the last thing before sleeping every night and from now on will only regret. The memory of Tara's face is a sheet of glass that has dropped down from the sky, and I crash into it like any dim-witted starling. I groan out loud. And all my skill deserts me and I skid backward and, forgetting the cardinal rule of Rollerblading, thrust an arm out behind me to break my fall. I fall down anyway, in the middle of tony Fifth Avenue, within shouting distance of the New School and Kenneth Cole and Emporio Armani, the way I fell as a child but not as effortlessly; a little kid expends no energy in falling, he just succumbs to gravity, which wants us all prone, but a grown-up struggles to remain upright, teeters, thrashes, goes rigid, dreading not just pain but embarrassment, and so suffers both in a measure that is directly proportional—say in a ratio of two to one—to the fury with which he tried to avoid them.

And this is exactly what happens to me, since the next thing I know I'm lying in the gutter while cars hiss by inches from my head, my whole left forearm is singing, and I am nevertheless waving it to stave off the hordes of good Samaritans who, actually, and I hate to say this about my fellow New Yorkers, are nowhere in sight, though perhaps the people who saunter past without looking at me are only *pretending* not to look at me out of exquisite tact. "I'm fine," I say to nobody. And I decide I must be, since I *can* wiggle my fingers, though just barely. That night I wrap the wrist in an Ace bandage and tell myself it's a sprain, but it keeps on singing its doleful tune and when I wake the next morning my forearm is blown up like Popeye's.

What I had turned out to be a simple fracture of my left radius. The cheery doctor who set it for me in the emergency room at St. Vincent's Hospital said, "I'll bet you were Rollerblading," and when I said yes, smirked. "I knew it, I just knew it. Rollerblader's radius. You're the thirteenth I've had this month."

"It's that common?"

"Common? I can diagnose these babies in my sleep! Fractured radius, hypertrophied quads. It's classic." He swathed my wrist in strips of soggy fiberglass, which he hardened with an ordinary blow-dryer. "The thing that gets me is why you guys don't take up running or something. You're a clumsy runner, the worst that can happen is you sprain yourself."

I got indignant. "I wasn't being clumsy, I was being guilty."

"Whatever. You want to see somebody in Psychiatry?"

"No thanks," I said. "I've got my own."

Am I overinterpreting? In the throes of guilt I have overdosed on pills and nearly whacked off an index finger with a meat cleaver (this right after I'd managed to deploy a gas-powered concrete saw that my friend Rob had loaned me with severe misgivings—"There's something about you and heavy equipment that just doesn't mix"—without a scratch). And on each occasion what I felt, beneath the shock and pain and humiliation, was a purr of satisfaction. It was not unlike what I feel when I finish paying my bills each month. It is the sensation of having received one's just deserts and choked them down to the last crumb.

A fractured wrist isn't all that much to complain about. If, on the day that Tara's face materialized reproachfully before me, I had fallen a little farther from the curb, directly in front of a speeding truck, say—then I *really* would have been in trouble. Because guilt can fuck up your life, but it fucks up your death even worse. According to Tibetan Buddhism, one's mental state at the terminal moment determines the condition of rebirth. If you die angry, you'll be reincarnated as a tusked demon in a hell where the very atmosphere is thick with rage. If you die ignorant, you'll come back as an animal that suffers dully through another lifetime; the texts don't specify what kind of animal, but I always imagine a yak straining up a mountain pass beneath enormous sacks of grain, being thrashed by a peasant who's forgotten the Buddha's teachings on kindness to all sentient beings. To die in a state of attachment guarantees rebirth as a *preta,* a hungry ghost, all toothless mouth and yawning gullet, condemned to yearn unappeasably for the world that is now barred to it. And if you die in a state of guilt? Let me quote from *The Tibetan Book of the Dead:* "Then . . . the Lord of Death will place round thy neck a rope and drag thee along; he will cut off thy head, extract thy heart, pull out thy intestines, lick up thy brain, drink thy blood, eat thy flesh, and gnaw thy bones; but thou wilt be incapable of dying. Although thy body be hacked to pieces, it will revive again."

Of course, any Buddhist will tell you that all these phenomena—the hells, the torments, the Lord of Death himself—are only hallucinations generated by the mind as it flickers out of existence. Or, more accurately, as it flickers into the *Bardo,* the antechamber between one life and the next. Buddhism was the first religion to recognize what a busy thing the mind is, and to ascribe to it the place that other religions gave to God. For Christians hell is a real destination, with real pits filled with real coals, and God is the one who sends you there. This can lead to resentment. Because even if you're absolutely sure that you, personally, are slated for heaven– maybe you've gotten a mailing that says "PRE-APPROVED"– you must know people whose chances are more iffy. You may even love them. And how can you ratify the justice, or honor the imperious heavenly judge, that condemns the people you love to roast miserably for eternity? Tibetan Buddhists never have to perform this moral high-wire act. God never enters the picture. They know that hell is the illusion of a consciousness that is so addicted to the dream of life that it will conjure up its own agony rather than awaken. *Pateo ergo sum:* I suffer, therefore I am.

For a long time I didn't know if Jews believed in hell. As a little boy I asked my mother and she said, "Of course not!"

"But what about Hitler? Or . . . or . . . Haman?"

"Them? Yes, *they* went. But they weren't Jewish."

"Okay, what about Finkelstein?" Finkelstein the landlord was Jewish and he was the most evil person I knew. It took him weeks to get the elevator repaired, and he threatened my poor mother when she was a day late in paying the rent. One winter the boiler failed and we went days without heat, cocooning ourselves in layered sweaters while our breath formed ragged white flags in the living room air. I came upon him in the lobby during this time, a pouting, round-shouldered man who was gleefully freezing us to death. As I slipped past him I muttered, "Let's play lynch the landlord." I didn't think he could hear me, but he seized my arm and whipped me around, so that I was staring up at his smudged glasses and the pale, terrified eyes behind them. "YOU GO TO HELL!" he sputtered. "YOU GO TO HELL, YOU!"

My mother had made me apologize, of course, but her opinion of Finkelstein hadn't changed. "That one? *Maybe* he'll go. I wouldn't be surprised."

My mother had both a vengeful streak and a startling capacity for forgiveness. When I told her that my father had terminal cancer, her first response was, "Well, I certainly never wished *that* on him." It was more than twenty years since he'd left her. Her friendships were perforated with injured silences; she was always breaking with people she accused of "taking advantage" of her. But she was too softhearted to be a true hoarder of grudges. "I thought you guys weren't speaking," I'd say after she'd tell me she'd seen a friend she'd eighty-sixed months before. "Oh, *she* came around," she'd say benignly. "I couldn't stay angry at her. You know me." As far as my father went, I'm sure my mother would have been perfectly happy with a broken leg.

But when I told her about my fractured wrist, she was horrified. "Oh, how could you? What were you doing?"

"I was Rollerblading."

"Rollerblading! Och, I knew it! I never should've let you."

"I'm forty-one, Ma. I don't think it's a question of 'letting' me do anything anymore."

"You don't have to remind me. But I told you it was dangerous. I told you and you wouldn't listen. And now look." For a moment I could hear the triumph in her voice, the luxurious pleasure of someone who has been justified by someone else's misery. An instant later she mastered herself. "Poor pussycat! What will you eat? Do you have any soup? Who's going to take care of you?"

A few years before this I would have said something like "Not you." We all make up stories about our parents, the way tribal peoples make up stories about the origin of the world, and my story about my mother was that she had never taken care of me. All her warmth and quivering solicitousness were just disguises for that fact, a cyclone spinning around an emotional vacuum. As evidence for this story I drew upon my memories of her in bed, wrapped custodially around her illnesses. I produced the incident of my scalding. "Look! Look!" I'd yell to anyone who'd listen. "I was literally boiled alive as a sacrifice to this woman's hypochondria!"

And of course I had the evidence that I *felt* uncared for; I'd felt uncared for all my life. Why else had I drugged and boozed and fucked myself halfway into the grave? There's a school of psychology—it was hugely popular in the 1980s—which maintains that any feeling is the artifact of some distant, buried truth. If you feel persecuted, it's because at some point you really were. If you feel violated, it's a sure indicator that Mommy or Daddy diddled you in the cradle. And if the primary feature of your emotional landscape, the brooding Stonehenge whose shadow blights the flowers and shrivels the grass, is the sense of being unloved—well, people don't just make this stuff up, do they? The moment I came upon this theory, in the office of a therapist I used to see when I was still full of the rancor that foams through every addict when he first gives up his drug, I ran with it, breathless and crying and exultant with self-pity. Because for some of us, finding an explanation for our unhappiness is preferable to happiness itself, especially if that explanation takes us off the hook and gives us permission to impale somebody else with a wet, red *thunk*.

Ethics aside, the trouble with blaming another person for your misery is that it makes you boring, boring to others and boring to yourself. Tattooists are very hard on the clients they call "weepers," the ones who announce every twinge and pang. And at the time I broke my wrist, even my analyst was sick of hearing me go off on my mom: "If I hear you say one more word about that poor woman, I am going to scream!" So I kept my mouth shut and tried to do the same with my mind when it grumbled that everything would've been different if it weren't for Her, and generally did my best to be cheerfully present and, I don't know, filial whenever the two of us spent any time together.

"Look at you!" she exclaimed one evening when I was up visiting. I'd just changed a lightbulb in her bedroom, which struck her as a very big deal for somebody with a fractured wrist. Her emphysema made it impossible for her to even climb up on the step stool. "It's like you're not handicapped at all! Who'd believe you could be so clumsy?"

I didn't argue with her. It would mean telling her about Tara and the guilt I felt at leaving her, and I never discussed guilt or girlfriends with my mother. All my life I'd been keeping secrets from her. I hadn't told her about my heroin habit until two years after I'd kicked. And she still didn't know about my tattoos, though that meant I had to wear a long-sleeved shirt every time I came over. I'd done the same thing when I was shooting dope, though back then it was tracks I was hiding.

When I was getting ready to leave, my mother said, "You could stay over. I hate to think of you shlepping all the way downtown with that wrist."

"No, no, Mom. It's okay. I can take care of myself." My fractured wrist wasn't much of an impediment. Really, it was more of a learning experience. I learned to cut the sleeves of my old shirts so I could wear them over my cast. I learned to shower with my left arm inside a garbage bag (the water pattered on it romantically and made me imagine that I was weathering a monsoon inside a tin-roofed shack in Port Moresby). I even learned to climb the ladder to my loft bed, which struck a lot of people as foolhardy but gave me a hot flush of accomplishment every time I'd managed to worm my way to the top.

Getting down was harder, though, and one night about six weeks after I'd cracked my wrist, I lost my grip. There was an instant in which I might have snagged the rungs with my other hand, but the instant went by, to be followed by another in which I fell backward, though the actual sensation was that of floating nauseously, innards bobbing, with enough time to look down and see that the floor below—and this really bothered me—needed vacuuming. First I hit the edge of my desk, a hefty slab of butcher block, and then the floor, so hard I heard the windows rattle. I yelled "Fuck!" and then couldn't yell anymore because all the breath had been knocked out of me and I couldn't draw any more inside. I was panting and groaning and my groans sounded like the groans of a ninety-year-old man strapped to a bed in a V.A. hospital, as hopeless and feeble and monotonous. Cursing sounded even worse, but I kept it up in between gasps. I was afraid that if I didn't make words of some kind, I might start crying. Something was piercing my back like the tines of a pitchfork. I thought I might have punctured a lung. My mother's lung had collapsed once, during what should have been a routine procedure in the hospital, and I was assailed by the memory of her face, eyes rolled up in panic as green-suited tormentors swarmed over her. I wondered if I was dying. My black cat Bitey strolled over and batted my hair with a paw. Her brother Ching cowered under the desk.

The telephone rang and I managed to wriggle over and pick up the receiver. "What happened?" It was my downstairs neighbor, trying to decide if she should be anxious or irate.

"Sorry," I wheezed. "Fell down." Then I added, "Not drunk." I was afraid she'd think I was. Why else do people fall down?

"My God! From your loft bed?"

"Uh-huh."

"Do you need an ambulance?"

"Uh-huh."

"Hold on, we're coming up."

I tried to tell her not to, but she'd already hung up. I was in my underwear and Maureen wasn't just my downstairs neighbor, she was also one of the editors I free-lance for; she knew Camille Paglia. So, still on my back, I crept—think of the Biblical injunction against the creatures that creep upon the face of the earth—over to the chair where I'd dropped my clothes and pulled them down to the floor and crawled into them with the astonishing agility of the Human Torso in Todd Browning's *Freaks,* who could roll cigarettes without benefit of arms or legs. When Maureen and her husband, Tim, let themselves in with the key I'd given them, I was sort of dressed. "Sorry," I groaned. "Late. Want tea?"

They kept me still until the medics came. These were two giants whose pink faces reared in and out of my field of vision as they shouted at me. "CAN YOU FEEL YOUR ARMS? CAN YOU FEEL YOUR LEGS? CAN YOU FEEL YOUR HEAD? DON'T MOVE! JUST TELL ME CAN YOU FEEL IT? CAN YOU FEEL IT?" It was like a gospel concert. The good news was that I could feel everything. The bad news was everything hurt. "Don't be scared," Tim said, and I tried to tell him that I wasn't, not really, it was just my *body* that was frightened, since I was hyperventilating and shivering and probably bubbling with adrenaline, but this was too complicated an idea to get across.

The EMS guys slid a stretcher under me like a spatula beneath an egg, strapped me to it, lifted. My ceiling glided past me, then the sloping underside of the stairwell, close enough to skim my nose, then a chilly arc of sky with its amber haze of streetlight, and then the stamped metal ceiling of the ambulance. A few minutes later I was gazing up at the fluorescent panels in a corridor of St. Vincent's—the E.R. was full—and I had to be content with this view for the next six hours. What I remember most about this time was trying to stay calm. If I was going to die, I wanted to die serenely, since I'd read enough of *The Tibetan Book of the Dead* to know the alternative—the demons, the ghosts, et cetera. And if I was supposed to live, I didn't want to disgrace myself in front of my employer and her husband or, when they finally left, before the strangers who kept coming to check my vitals and insurance information (being hospitalized in America in the 1990s isn't much different from applying for a mortgage, except that you're usually dressed worse and the personnel are more skeptical of your creditworthiness).

I tried counting my breaths, one to ten, one to ten, but this is problematic when you can't breathe. Soon my concentration broke and pain came barging in to fill the vacuum, back, chest, flanks, hips, every part throbbing, every nerve path humming with a single message, as though the community of neurons, usually so contentious and polyphonic, had suddenly become unanimous on that one point. I began to pray, out loud, since the hallway was empty. What I had in mind was the Saint Francis Prayer: "Lord, make me an instrument of thy peace. Where there is darkness, let me bring light. Where there is hatred, let me bring love. Where there is"—oh shit, what comes next?—"Grant that I may seek to comfort rather than to be comforted, to understand than to be understood, to—" Oh, fuck, it hurts!

I might have done better if I'd memorized some of *The Book of the Dead,* the part that the monk is supposed to chant to the dying person to usher his mind gently past the lures and terrors of rebirth and into the Void: "O nobly-born, the time hath come for thee to seek the Path. Thy breathing is about to cease. Thy *guru* hath set thee face to face with the Clear Light . . ." The sentiments of Saint Francis were too lofty for me. I wasn't interested in selflessness, I was interested in cessation, and although the cessation that Buddhism has in mind is in fact the cessation of self, I wasn't in the frame of mind for comparative theology. I just wanted to stop suffering, and whatever else I believe, I'm enough of a Buddhist to know that life is suffering and that the answer to suffering is to stop the wheel of life, just stop it. Stop it.

Which is what I muttered through clenched teeth when two thugs—without their lab coats they would have been ringers for the guys you see stoking the boiler in every Ship of the Damned movie ever made, all they needed was eye patches—trundled me into X ray and demanded that I remove my earrings, which I kept telling them was impossible, seeing that one of my arms was in a cast and the other incapable of moving more than a few inches

without sending me into convulsions. But they were merciless—
maybe they thought my earrings would *resonate* out of my earlobes—and we kept arguing back and forth with diminishing
politeness (belligerence seems to be one of the last ways in which
helpless people reassure themselves that they aren't) until I finally
yelled at them that they could take out the fucking rings their own
damned selves because if they waited for me to do it, they'd have
to go on waiting until I was cured or dead.

Just stop it, I whimpered at around six in the morning, seven
hours after my admission and nine since my last piss, when an
apologetic Filipino nurse with the high, bony forehead of a great
composer informed me that since I wouldn't produce any urine—
couldn't, I corrected him, *couldn't,* it wasn't as though I wasn't trying, but *you* try pissing when your entire body is calcified with
pain—he was going to have to catheterize me, and he came at me
with the vinyl hose and a tube of some local anesthetic, which
might have appealed to some people (I once interviewed a fellow
who'd pierced his urethra and stretched the holes until he could
wiggle his little finger through them—I declined the opportunity
to watch him demonstrate—and insisted that it was the greatest
sexual experience since the invention of the blow job) but sent
me skittering over the threshold of personhood and into the
zone where I was just a *patient,* a "poor thing," that's what they
call you, "poor thing," a random aggregate of functions and com-
plaints like the five *skandhas* or "heaps"—form, sensation, perception, emotion, consciousness—that Buddhists believe make up
the illusion of identity, a body that moaned and cringed and finally wept as a gloved hand seized a bit of its flesh and jabbed a
tube inside it, though I suppose a truer word would be "inserted."
Still, it felt like jabbing to the patient, who was incapable of
imagining a misery greater than the one he was locked in at that
moment, incapable of anything but anguish and shame and a
touch of awe at the volume of urine that was spurting out of it

or him or do I mean *me?* Who knows? Who cares? Just stop it!
STOP IT! STOP IT!

Six hours later my caregivers deposited me in a room where
they pumped me full of Fentanyl via a needle the size of a dueling
rapier that they plunged directly into my spine. It's the same procedure that's used on women in labor. "No narcotics," I pleaded,
but in the most halfhearted way: I was dying for that shot. "You're
not breathing," a doctor scolded me. "We've got to get you breathing, and that means we've got to give you this epidural to make
you comfortable. Otherwise, my friend, you're in for a bout of
pneumonia and we don't even want to *think* about that." I had a
moment to worry that the highly paid technician on the delivering
end would misjudge his aim a quarter-inch and paralyze me for life
and another to fret that this narcotic kiss would send me back into
active addiction—it occurred to me that my dope-hungry subconscious had engineered the fall toward precisely this end, that it had
been willing to crack nine bones for a single taste of its drug of
choice. Then I was sinking into the arms of a nurse and the sweet
nausea of a synthetic opiate. Years and years since my last shot and
I still equated that queasiness with joy. "Nooo, it's too good," I
sighed. Then everything stopped.

For a long time I have been in the habit of saying prayers of
thanksgiving. This is hard for someone who isn't sure if he believes in God or what sort of God he believes in, but it's useful because it makes a habit of gratitude, which seems to be one of those
things that requires external reinforcement, like flossing. So when I
came to in my hospital room, I immediately said thank you. I was
grateful to still be alive. I was grateful that I could move my arms
and legs and, a day later, limp to the bathroom with my IV rattling
behind me like a spindly robot dog. I was grateful to be out of
pain, or at least not immersed in it the way I had been. You appreciate narcotics in a whole new way when you actually need them.
Most of all, I was grateful for the people who came to me, usually

without my asking, since I've never been good at asking, scared of imposing on others or of indebting myself, and made themselves useful in a matter-of-fact way that would have baffled me when I was little and used to people crying "Here, darling, see what I brought you!" when they so much as handed me a glass of water, but which as a grown-up is the only form of love I can recognize, or do I mean accept?

Maureen and Tim picked up my mail and fed my cats. Flipper brought me clean clothing; his wife, Kathy, made phone calls for me; Linda and Lauren and Nicole visited with books and gourmet meals that I couldn't bring myself to eat but that proved useful for sweetening up the nurses; Francis and Lorenzo and David and Teru offered spiritual counseling and reassurance ("Well, of course you took the Fentanyl. You wanted to *breathe,* no? Tell me, is it as good as Dilaudid?"). Rob made up a bed for me on the sofa when I finally came home.

The one person who didn't come rushing to my bedside was my mother, but this was through no fault of hers. "What do you want me to tell her?" Kathy asked when we'd gone through the list of people she was supposed to notify of my new status.

"Don't tell her anything, for God's sake! Don't call her."

"So *you'll* call her?"

"Of course I'm not going to call her. You think I want to give the poor woman a heart attack?"

"She's not going to have a heart attack. You just fractured some bones."

"She's going to have a heart attack when she sees my tattoos." I yanked up the sheets to see if I could keep them hidden. "Shit, it's not going to work. Don't look at me like that, Kathy. I used to go six months without talking to the old lady. Believe me, she'll live if she doesn't hear from me for a week. She probably won't even think twice about it."

But on the day before I was released from St. Vincent's, the telephone rang and when I picked it up, my mother was speaking to me. "I knew it. I knew something had happened to you!"

"Oh God, I'm sorry. Who told you?"

"You think I don't know when my own son is sick?" For a moment she was so pleased with herself that she forgot to be angry.

"I'm not sick."

"Then what are you doing in the hospital?"

"I fell."

"And you didn't call me."

"I was going to. I didn't want you to worry."

"And I don't worry if I don't hear from you for a whole week? What did you break?"

"A few ribs."

"What if it had been your head? I should have found out in the obituary? When are visiting hours?"

"Mom, it's cold outside. Think of your breathing. They're letting me out tomorrow. Why don't you wait till I come home?"

"Of course I'll wait. I'll wait forever if that's what you want. You'd think it would kill you for your own mother to visit you in the hospital. Why do you always shut me out?"

What answer could I have given her that she wouldn't have perceived as an attack? And that wouldn't in fact have been one? A few years before this my mother had come down to Baltimore for Thanksgiving. It was the most time we'd spent together since I was sixteen. On the fourth day we went to a shopping mall, which made my mother feel the way other people do when they first see the Rockies or the Grand Canyon: here was the *real* America. We were about to drive back home when she saw some expression cross my face, who knows what it was, and asked me, "What are you feeling?" I suppose I'd spent too much time in therapy, where a phrase like that functions as the starting gun for breakneck sprints of autovivisection. Or maybe what I was really feeling was mean. Without thinking, I answered, "I feel like I need to be alone for a while." My mother started crying and flung herself from the car. Luckily it was still parked in the Timonium mall. "Fine! Be alone, then!" She might have stomped all the way back to New York, or at least tried, a short, sturdily built woman whose hair was still black, sobbing and wheezing and stopping to huff an angry cigarette every few hundred yards, if I hadn't followed her out into the twilit parking lot and pleaded and apologized the way I had so often when I was little. There are people with whom you cannot afford to be honest, and this has less to do with their limitations than with your own. How could I tell my mother that in her presence I always felt like a testy eight-year-old leaning against the door of his room with all his might while she hammered on the other side? "Leave me alone!" the boy kept howling. "Stay out of my *stuff!*"

I don't remember what stuff I wanted to keep her out of back then: horror movie magazines, maybe, or the mummified mouse that Erich Erdoes had given me for Christmas, a brittle juju of bone and matted fur that would have made my mother cry out with disgust before she made me flush it down the toilet. If you want to know the truth, I wasn't thrilled to have the thing, either. Every time I came across it in my sock drawer, entombed in its matchbox with its paws drawn up to its chest and its incisors bared like little yellow awls, I felt sick. But it was mine; it was my secret thing, and I wanted her to stay away from it. It must be deeply indicative of my nature that the things I kept hidden from my mother always had that double *mana,* an aura that made them precious and loathsome at the same time: the glassine sachets of dope, the pornographic playing cards, the needles that I scoured between uses and wrapped in cotton and secreted in a children's book I'd painstakingly hollowed with a matte knife, all my filthy treasures. They were things I could tell her about only after they'd been discarded like the idols of a discredited religion, fallen stones overgrown with lichen that you have to look at for a while before you realize that they were once the heads of gods—and that the charred sticks scattered at their base were once the bones of children.

Now I had only one secret left and it was one I couldn't discard, not even if I wanted to.

"Mom, I've got to tell you something." It was a few days after our telephone conversation, and my mother had come downtown to visit me, stopping at a supermarket on the way. The first thing I saw when I answered the door was a delivery boy who was bent almost double beneath cases of canned soup and kasha and orange juice and dried fruit, the last item because my mom equated illness of any kind with constipation.

"You're not using drugs again?" She breathed heavily with emotion, or perhaps only because my apartment was one flight up and filled with cat hair. Bitey and Ching terrified her and they must have sensed it because they kept weaving around her ankles and purring madly. "Shoo! Get away from me! Don't be offended, it's nothing personal. Don't tell me you're using drugs again!"

"No, I'm not using again. I want to explain something to you."

"Go right ahead. You've certainly got a lot to explain."

"I know. I'm sorry. Look, when I didn't call you last week, it wasn't because I didn't want you there—"

"You could have fooled me," she said grimly. "And I don't know why it would have been so painful to you. Most people want to have their families by them when they get sick. Only you have to be different. Can you explain that to me? Why you always have to be different?"

"I'm *trying* to explain. Look, it's just that there was something I didn't want you to see just then. I didn't want to upset you."

"Is there something wrong? Do you have a disease? Please don't tell me you have a disease! I don't need to hear that."

"Ma, I'm fine. I don't have a disease. I have . . . I have . . . *tattoos.*"

"Tattoos! Since when? *I* never saw a tattoo on you!"

"That's what I'm saying. I hid them. I've had them for years."

"Years? That's impossible! I would have known. Where?"

"On my arms, for starters."

"Arms? You've got more than one?"

"Yes."

"How many?"

I phrased it as a question, as though I was willing to revise my count downward if it proved to be too much. "Six?"

"Six? No! I don't believe it! Let me see."

"You don't want to see."

"What, are they dirty?"

"They're not dirty. They're art, for God's sake! All right. Here." I decided that the Dayak design on my left biceps would be the least upsetting to her. It was painful reaching over to roll up my sleeve—it would be weeks before I had more than the most constricted range of motion—and it took some doing to work my shirt over my cast, but at last I turned and displayed it to her, feeling sheepish and pugnacious at the same time. She examined it silently. My mother and I had the same face, the kind that registers the faintest blip of feeling. But at certain times she had the ability to make her screen go blank.

"So?" I asked.

"You think I'm shocked? I'm not shocked." She lit a cigarette. "Disgusted, maybe. But not shocked."

I wonder if Freddy would have liked this story. A lot of tattooists seem to secretly crave legitimacy and rapprochement, like the death-row inmates in Merle Haggard songs who just want to see their mamas before they die. They make their living, and to a large extent define their personalities, affronting the citizenry; they are constantly drawing a line between themselves and the people they call "blanks." But get one of them alone for a while and he's likely to tell you a story whose whole point is to prove what a softy he is at heart. At the same convention I met a guy named Toad from Anaheim who told me how he'd once tattooed a fourteen-year-old boy who was dying of leukemia. "All he wanted was to be tattooed with an Indian," Toad said. There was a throb in his voice. "I don't know if he was part Indian himself or he just liked the idea. He sure didn't look like an Indian. His folks had gone all over L.A. and everybody had turned 'em down on account of the kid being underage and all. But they came to me and I told 'em, 'Hey, you just sign me an affidavit and give me a note from the little guy's doctor, and no problemo.' And that's what they did. I gave that kid the nicest Indian chief you ever saw. And when he tried to pay me, I said, 'That's all right, son. You just take that money and spend it on something you want. This tat's on old Toad.' "

But I didn't tell my story to Freddy or anyone else I met in Amsterdam. Its chief drawback was that I never showed my mother all my tattoos. My stigma would have freaked the hell out of her, I'm sure. And if she'd ever seen the falling angel on my right shoulder blade, she probably would have decided that I was a closet Satanist.

Speaking of Satan, I had a lot of free time after my accident, or really a lot of time in which I couldn't do much but read, swooning on my chaise longue with my crazed rib cage cushioned like a mending vase. And I began looking through the literature for an answer to the question I'd asked my mother when I was little: Do Jews go to hell? What I discovered is that this is yet one more of the things Jews can't agree on. Hell isn't even mentioned in the Torah. The closest thing you find is Sheol, a dusty gray underworld that's as inclusive as the Hard Rock Café and, I'm sure, as dreary: Anyone can get in; everyone *will*. You have to foray deeper into the Bible and from there into the multistoried annex of the

Talmud before you come across the idea of separate facilities for the righteous and the wicked.

Now, I think there's a reason why this idea enters Judaism late in the historical record. In the first five books of the Hebrew Bible, God is present in the midst of Israel and meddling violently in its affairs. Aaron's sons perform a sacrifice improperly and He incinerates them on the spot. Korah grumbles against Moses, and Yahweh splits the earth beneath his feet. The Torah's justice is swift and unequivocal, dealt by a God whose trigger finger is as itchy as Dirty Harry's. But in the succeeding centuries, God intervened less and less frequently in the lives of His chosen people. Long before the Book of Job it must have become distressingly clear to the Hebrews that the sinful thrived and the blameless suffered. And, because they couldn't bear—or possibly even envision—a universe in which God no longer judged man, they simply postponed His judgment. And if the question that had preoccupied their ancestors was "Who shall live and who shall die?" it now gave way to another question, one that could be answered only after death: "Who is saved and who is damned?"

According to the Talmudic School of Shammai, the souls of the dead belong to three classes: The perfectly righteous are immediately granted Eternal Life; the irredeemably wicked are plunged into the fires of Gehenna and consumed there; but the vast majority of the dead are tepid sinners. The latter are sent to Gehenna, but only for a time, and what they pass through in those molten cauldrons is not so much punishment as purification: The prophet Zechariah compared it to the refining of silver. In time the smelting is complete. The purified souls rise shining into Paradise. To believe some sources, one of the chief attractions of Paradise is that it is situated next door to hell, is separated from it, in fact, only by a low wall. So in between singing psalms and basking in the divine Presence, the sanctified dead get to peer down at the torments of those who took their places in the Pit, like high-school seniors serenely contemplating the hazing of incoming freshmen.

There is another school of Talmudic thought that maintains that one day human beings will attain perfect righteousness *while still on earth* and on that day Gehenna will cease. I would like to see that. I know that at best I am a tepid sinner and slated for some strenuous dues-paying in whatever world that is to come. But, more than that, the whole idea of heaven and hell offends me. It re-creates in the next life the same divisions that are so maddening in this one. Is all I have to look forward to more courts and prisons? More fabulous clubs with lines of preterite cowering before the bouncers at their door? Somewhere there has to be a bliss that isn't contingent on someone else's misery. The early Buddhists believed that the highest goal was the cessation of birth and death that is known as Nirvana. But in time some felt that this solitary slipping out of existence was rather selfish. And it was decided that it was more commendable to take up the path of an enlightened being, or bodhisattva. A bodhisattva has attained all the conditions necessary for Nirvana: He could step off the wheel of life at any moment. But he chooses to remain, to go on being born and suffering and dying until all sentient beings are rescued with him. In Judeo-Christian terms, a bodhisattva is someone who refuses to go to heaven as long as a single soul is still in hell.

I recovered completely from my fall. A half a year after I got my seventh tattoo I was visiting friends in Los Angeles. Every day I'd drive the freeway to Manhattan Beach and Rollerblade up to Santa Monica and back. I loved swooping beside the Pacific while the waves reared and broke and the sun beat down on my shoulders. I took the distance in long, scissoring strides, my arms swinging. And I exalted in the wholeness of my body, this amazing thing that had survived vodka and heroin and cocaine and cigarettes and the sudden breakage of much of its vital infrastructure, not to mention the ordinary erosion of forty-two years, a span of time that not so long ago would have made me an old man.

One afternoon I came back to the house where I was staying and the phone rang, and when I picked it up my mother was speaking to me.

"Oh, it's you. I thought you'd be out. Is it nice there?"

"It's beautiful. Eighty degrees. Are you all right?"

"No, not so good. I'm in Mt. Sinai. Dr. Greenhut made me go."

"He made you?"

"He made me go. I didn't want to. But my breathing was bad and I was having palpitations, and when I came to his office Greenhut took one look at me and said, 'Mila, you got to go to Mt. Sinai right this minute.' He wanted to call me an ambulance, but I said no. I didn't even have a nightgown with me."

"What do they say is wrong?"

"On the CAT scan they found a spot. In my lung."

I must have severely disassociated for a moment—I mean to the point of schizophrenia—because at the same time my mother said this, I heard another voice whispering inside my head, and it was saying words that I later recognized as coming from the Book of Job: *And I only am escaped alone to tell thee.*

"Oh, Jesus. I'm so sorry, Ma."

"Greenhut said it might just be a shadow." More than anything, it was her attempt at insouciance that frightened me. I was used to a mother who knew that every sniffle was a sign of cancer.

"I'm coming back," I said.

"I'm sorry. I don't want to spoil your vacation. Maybe you should wait until they find out more."

"It's all right. There's nothing to be sorry about. I'll be there to-morrow."

I wish I could say that I felt as matter-of-fact as I tried to sound. Inwardly I boiled. For a while I rehearsed every false alarm in our long history of emergency—the canceled trips, the interrupted trysts, the pleasures sacrificed to her frailty—because in my particular version of events my mother had always gotten sick whenever things were finally about to go my way. I recalled all the nights I'd spent sleepless with fear for her. I'd grown up in the shadow of her illness as some people grow up in the shadow of a volcano, always listening for that first rumble, always waiting to flee the lives they've stitched together on its slopes. Under such circumstances one starts to see the malignity in things: I saw it in her. She was my antagonist, my thwarter. But of course a false alarm was what I was praying for. It was so much easier to rage at my mother than it would be to mourn her. And then I remembered that this story was just my story and that I could no longer afford to confuse it with the truth. The truth was that what was happening now was happening to my mother and not to me. I was just a spectator.

When I next saw her she was lying in a hospital bed, festooned with tubes and wearing a nightgown—one of the ones she'd brought from home; she couldn't stand the *shmattes* the hospital gave you, with their open backs that gave anybody who wanted a good look at your *popo*—and a red housecoat that might have been the same one I remembered her wearing when I was small. Over the next three months she would leave the hospital and go back in, but I never saw her in a dress again. There'd been a time when seeing my mother in her bedclothes had made me embarrassed and angry; here she was again, refusing to maintain the decencies. But now it was clear that it was too hard for her to dress herself. Along with lung cancer, my mother had emphysema, remember, and in the later stages of that disease everything is difficult. The walls of the lungs cling together like plastic wrap: The greediest breath admits only a thimbleful of air. In her last months my mother couldn't pick up a teaspoon without gasping for minutes afterward.

It became evident that I would have to feed her. At first I was awkward at it. My hand shook and I'd end up spilling half the food on her nightgown until she shook her head in disgust. "Enough. I can't anymore. You're ruining my good clothes. Who's going to wash them, can you tell me?" My mother's cousin Rosa was better at it. She knew how to tear a grapefruit into dripping petals and drop them one by one into my mother's mouth, the way you'd hand-feed a baby bird, while she murmured comfortingly in Russian. One night, watching them, I was suddenly sick with jealousy. Rosa had immigrated only a year before; we hardly knew her. Who was she to be feeding my mother grapefruit and consoling her in a language my mother wasn't even supposed to know?

"Since when do you speak Russian, anyway?" I'm sure I sounded peevish.

"I don't know. Mama and Papa spoke at home when I was little. All of a sudden I just remember. Isn't that peculiar!"

Of course, this is what's supposed to happen as people near their death. It's as though relativity applied to human time as well as to its roomier galactic counterpart. The time that remained to my mother was narrowing, and this was sending ripples through the time she'd already passed through. Her life was being coiled like the dough on a baker's board, its ends braiding together before they were finally pinched shut. When I entered her room in those last months she'd gaze up at me with the startled eyes of a child who's been awakened from a nap and then smile with the unabashed pleasure most grown-ups spend half a lifetime learning to conceal and then forget. "Oh, it's you! I'm so glad you came. Tell me a story."

"What kind of story?"

"Oh, what you did today."

There wasn't much to tell her. I was spending my days at the hospital or on the phone with doctors and social workers. I couldn't make up anything more entertaining: The hospital's overheated air was lethal to my powers of invention. Instead I read to her. She liked listening to Gore Vidal's memoirs, though I was troubled by the way his voice imprinted itself on mine, so that I found myself reading aloud in the inflections of an aging world-weary queen, assassinating other people's characters with every jeweled sentence.

Once I tried to tell her how sorry I was for all the years I'd wasted avenging myself upon her, but she became impatient. "No, no. You told me already. I don't need to hear it again. Please, Peterle. You had a little trouble, and now thank God it's over. Whatever you did means nothing now. You've made it all up to me. You've been wonderful."

"*You've* been wonderful. I couldn't have had a better mother."

"No, don't!" she cried. A look of agony passed over her.

"You were the best. I remember how you played with me when I was little. The birthday parties, the big cakes. Remember that cake you got me for my seventh birthday? It was shaped like a big number seven. It was amazing, I'll never forget it. You were so good to me."

"Not so good." She spoke slowly, between sobbing breaths. "Not good enough. I didn't pay attention. You could have died."

"When? What are you talking about?"

"When the nurse—" She made a grasping motion, as though trying to pluck words from the air. "When she burned you. With the tea. You almost died."

"Oh," I said. "But what could you have done? You were sick, Ma, remember? I do. I remember it perfectly. You were lying in bed and the nurse was bringing you tea and I ran right into her. POW! You should have seen the look on her face! What a spaz I was, even then! There was nothing you could have done. And anyway, I got through it just fine, didn't I? I'm right here."

The next morning my mother's doctor called and told me that she'd come down with pneumonia during the night. "It seems to be especially virulent. With the nodule in her lung—" He couldn't bring himself to say "tumor"; I could hear him nerve himself up to

the word and then sidle past it. I'd hate to be a doctor. They spend
years trying to keep their patients alive forever and sooner or later
they fail, they all do, all the time. And then they have to confess it.
"With the nodule in Mother's lungs, we can't aspirate. You understand what I'm saying."

I said I did. And I went up to the hospital. When I first saw my
mother, her eyes were closed—her eyelids were a terrifying bluish
violet—but they fluttered open for a second when I sat down beside
her on the bed and placed my hand on her forehead. It was damp
and burning. "Mom, can you hear me?" I thought I could hear her
groan, groan like someone being crushed beneath tons of earth,
but this was just the sound of her breathing. "I'm here. I'm right
here with you. You're going to be all right." I realized that I was
lying to her. "I'm not going away."

I have some trouble telling this story. It is so manifestly *my story,*
and I fear I may be using my mother only as a character in it, a
prop for my own aggrandizement. It's so hard to tell stories about
your life without subsuming the innocent people who had the bad
luck to stumble into it. I apologize to them all. I wish I could exit
this story now; I wish I could shut up the way you ought to in all
decency when you realize you've been monopolizing the conversation in your usual loudmouthed way. I would like to give this story
to my mother, to let her have the last word in it. But she cannot
speak. And I can't imagine what she would have said while she lay
with her heart being pumped full of epinephrine and her veins
being flushed with glucose and antibiotics. At one point a specialist
told me that her only chance at surviving was by being ventilated.
A long tube would be thrust down her throat and into her lungs,
where it would be inflated by an outboard motor. She would become the unconscious receptacle for a breathing machine. My
mother's father had died on a ventilator, and she could never forget the look in his eyes as he tried to speak around the plastic bit in
his mouth. "I never should have let them do it. Please, Peter, what-

ever happens, don't let them do that to me." I repeated these instructions to the specialist, but he assured me that the ventilation would only be temporary: Either my mother would pass through the crisis within the next twenty-four hours or die regardless, though somehow I doubt he actually said "die." I went in to talk to her. She was already being prepped; she was naked beneath the thin sheet; her lips were stained with disinfectant. "He says it's your one chance, Mom. He says it's just for a while. Can you hear me, Mom? Can you tell me what you want?" But she couldn't tell me, and so I had to guess: I had to imagine what her story would be had she the voice to tell it. And I told her doctor to go ahead and insert the tube.

The next day my mother and I were alone in a cubicle in the Medical Intensive Care Unit, with curtains screening us from the nurses' station and the neighboring cubicles where other people, strangers, all of them, waited and died and grieved. I suppose some of them got better, too, but my overwhelming impression was of a place where people died to soothing beeps and hisses that might have been the sounds of a rain forest, where the light filtered greenly through the treetops and the animals were harmless and shy. I'd run out of things to say. My hand was stiff from holding hers. More and more I found myself looking not at my mother but at the monitors that registered her waning.

So I began to read aloud from the *Bardo Thodol, The Tibetan Book of the Dead*. As I've said, this book is meant as a map for the dying: Its instructions steer the retreating soul or mind past the seductive lights of different incarnations, the aforementioned hells as well as the more appealing realms of the gods. Most of us would probably be pretty happy to find ourselves reborn in a Buddhist paradise, crowned and blue-skinned and screwing blissfully for aeons with other celestial beings. But even gods yearn and suffer. So *The Book of the Dead* tries, in its complicated way, to guide the hearer entirely off the wheel of birth and death and into the Void, the still, luminous place we left when we began to believe in the illusion of our own existence.

" 'O nobly-born Mila Trachtenberg, listen,' " I read. " 'Now thou art experiencing the Radiance of the Clear Light of Pure Reality. Recognize it. O nobly-born, thy present intellect, in real nature void, not formed into anything as regards characteristics or color, naturally void, is the very Reality, the All-Good.' "

You were supposed to read this to the dying person three times, but on my second go-round a nurse came into the room, and I paused long enough to realize that I had only the vaguest clue as to what any of it meant. And that my mother, assuming she could hear me, would have no clue at all. I had an image of her sitting up and spluttering, "Void? What void? What are you saying? That I've got nothing on my mind?"

I'm sorry that I didn't know more about Jewish death rituals then. They might have been more comforting, if only because their memory was encoded in both our genes. Among the Orthodox, the dying person is attended by representatives of the Holy Society, who read aloud from the Scriptures and particularly from the 119th Psalm, the one that begins "Blessed are the perfect in every way, who walk in the law of the Lord." The idea is to encourage the soul as it struggles with the Angel of Death. There's no question about the outcome of this contest. The dying person is naked and alone. The angel wields a sword and acts on the orders of the Most High. I knew He wanted us all dead. The chanting just evens the odds for a little while.

What I ended up doing was singing. My mother used to love to hear me sing when I was little and less easily embarrassed than I am now. I sang for what felt like hours, while people came in and out of the room, the nurses and doctors who took my mother's vitals, the relatives who just came to keep her company. *Two drifters, off to see the world.* I tried not to look at them; I would have gotten inhibited. I kept my eyes on my mother's face, wondering if the faint tugging of her lips might be a sign of pleasure. *I'll be so alone without you.* My repertoire was limited to ballads, love songs, mostly. I didn't stop to wonder whether it was strange to sing a love song to my mother, though once this thought would have been enough to strike me dumb on the spot. *I'll see you in my dreams.*

Toward two that afternoon my friend Sheila came to help me. We started with an old Irish song we both knew, "The Lily of the West." But then we were at a loss. My mother's forehead furrowed as though she was waiting impatiently for the next selection. The monitor above her bed chirped more quickly. " 'Amazing Grace'?" Sheila asked. I nodded. *Amazing grace, how sweet the sound that saved a wretch like me.* Something was changing in the room. It wasn't the proverbial hush, since all around us expensive machines were doing their jobs with noisy urgency. It was the sound of the forest in the moment before a monsoon, when every surface pants for the relief of rain. I squeezed my mother's hand and sang more loudly. *'Twas grace that taught my heart to fear, 'twas grace my fear relieved.* Just as we got to the last line, the beeping became a prolonged trill, a sort of birdcall. I said the *Shema,* the prayer that Jews are supposed to say on their deathbeds. I kissed my mother on her eyelids. And then medical personnel burst through the curtains and she passed from my hands into theirs, though they didn't keep her long; she was already gone.

You rarely see anyone with "Mom" tattooed on him anymore. And rarer still are those sentimentally realistic portraits that people used to have copied from photographs and inked on them as permanent reminders of their vanished ones. We are no longer supposed to be so visibly attached to the dead. When people ask me about the falling archangel on my left shoulder blade, I sometimes say it's a memorial to my mother. No one needs to know that I had it done nine months before she died. When I got it on that crowded floor in Amsterdam, where somber burghers once squandered fortunes bidding for tulips, I thought I was documenting one kind of fall, but I actually may have been anticipating another, one that was longer and more permanent. My ribs don't hurt at all these days.

Sometimes I wonder who that angel really is. Maybe it's my mother, though not even in the hyperbole of mourning would I ever call her an angel. She was just a woman who loved and suffered and liked to be told stories. I miss her. Maybe it really is Lucifer. Milton tells us that Lucifer was the first to fall and dragged us down behind him. But I can imagine a Gnostic gloss in which the Bright Son of Morning is ejected from heaven only later on, not because he tempted Adam and Eve, but because he questioned their fearful punishment. "For God's sake, it was just a goddamn apple!" he yells up at the Throne. And the next thing the trapdoor has snapped open beneath his feet and he is falling. As I said, I have a quarrel with any God who would carve his creatures up into the preterite and the saved, designating some for hell and others for a paradise in which they get to praise Him for eternity. I say the Kaddish for my mother every day, but it irks me that its words have nothing to do with the dead but are simply a further buttering-up of the Almighty. It's childish of me, I know.

I have no desire to go to heaven—and God probably has no desire to have me there, with my ceaseless grousing. I would prefer to simply be extinguished, to silence the muttering of self, the thing that preens and craves and hungers and tells itself stories in order to live. I would be a Buddhist if Buddhism's vision of release didn't sound so technical, a dance chart I could never follow. When I think of the release I'd like, I keep returning to the speech Sonia has at the end of *Uncle Vanya,* when it becomes clear to her that all the modest hopes she's harbored for her life are really too much to hope for: "We shall rest!" she says. "We shall hear the angels, we shall see the whole sky all diamonds, we shall see how all earthly evil, all our sufferings, are drowned in the mercy that will fill the whole world. And our life will grow peaceful, tender, sweet as a caress. I believe, I do believe. . . . In your life you haven't known what joy was; but wait . . . wait. We shall rest. . . . We shall rest."

ABOUT THE AUTHOR

Peter Trachtenberg is the author of *The Casanova Complex*. His articles and short stories have appeared in *Chicago, Triquarterly, Poets & Writers, BENZENE,* and other periodicals. He has won the Nelson Algren Award for Short Fiction and a fellowship in fiction writing from the New York Foundation for the Arts. He lives in New York City and is at work on a novel.